The Politics of Property Rights Institutions in Africa

Why do some political leaders create and strengthen institutions such as title registries and land tribunals that secure property rights to land, while others neglect these institutions or destroy those that already exist? How do these institutions evolve once they have been established?

This book answers these questions through spatial and temporal comparison of national and subnational cases from Botswana, Ghana, and Kenya, and, to a lesser extent, Zimbabwe. Ato Kwamena Onoma argues that the level of property rights security that leaders prefer depends on how they use land. However, the extent to which leaders' institutional preferences are translated into actual institutions depends on the level of leaders' capacity. Further, once established, these institutions through their very working can contribute to their own decline over time. This book is unique in revealing the political and economic reasons why some leaders, unlike others, prefer an environment of insecure rights even as land prices increase.

Ato Kwamena Onoma is Assistant Professor of Political Science at Yale University. After receiving his PhD from Northwestern University, he was a Postdoctoral Fellow at the Niehaus Center for Globalization and Governance at Princeton University. His work is featured in *Explaining Institutional Change: Ambiguity, Agency, and Power*, a collection of essays edited by James Mahoney and Kathleen Thelen (2010, Cambridge University Press).

The Politics of Property Rights Institutions in Africa

ATO KWAMENA ONOMA

Yale University

CAMBRIDGE
UNIVERSITY PRESS

CAMBRIDGE
UNIVERSITY PRESS

32 Avenue of the Americas, New York NY 10013-2473, USA

Cambridge University Press is part of the University of Cambridge.

It furthers the University's mission by disseminating knowledge in the pursuit of education, learning and research at the highest international levels of excellence.

www.cambridge.org
Information on this title: www.cambridge.org/9781107546196

First published 2010
First paperback edition 2015

A catalogue record for this publication is available from the British Library

Library of Congress Cataloguing in Publication data

Onoma, Ato Kwamena, 1975–
The politics of property rights institutions in Africa / Ato Kwamena Onoma.
    p.   cm.
Includes index.
ISBN 978-0-521-76571-8 (hardback)
1. Right of property – Africa, Sub-Saharan.   I. Title.
KQC194.5.O56   2009
333.30967–dc22   2009032726

ISBN 978-0-521-76571-8 Hardback
ISBN 978-1-107-54619-6 Paperback

To D. A. Akyeampong and G. K. Tetteh of Senya Bereku. And also to the memory of the late Mzee Frank Mcharo of Taita Mwatate.

Contents

List of Maps and Tables

Acknowledgments

This book explains variations in how political leaders deal with institutions that govern property rights in land. It further investigates how these institutions, including title registries, land tribunals, and rules about how to transact in land, change over time. I received a lot of help from many people in pursuing this project. While I acknowledge a few people here, I am very grateful to all of those who in different ways contributed to the fruition of this project.

I benefited greatly from the help of many in conceptualizing, researching, and writing this book. My dissertation committee members, William Reno, Edward Gibson, Kathleen Thelen, and Souleymane Diagne provided me with support and freedom to develop my thoughts on this project. Jeffrey Winters, Ben Ross Schneider, David Schoenbrun, Andrew Roberts, and Michael Wallerstein helped me develop the initial ideas that informed my dissertation proposal. I also received critical support and comments from colleagues and friends at Northwestern University, including, but not limited to Praise Zenenga, Roshen Hendricksen, Sarah Benoit, John Bennett, Barbara Murphy, Mshai Mwangola, Birol Baskan, Godwin Murunga, Judith Singleton, Meida Villafana-McNeal, Nana Akua Anyidoho, Nathalie Etoke, and David Donkor.

Once I started work on transforming the dissertation into a book manuscript, Rachel Riedl, Soo Yeon Kim, Vineeta Yadav, Tim Bartley, Nancy Bermeo, Robert Keohane, Atul Kohli, Jennifer Widner, Ellen Lust, Elisabeth Wood, James Scott, Peter Swenson, and Abbey Steele read and commented on various parts and drafts of my manuscript. Christopher Udry and John Roemer generously agreed to listen to and comment on my renderings of various parts of the manuscript. Members of the Workshop on Institutional Change organized at Northwestern University in October 2007 and of the 2007–2008 Comparative Politics Workshop at Yale University also gave me feedback on various aspects of this manuscript. I also thank two anonymous reviewers for Cambridge University Press for very useful comments on this manuscript. Mary Barrosse-Antle and Alexandra Hartman provided valuable research assistance as I finished work on the manuscript. Stacey Maples of Yale University's Map Department generously provided me with the maps in this volume.

A lot of people made my field research in Botswana, Ghana, and Kenya possible. Even though I cannot name those that I interviewed for reasons of confidentiality, I am very grateful for the multiple ways in which they helped my research, welcomed me into their homes, helped me contact people, and gently pointed me toward important issues. This book would not have been possible without their help.

Moses and Juliana Acquah and Edem Avudzivi provided me with bases from which to launch my forays into the field in Ghana. My colleagues at Northwestern, Godwin Murunga and Mshai Mwangola, ushered me gently into the world of Kenyan politics. In Kenya, my friends Alfred Anangwe, Susan Mwangi, Steve Omondi, Peter Wafula Wekesa, and Aggrey Nganyi taught me a lot about Kenya and life. Emma and Ngari Githuku of Nairobi, the Mwangola and Mcharo families of Taita Taveta, and Peter ole Kilesi of Dol Dol opened their homes to me. Kenneth Waturu Wahome, Francis ole Merinyi, and Liverson Mwangombe helped me discern the complex web of land politics in Kenya. Masego Seema, Mma Masego, Punie, Kabelo, and Thabo Seema of Mahalapye and Matlhogonolo Lekaje of Masunga provided me with homes and families in Botswana. The friendship of colleagues and friends such as Bowelo Kesiane, Lorato Chwene, Nonofo Munyalo, Anas Nyamekye, Nicholas Kilimani, and Brian Eaton helped me adjust to southern African life.

Dr. Acquah of the Department of Economics at the University of Botswana was a constant mentor. Faustin Kalabamu and Dr. Forche at the University of Botswana provided me with much needed intellectual support and direction. Divine Fuh started out as my contact person in Botswana and became a brother.

The Department of Political Science at the University of Ghana, Legon; the Department of Political and Administrative Studies at the University of Botswana in Gaborone; and the Department of History, Archaeology, and Politics at Kenyatta University in Nairobi all provided me with valuable institutional affiliation and support during my field research.

Field research for this book was made possible by a generous Social Science Research Council International Dissertation Research Fellowship and generous summer research grants from the Center for International and Comparative Studies and the Program of African Studies at North-western University. The Council for the Development of Social Science Research in Africa (CODESRIA) funded my participation in workshops in Dakar at which I was able to share and receive comments on my work.

I thank Cambridge University Press for allowing me to reproduce here significant amounts of my chapter titled "The contradictory potential of institutions: the rise and decline of land documentation in Kenya" from the volume *Explaining Institutional Change: Ambiguity, Agency, and Power*, edited by Kathleen Thelen and James Mahoney.

I thank my partner Yaba Ndiaye for her love, support, and encouragement. She read and commented on various parts of this manuscript. She also displayed immense patience and tolerance in listening to and commenting on my ideas at various stages of development. Our daughter Adjoa N'guidé provided the comic relief that I so badly needed as I worked on the final stages of this project.

Abbreviations

AASA	Akyem Abuakwa State Archive
AMA	Accra Metropolitan Assembly
BDP	Botswana Democratic Party
CPP	Convention Peoples Party
DLAS	Department of Land Adjudication and Settlement
GEMA	Gikuyu, Embu, and Meru Association
GREDA	Ghana Real Estate Developers Association
GSU	General Service Unit
KANU	Kenya African National Union
KNA	Kenya National Archives
LBC	Land-Buying Company
MDC	Movement for Democratic Change
NDC	National Democratic Congress
NLM	National Liberation Movement
NPP	New Patriotic Party
OASL	Office of the Administrator of Stool Lands
PNDC	Provisional National Defense Council
SFT	Settlement Fund Trustees
SHHA	Self-Help Housing Agency
SLIMS	State Lands Information Management System
TGLP	Tribal Grazing Land Policy (1975)
TLIMS	Tribal Lands Information Management System
UGCC	United Gold Coast Convention
ZANU-PF	Zimbabwe African National Union-Patriotic Front

MAP 1. Map of Botswana.

MAP 2. Map of Ghana.

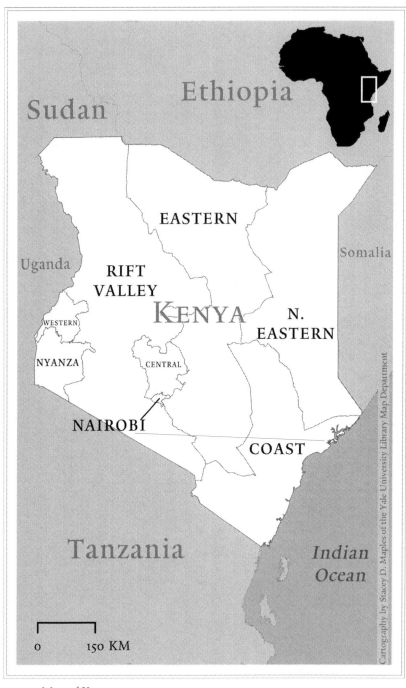

MAP 3. Map of Kenya.

Divergent Attitudes Toward Property Rights Institutions

Kihika Kimani was an ingenious political leader. A small-time business-man and aspiring politician with little actual clout, he lost his 1969 bid to unseat Fred Kubai, the veteran MP (Member of Parliament) for Nakuru[1] East in Kenya. Smarting from the defeat, he decided to harness the abundant possibilities for amassing and deploying political power presented by property rights in land to achieve his ambitions.[2] He established the Ngwataniro land-buying company and convinced thousands of peasants in Nakuru to buy shares in it. The revenue from sales was supposed to then be used to buy large farms from departing white settlers, which would then be subdivided and distributed to shareholders.[3] Registered in 1972, Ngwataniro had grown by 1975 to become a large company of more than 30,000 shareholders with assets ranging from ranches and farms covering tens of thousands of acres to schools.[4]

---

[1] At the heart of Kenya's Rift Valley, Nakuru District is the country's bread basket. It was the bastion of white settlers before many influential black politicians and bureaucrats bought up the farms of departing settlers.

[2] "Campaign against JM rumors," *Weekly Review* (Nairobi), May, 5, 1975.

[3] Nick Gatheru Wanjohi, "The politics of land, elections, and democratic performance in Kenya: a case study of Nakuru District," *Institute for Development Studies, University of Nairobi Working Paper 412* (1985), p. 13; Kenya, *Report of the Commission of Inquiry into the Land Law System of Kenya on Principles of a National Land Policy Framework, Constitutional Position on Land, and New Institutional Framework for Land Administration* (Nairobi: Republic of Kenya, 2002), p. 38 of Appendix.

[4] "Ngwataniro at crossroads as internal problems surface," *Weekly Review* (Nairobi), December 12, 1977; "Campaign against JM rumors," *Weekly Review* (Nairobi), May 5, 1975; and "Shocking revelations," *Weekly Review* (Nairobi), March 30, 1979.

Kimani then used Ngwataniro to rise to the heights of local and national power. He used funds from shareholders to conduct his political campaigns, although this led to massive losses for the company and the nonreceipt of land by many shareholders.[5] He bought political support by·giving company lands to many people who had no shares and punished political opponents who had shares by depriving them of land. He continuously forced shareholders to comply with his political demands by threatening their land rights. He even influenced the voting character of constituencies by trucking large numbers of Ngwataniro members around Nakuru District with promises of land and threats to property rights during the revision of the voter rolls in 1977.[6]

Exploiting property rights in these skilled ways, Kihika Kimani was able to achieve a political feat of enormous proportions. In the 1974 elections, he successfully executed an audacious plan that replaced three of four Nakuru MPs and many civic councillors with Ngwataniro members.[7] The only MP that survived this Ngwataniro tide was Mark Mwithiga, MP for the Nakuru Town constituency. But Mwithiga was later jailed by the Nakuru police for assault. (The police commissioner was a member of Ngwataniro.) Mwithiga then won the by-election held for his seat from jail, but ultimately he was defeated in a second by-election.[8]

The Nakuru mayor, Mburu Gichau, and Rift Valley provincial commissioner, Isaya Mathenge, were also Ngwataniro members.[9] By the late 1970s, Kihika Kimani had acquired unparalleled power. At the height of this power, he even ventured into national politics. He attempted to prevent Vice President Moi from automatically succeeding President Kenyatta by organizing a movement to change the constitution of Kenya.[10]

---

[5] "Mr. 100 percent," *Weekly Review* (Nairobi), January 12, 1979; "Ngwataniro at crossroads as internal problems surface," *Weekly Review* (Nairobi), December 12, 1977; and "Kimani rule in Ngwataniro ends," *Weekly Review* (Nairobi), April 27, 1979.

[6] "Ngwataniro at crossroads as internal problems surface," *Weekly Review* (Nairobi), December 12, 1977.

[7] "Campaign against JM rumors," *Weekly Review* (Nairobi), May 5, 1975; and "Mr. 100 percent," *Weekly Review* (Nairobi), January 12, 1979.

[8] Ibid.

[9] "Shocking revelations: company allegedly lost millions of shillings," *Weekly Review* (Nairobi), March 30, 1979; and "Campaign against JM rumors," *Weekly Review* (Nairobi), May 5, 1975.

[10] "1977 limping to the finish in Kenya," *Weekly Review* (Nairobi), December 26, 1977.

Kihika Kimani's blatant exploitation of property rights to harness personal power highlights some of the ways in which a number of political leaders in African societies have undermined property rights on the continent. They have arbitrarily enforced and abrogated rights, subversively exploited land documents, and installed themselves as the final arbiters of property claims, avoiding independent courts that would decide on land claims. All of this has taken place while African leaders in other countries have fervently worked toward creating and strengthening institutions such as land tribunals, title registries, land boards, village committees, and the enforcement mechanisms that secure land rights.

Global demand for raw materials, the expansion of commercial agriculture, climate change, population growth, and rapid urbanization have all led to land scarcity, rising land values, and the commercialization of land in many African societies.[11] Using national and subnational units of analysis, this book explains why political leaders in Botswana, Ghana, and Kenya have created different institutional environments to reap the potential power and wealth thereby provided.

Why do some leaders create and reinforce institutions that govern property rights in land while others neglect or undermine these same types of institutions? For instance, state officials in Kenya up to 1990 (1963–1990) and the leaders of Botswana strengthened institutions that govern property rights in land in their bid to harness political and economic benefits from rising land values.[12] Colonial and postcolonial Ghanaian state leaders as well as government officials in Kenya since 1990 (1991–2000) have either neglected or further subverted existing property institutions as they have exploited similar benefits.[13] The divergence across these cases

---

[11] Christian Lund, *Local Politics and the Dynamics of Property in Africa* (New York: Cambridge University Press, 2008), p. 10; and Jon Unruh, "Refugee resettlement on the horn of Africa: the integration of refugee and host land use patterns," *Land Use Policy* 10 (January 1993), p. 65.

[12] Faustin Kalabamu and Siamsang Morolong, *Informal Land Delivery Processes and Access to Land for the Poor in Greater Gaborone, Botswana: Informal Land Delivery Processes in African Cities 3* (Birmingham: International Development Department, School of Public Policy, University of Birmingham, 2004), p. 47.

[13] Internal Displacement Monitoring Center (IDMC), "'I am a refugee in my own country:' conflict-induced internal displacement in Kenya" (Geneva Switzerland, December 19, 2006), pp. 13–20. http://www.internal-displacement.org/8025708F004BE3B1/ (httpInfoFiles)/AF919E45D789BD0BC125724900350687/$file/Kenya%20Special% 20Report%20Dec06.pdf. (Accessed June 4, 2007.)

is all the more interesting because of the long history of advocacy efforts by international institutions such as the World Bank to persuade all three of these countries, among others in Africa, to undertake institutional reforms aimed at securing land rights.[14]

Also, once established, how do these institutions change over time? In examining these specific questions, this book reflects on the broader question of uneven political economic development across the African continent. Why have rising land values spurred by various global and local factors coincided with sociopolitical stability and economic growth in some societies, but with sociopolitical instability and lack of economic growth in others?

First, this book argues that the ways in which leaders extract value from land and the extent of their capacity explains variations in their treatment of institutions that govern land rights. Leaders who accrue gains from land indirectly through the productive exploitation of land for agriculture or real estate development, for instance, have a preference for strong institutions that secure rights. Whether or not they create such institutions depends on the extent of their influence. Leaders whose gains from land are accrued directly[15] and are not mediated by the productive use of land have no such interest in securing property rights.

Involved in activities such as the sale of land and the exchange of land for political support, weak institutions for governing rights are what sometimes facilitate the activities of these leaders. The extent to which these leaders subvert institutions is also dependent on the extent of their power and influence.

Second, this book argues that while exogenous changes to the political leadership and the environment that leaders face often cause institutional change, such change can also come from the endogenous working of these institutions. These institutions – by their functioning – can contribute in major ways to their own decline.

As the account of Kihika Kimani's exploits at the beginning of this chapter indicates, property rights are critical to understanding high as well as low politics in many developing countries. Writing in 1949, Meek noted insightfully:

---

14 Camilla Toulmin and Julian Quan, "Evolving land rights, tenure, and policy in sub-Saharan Africa," in Camilla Toulmin and Julian Quan, eds. *Evolving Land Rights, Policy, and Tenure in Africa: Issues* (London: IIED: Natural Resources Institute, 2000), p. 2.

15 I thank Peter Swenson for suggesting the terms "direct" and "indirect" to characterize these modes of exploiting land.

It would be impossible to exaggerate the importance of the subject of land tenure in the [British] colonies. . . . Land is, for the most part, the only form of capital and its exploitation the only means of livelihood. Such manufacturing industries as exist are almost solely concerned with the products of agriculture. Land therefore has something of a sacred character and rights over land are more jealously treasured than any other form of rights.[16]

The economic significance of land rights has continued to this day, providing an excellent window into the wider political economy of African countries.[17] The economic implications of property rights institutions have received the lion's share of attention in the growing literature on property rights. Secure rights and related instruments such as titles are thought to encourage and facilitate greater investment in economies. They are said to remove uncertainties over whether investors would be able to hold land long enough to reap the fruits of their investments, reduce the cost of private protection of parcels to free up resources for further investment, and allow the use of land as collateral for loans.[18]

The political repercussions of property rights, which have received less attention in the literature, are even more important. Disputes over land rights are some of the biggest sources of intrastate conflicts in African countries. Cote d'Ivoire, the Democratic Republic of Congo, Zimbabwe, Nigeria, Western Sudan, and Kenya, among others, have been plagued by conflicts of varying intensities arising at least partly from disputes over land rights.[19] In Kenya's Rift Valley Province, postelection violence that claimed hundreds of lives in Nakuru, Uasin Gishu, and Kericho

[16] Charles Kingsley Meek, *Land, Law, and Custom in the Colonies.* 2nd ed. (London: Oxford University Press, 1949), p. v.

[17] Christian Lund, *Local Politics*; Camilla Toulmin and Julian Quan, "Evolving land rights," and Sara Berry, *Chiefs Know Their Boundaries: Essays on Property, Power, and the Past in Asante, 1896–1996* (Cape Town: David Philip, 2001).

[18] World Bank, *Building Institutions for Markets: World Development Report, 2002* (New York: Oxford University Press, 2002), pp. 31–35; Markus Goldstein and Christopher Udry, "The profits of power: land rights and agricultural investment in Ghana," *Economic Growth Center Paper 929* (November 2005); and Hernando de Soto, *The Mystery of Capital: Why Capitalism Triumphs in the West and Fails Everywhere Else* (London: Bantam, 2000), pp. 6–7.

[19] Séverine Autesserre, "Local violence, national peace? Postwar 'settlement' in the Eastern D.R. Congo (2003–2006)," *African Studies Review* 49 (December 2006); Dwayne Woods, "The tragedy of the cocoa pod: rent-seeking, land, and ethnic conflict in Ivory Coast," *Journal of Modern African Studies* 41 (April 2003): 641–655; "Nigeria: lives lost, villagers flee over 50-year conflict," *Vanguard* (Lagos), June 9, 2007, http://allafrica.com/stories/200706090020.html. (Accessed June 11, 2007.); IDMC, "I am a refugee;" "Menace of land guards evokes fear in capital," *Africanews* 40–42, July 20, 1999, http://lists.peacelink.it/afrinews/msg00022.html (Accessed April 18, 2007.);

districts in 2008 was in many ways motivated by historical conflicts over land, even if the proximate cause was the fraudulent election of December 2007.[20] Land rights are also at the core of political control and empowerment in these societies. The lure of access to and protection of land rights is one that the powerful and landed often employ to control the political activities of less powerful members of society.[21]

For these reasons, the politics of property rights are vital to understanding the wider political economies of postcolonial African countries. State- and local-level political struggles are almost always played out in the land arena. National and subnational political order and disorder can often be gauged through the level of order in the land market. The winners and losers in national and local politics are often the same as the winners and losers in the land market. Important national political transformations are also reflected in transformations in land market struggles.

CASE SELECTION AND STUDY DESIGN

To explain variations in how leaders treat institutions that govern land rights and why these institutions change over time, this book blends spatial and temporal comparisons of national and subnational units of analysis to assess alternative explanations and demonstrate the analytic utility of the explanation put forward here. The cases are drawn from Botswana, Ghana, and Kenya. The main period under review ranges from the late 1950s, when Ghana secured independence, to the late 1990s. The need to contextualize analysis, however, requires the discussion to not only look farther back into the colonial histories of these societies, but also to reflect on more recent developments since the late 1990s.

The choice of these three countries to examine was partly influenced by similarities between them that allowed me to control for certain obvious alternative explanations. Each is a relatively successful African country that has largely escaped the protracted postcolonial civil wars that have

---

and Kenya, *Report of the Judicial Commission Appointed to Inquire into Tribal Clashes in Kenya* (Nairobi: The Commission, 1999).

[20] "Kenya's geographical and political rift," *BBC News*, January 28, 2008. http://news.bbc.co.uk/2/hi/africa/7213211.stm. (Accessed February 25, 2008.)

[21] Jean-Marie Baland and James Robinson, "How does vote buying shape the economy?" in Frederic Schaffer, ed. *Elections for Sale: The Causes and Consequences of Vote Buying* (Boulder, CO: Lynne Reinner, 2007), p. 123.

affected some other African nations. This relative peace has allowed for potential property rights reforms. Further, all three countries have faced pressures for tenure reforms from the World Bank.[22] Despite these similarities, there are nonetheless wide variations in the ways leaders have handled property rights institutions across and within these countries, which allows for causal analysis.

Chapter 2 lays out the theoretical arguments in this work. The discussion explores varying institutional choices by leaders and examines how endogenous factors have contributed to change in these institutions once they have been established. Chapters 3, 4, and 5 account for divergent institutional choices. Chapter 3 undertakes a cross-national analysis of responses by state leaders in Botswana and Ghana. Successive Botswana Democratic Party (BDP) governments have invested heavily in creating and strengthening institutions that govern land rights across their country. In Ghana, generations of colonial and postcolonial leaders have refrained from trying to create such institutions in most of the country, concentrating on only a few enclaves where they still have not attained much success in reinforcing institutions.

The selection of these two cases is partly informed by the puzzling nature of the divergence between them, which defies several plausible alternative explanations of political economic outcomes in developing countries that would lead us to expect similar outcomes in the two countries. Both countries were colonized by the British, who employed a similar method of indirect rule and left the administration of land throughout most of the country in the hands of traditional leaders.[23] Because of these similar colonial histories, one might be led to expect similar postcolonial trajectories in the governance of land rights. This is particularly so given

---

[22] Camilla Toulmin and Julian Quan, "Evolving land rights," p. 2; Elisha Atieno-Odhiambo, "Hegemonic enterprises and instrumentalities of survival: ethnicity and democracy in Kenya," *African Studies* 61 (February 2002), p. 240; L. Wily, *Land Allocation and Hunter-Gatherer Land Rights in Botswana: The Impact of the TGLP* (London: Anti-Slavery Society, 1980), p. 16.

[23] Ross Molosiwa, *Botswana: An Official Handbook*, 5th ed. (Gaborone: Publicity Unit the Department, 1999), p. 40; A. Adu Boahen, *Ghana: Evolution and Change in the Nineteenth and Twentieth Centuries* (London: Longman, 1975); Kathryn Firmin-Sellers, *The Transformation of Property Rights in the Gold Coast* (New York: Cambridge University Press, 1996), p. 21; Faustin Kalabamu and Siamsang Morolong, *Informal Land Delivery*, p. 43; and Charles Ilegbune, "Concessions scramble and land alienation in British Southern Ghana, 1885–1915," *African Studies Review* (December 1976), p. 19.

the literature that has often sought to explain postcolonial outcomes in countries in terms of their colonial masters and modes of colonial governance.[24] It is important, therefore, to understand the divergence.

There are good demand-side as well as supply-side reasons to expect Ghanaian leaders to have done more to create and propagate institutions that secure land rights around their country than the leaders of Botswana. Pressure on land and calls for legal reforms have been far more intense in Ghana than in Botswana because of population density. Ghana, which has an area of 228,000 square kilometers (about half the size of Botswana), has about twelve times Botswana's 1.7 million people.[25] Further, the nature of the resource bases of these two states suggest that Ghanaian leaders should be more willing to supply these demanded institutions.

Botswana is heavily dependent for its revenues on diamonds mined from a few locations in the country such as Orapa, Letlhakane, and Jwaneng.[26] The gold, diamonds, and cocoa on which Ghanaian state revenues heavily depend are far more dispersed throughout the southern half of the country. Given this difference, one would expect Batswana leaders to focus on the enclaves from which the state draws resources and to be less enthusiastic about building institutions across their country. Ghanaian elites should be more eager to reinforce institutions across the country since the state draws revenue from a greater part of the country. So, why is the opposite true?

Given the longstanding unwillingness of the Ghanaian government to establish strong institutions that govern land rights in most of the country, Chapter 4 explores how subnational leaders operating within this relatively laissez-faire environment have handled institutions. This is not an excuse to exclude the Ghanaian state from analysis. It is only an attempt to explain why local land institutions within the larger political institutional context of the state vary.

---

[24] Kathryn Firmin-Sellers, "The reconstruction of society: understanding the indigenous response to French and British rule in Cameroon," *Comparative Politics* 34 (October 2001); Michael Crowder, "Indirect rule: French and British style," in M. Klein and G. Wesley Johnson, eds. *Perspectives on the African Past* (Boston: Little, Brown, 1972); and Kathryn Firmin-Sellers, "Institutions, context, and outcomes: explaining French and British rule in West Africa," *Comparative Politics* 32 (April 2000).

[25] Ross Molosiwa, *Botswana*, 13; and World Bank, *African Development Indicators, 2004* (Washington DC: World Bank, 2004), pp. 5–6.

[26] See the Government of Botswana site, http://www.gov.bw/index.php?option=com_content&task=view&id=63&Itemid=74 (Accessed June 27, 2007.)

This book studies two traditional areas: Akyem Abuakwa and the Ga Traditional Area. In Ghana traditional areas are entities under the leadership of traditional hereditary paramount chiefs, also often called kings, who are not part of the state bureaucracy. The boundaries of these entities are not strictly determined by state officials, but they can often be traced to precolonial kingdoms. While most of the powers of these chiefs have been usurped by the state, the power to allocate land in around 75 percent of Ghana's territory is one of chiefs' powers that are still recognized by the Ghanaian constitution.[27] Chiefs in the Ga Traditional Area have consistently undermined property rights institutions, in stark contrast to Akyem Abuakwa chiefs' efforts at strengthening institutions since the 1920s. Explaining this subnational variation allows us to capture and examine the more variegated character of institutional responses to similar economic and political opportunities within a single country.[28]

The particular cases of Akyem Abuakwa and the Ga Traditional Area were chosen because they allow use of a dynamic comparison design that utilizes both temporal and spatial frames of comparison to increase the internal validity of causal analysis. As explained by Gerring and McDermott,[29] dynamic comparison exploits one case (the largely urban Ga Traditional Area), where the key independent variable (how chiefs exploit land) is held constant over time, and another case (the predominantly rural Akyem Abuakwa), where the key independent variable changes over time. The discussion then compares and accounts for outcomes before and after the change in the key explanatory variable.

This design permits control for various alternative explanations, including the causal effects of a rural versus urban environment. The rural character of Akyem Abuakwa has been constant, but the way in which traditional elites have exploited land and handled property rights institutions has varied over time, casting serious doubts on whether the rural nature of Akyem Abuakwa is responsible for recent outcomes.

[27] Michael Roth, Jeffrey Cochrane, and R.K. Kasanga, *Land Markets and Legal Contradictions in the Peri-Urban Area of Accra Ghana: Informant Interviews and Secondary Data Investigations*, *LTC Research Paper*, 127 (Madison, WI: Land Tenure Center University of Wisconsin-Madison, 1996), pp. 5–6.

[28] For more on the benefits of subnational analysis, see Richard Snyder, "Scaling Down: The Subnational Comparative Method," *Studies in Comparative International Development*, 36 (Spring 2001), 93–110.

[29] John Gerring and Rose McDermott, "Internal validity: an experimental template," in John Gerring, ed. *Case Study Research: Principles and Practice* (New York: Cambridge University Press, 2007).

Both traditional areas have been incorporated into the global political economy for a long time, ensuring similar rising land values, the commercialization of land, and the proliferation of distributive conflicts over land.[30] Also, at least 70 percent of the land in both areas is customary land legally controlled by traditional chiefs and lineage heads who, by law, are supposed to only be custodians that grant user rights.[31] Further, the capacity of chiefs in both areas has been similarly curtailed by the creation of the Ghanaian state. These similarities allow us to hold rising land values, distributive conflicts, types of formal land tenure arrangements, and the capacity of political leaders constant across cases.

In Chapter 5, Kenya is studied because it provides a very interesting case of path switching that allows temporal comparison of two periods in the country's postcolonial history. In the first period, which we call Early Kenya (1963–1990), senior state officials of the Kenya African National Union (KANU), which ruled the country from independence in 1963 to the multiparty elections of 2002, reinforced property rights institutions. Interestingly, the same group of leaders in a second period (1991–2000), which we call Late Kenya, switched and significantly subverted the very institutions that they had created.

The case of path switching by Kenyan leaders from reinforcing to subverting institutions is excellent for causal analysis. It offers controls for many potential explanations that remain constant before and after the switch, allowing me to focus on the causal weight of changing factors. The KANU party dominated national politics in Early and Late Kenya.[32] National ruling elites owned vast tracts of land in both Early and Late Kenya.[33] Kenya's heavy dependence on land-intensive agriculture and tourism sectors remained constant in both periods. Given so many continuities between the two periods, why did national ruling elites in Kenya switch to subverting property rights institutions that they had earlier invested in creating and reinforcing? The explicitly temporal nature of the analysis here also allows us to demonstrate the causal significance of some of the relationships laid out in other chapters that are more involved in spatial comparison.

---

[30] Claire Robertson, *Sharing The Same Bowl? A Socioeconomic History of Women and Class in Accra, Ghana* (Bloomington: Indiana University Press, 1984), pp. 27, 49–50; and Charles Kingsley Meek, *Land, Law and Custom*, p. v.

[31] 1992 Constitutions of the Republic of Ghana, p. 267.

[32] Frank Holmquist, Frederick S. Weaver, and Michael D. Ford, "The Structural Development of Kenya's Political Economy," *African Studies Review* 37 (January 1994).

[33] "Who owns what in Kenya," *Weekly Review* (Nairobi), March 8, 1991.

Chapter 6 also deals with Kenya, but it shifts from the emphasis on the dominant themes of institutional choice and stability that inform most of this work to reflect on institutional change. It examines the ways in which gradual endogenous change contributes to transformations in institutions that display clear positive feedback effects. Departing from the focus on the activities of rulers in the rest of the book, Chapter 6 also examines the ways in which less central actors exploit opportunities partly created by the very institution of land documentation in ways that ultimately contribute to its decline. This adds to the literature on endogenous contributions to institutional change.

This work is situated within the broader political economic literature in the concluding chapter.

DISORDER AND POLITICS IN AFRICA

Reflections in this work on the deliberate subversion of institutions to facilitate various political and economic ways of exploiting land bring to mind a rich literature on the political uses of disorder in postcolonial Africa. This literature reflects on the ways in which political consider-ations have motivated African leaders to deliberately choose economi-cally and socially ruinous policies. Bates's[34] seminal 1981 work can be regarded as one of the original works in the field. He was interested in why states in sub-Saharan Africa have tended to pursue agricultural policies that have involved, among other things, buying export crops from farmers at very low prices and setting controls on the prices at which farmers can sell food crops to urban populations. These policies have contributed to the devastation of agricultural sectors in many countries. Bates's answer was that, while economically inefficient, these policies have allowed states to appease restive urban constituencies on whose quiescence states have depended for their survival.[35]

Many social scientists working on the political economy of Africa have followed in Bates's footsteps by reflecting on the deliberate political cre-ation and exploitation of disorder and ruinous economic policies in Africa by state leaders who have been motivated by political realities. Chabal and Daloz's *Africa Works: Disorder as Political Instrument*; Bayart, Ellis, and Hibou's *The Criminalization of the State in Africa*; Reno's *Warlord*

---

[34] Robert Bates, *Markets and States in Tropical Africa* (Berkeley: University of California Press, 1981), p. 4.
[35] Ibid.

Politics and African States; and van de Walle's *African Economies and the Politics of Permanent Crisis* are all examples of such work.[36]

This book draws on the insights in much of the literature into the political production and uses of disorder. But it also departs from the literature in significant theoretical and methodological ways. Unlike other works in the literature, this is *not only* a story about how political considerations cause leaders to make economically irrational decisions; this is a book about the ways in which political considerations push some leaders to make socioeconomically beneficial decisions and others to make socioeconomically destructive ones.

In many of the works cited here, politics in Sub-Saharan Africa is presented as something that *necessarily* bears disruptive and perverse fruit. A logical conclusion to draw from such a premise is the highly problematic but very popular view that the suspension of politics is the solution to the problems facing societies on the African continent. We saw this in the justification of military coups that blamed social ills on the "politics" played by the ousted rulers. This is also evident in the reversion to technocratic change teams by international financial institutions such as the IMF (International Monetary Fund) and World Bank as they have sought to institute macroeconomic and political reforms.[37] These technocrats, well shielded from "murky" politics, have often been seen as the only hope for bringing about positive political economic reforms. The urge to suspend politics can even be seen in the advocacy by scholars such as Stephen Ellis of new international trusteeships (which some call the new colonialism) as a cure for the ills facing some African countries.[38]

In the pairwise comparisons made in this book, politics does cause some leaders to make economically sound decisions. It is important to emphasize this point. The supply of secure property rights in places such

---

[36] William Reno, *Warlord Politics and African States* (London: Lynne Reinner, 1998); Patrick Chabal and Jean Pascal Daloz, *Africa Works: Disorder as Political Instrument* (Bloomington: Indiana University Press, 1999); Nicholas Van de Walle, *African Economies and the Politics of Permanent Crisis* (New York: Cambridge University Press, 2001); and Jean-François Bayart, Stephen Ellis, Béatrice Hibou, *The Criminalization of the State in Africa* (Bloomington: Indiana University Press, 1999).

[37] Thandika Mkandawire and Charles Soludo, *Our Continent, Our Future: African Perspectives on Structural Adjustment* (Trenton, NJ: Africa World Press, 1999), p. 26; Thandika Mkandawire, "Crisis management and the making of 'choiceless' democracies," in Richard Joseph, ed. *State, Conflict and Democracy in Africa* (Boulder: Lynne Reinner Publishers, 1999), p. 126; and Adebayo Olukoshi, "The elusive Prince of Denmark: structural adjustment and the crisis of governance in Africa," in Thandika Mkandawire and Charles Solubo, eds. *African Voices on Structural Adjustment* (Trenton, NJ: Africa World Press, 2003).

[38] Stephen Ellis, "How to rebuild Africa," *Foreign Affairs* 84 (September–October 2005).

as Botswana, Early Kenya, and Akyem Abuakwa was not due to the absence of political considerations, but instead on the presence of certain types of political considerations. Unlike the works on the political uses of disorder cited above, (African) politics are not always seen as motivating the choice of socially destructive policy paths. This opens up the possibility of studying which types of politics lead to suboptimal outcomes and which types of politics lead to more socially beneficial policy choices. This is the fundamental goal of this book.

There is also a related significant methodological difference. Most of these works on the political manufacture and uses of disorder treat Sub-Saharan Africa as a homogenous unit. The dependent variables with which each of these works deals – whether it is the study of failed agricultural policies, the criminalization of the state, or the subversion of economic reform programs – do not vary across their study. This creates a potentially serious methodological challenge. Since the explanatory variables are also mostly constant across cases, the internal validity of such analyses is not obvious.[39]

Then there are the problems that arise from efforts at homogenizing a continent that is, in most ways, quite heterogeneous. van de Walle's[40] work presents an arresting example. The book sets out to "identify and explain patterns, which have kept Africa for several decades mired in a seemingly permanent crisis."[41] But North Africa, South Africa, Botswana, Mauritius, Ghana, and Uganda are all summarily excised to facilitate the homogenization of a continent that is obviously anything but homogeneous. This refusal to exploit heterogeneity in causal analyses of the political economy of Africa is at times perplexing. But this study avoids these problems by considering cases with varying outcomes.

In both a theoretical and a methodological sense, this book has more in common with Boone's recent work on the *Political Topography of the African State*.[42] Her work also displays clear variations in the outcomes to be explained.

In Boone's work, all leaders do not jettison the institutionalization of the state in every area of their country. Further, theoretically, she does not portray the political context that leaders are located in as one that always

---

[39] For further discussion of this methodological point see Gary King, Robert Keohane, and Sidney Verba, *Designing Social Inquiry* (Princeton: Princeton University Press, 1994), pp. 147–49.

[40] Nicholas van de Walle, *African Economies*.

[41] Ibid., p. 19.

[42] Catherine Boone, *Political Topographies of the African State: Territorial Authority and Institutional Choice* (New York: Cambridge University Press, 2003).

causes them to further erode and deinstitutionalize the state. Instead, like this work, she shows how varying rural social structures (political relations) lead some state leaders to fashion power-sharing arrangements, some to usurp rural authorities, others to avoid incorporating these rural bosses, and still others to administratively occupy far-flung regions.[43]

Further, much of the literature on the political exploitation of disorder has focused on postcolonial African leaders, giving the impression that it is another malaise of the postcolonial era. As is evident in our analysis in Chapter 3 of the decisions of colonial leaders concerning property rights institutions in Ghana, the sacrifice of economically beneficial institutions for political ends is not an innovation of postcolonial leaders.

In his seminal work, Mahmood Mamdani makes this same point in an emphatic manner by noting the "moral surrender" and shift by colonial authorities from "a civilizing mission to a law-and-order administration" rooted in the "decentralized despotism" of indirect rule in much of colonial Africa.[44] In most areas of British colonial Africa, this surrender included deliberate efforts at preventing the evolution of tenure and administration systems beyond the classification of and as a communal resource to be governed by chiefs.[45]

INSTITUTIONS THAT GOVERN PROPERTY RIGHTS IN LAND

The concrete ways in which political leaders handle institutions that govern property rights in land constitute the dependent variable in this study. This is a deviation from many analyses that examine subjective feelings of security by landholders. This choice has its costs and benefits. The security of land rights is the effect of multiple factors, including deep-rooted social practices and customs as well as population density and access to land. By not focusing on actual levels of tenure security, the research presented in this book does not consider these other factors. Thus, the character of institutions that govern property rights in land, the subject of this work, will only partially overlap with subjective feelings of security in an area. On the other hand, this choice makes research more feasible

---

[43] Ibid., p. 33.

[44] Mahmood Mamdani, *Citizen and Subject: Contemporary Africa and the Legacy of Late Colonialism* (Princeton, NJ: Princeton University Press, 1996), p. 109.

[45] Ibid., pp. 51–52.

TABLE 1.1. *Institutions that Govern Property Rights in Land*

Form	Functions
Laws, norms, rules, and policies	State proper ways of transacting
Registries, survey departments, councils of elders, land overseers	Keep information on interests, dimensions, and locations
Courts, tribunals	Adjudicate land disputes
Police, task forces, village committees, boards	Enforce and monitor compliance with rules concerning rights

because concrete steps at reform, such as changes in laws and administrative structures, are easier to capture than actual levels of security of tenure.

As shown in Table 1.1 above, institutions that govern property rights in land are best understood as a bundle composed of four distinct but related components. The first component is made up of rules that indicate the proper ways of transacting in land rights.[46] These rules may be formal laws or informal norms. The second component is a set of institutions that collects, maintains, and makes available to the public information on interests in and the geographical attributes of land parcels.[47] These institutions may take forms ranging from elders who act as human archives to survey departments and fully digitized land title registries. Institutions that adjudicate land disputes constitute the third element. These institutions include the normal courts, special land tribunals, councils of elders, and administrative bodies tasked with adjudication. The final component is made up of institutions that enforce the decisions of administrative and adjudicatory bodies concerning land rights.[48]

The four components are closely related because each influences the effectiveness of the others. For instance, murky rules governing land transactions often lead to a proliferation of disputes that impact the workings of tribunals that hear land cases, and they make it almost impossible to have proper and credible records on land interests.

---

[46] Botshelo Mathuba, *Land Administration in Botswana*. (Paper prepared for the National Conference on Land Reform, Namibia, 1991.)

[47] L. K. Agbosu, "Towards a workable system of title registration for land in Ghana," in A. K. Mensah-Brown, ed. *Land Ownership and Registration in Ghana: A Collection of Studies* (Kumasi, Ghana: Land Administration Research Centre University of Science and Technology, 1978), p. 33; and Callistus Mahama and Martin Dixon, "Acquisition and affordability of land for housing in urban Ghana: a study in the formal land market dynamics," *RCIS Research Paper Series*, 10 (October 2006), p. 38.

[48] L. K. Agbosu, "Towards a workable system," p. 33.

These institutions, even at their functional best, only minimize disputes over land rights and allow for their fast and peaceful resolution. The question of the effectiveness of these institutions is one of degree and should not be seen as a dichotomy between societies in which land rights are secure and those in which they are not secure. Land rights are in question even in advanced industrial democracies such as the United States, as never-ending debates and struggles over eminent domain demonstrate.[49]

This book treats these institutions primarily not as structures for ensuring social justice, but as instruments for ensuring the security of rights. Even though institutions that secure property rights are often advocated as a means of ensuring social justice,[50] they can be, and often are, used to distribute land in unfair ways or to make unfair distributions of land more secure.[51] This was the case in settler colonies such as South Africa, Zimbabwe, Namibia, and Kenya where white settlers fashioned these instruments to legitimize and calcify their seizure of lands from blacks.

Even though title registries and survey departments are supposed to only capture and record realities, they have a lot of flexibility as to how they document and record social facts.[52] These institutions also inadvertently create room for shrewd and well-connected state functionaries to cleverly steal land from the less powerful and knowledgeable.[53] Requiring people to produce documentary evidence for their landholdings, for instance, can be a good way of invalidating the claims of many in societies where the documentation of land rights did not already exist. Those with knowledge of and access to title registries can then make out indefeasible

---

[49] Ben Arnolby, "Topping 2006 ballot initiatives: eminent domain," *Christian Science Monitor*, October 5, 2006, http://www.csmonitor.com/2006/1005/p01s02-uspo.html (Accessed February 2, 2007.)

[50] Nelly Stromquist, "The impact of structural adjustment programs in Africa and Latin America," in Christine Heward and Sheila Bunware, eds. *Gender, Education and Development: Beyond Access to Empowerment* (London: Zed Books, 1999), pp. 17–28.

[51] Joel Ngugi, "Re-examining the role of private property in market democracies: problematic ideological issues raised by land registration," *Michigan Journal of International Law* 25 (2004), pp. 471–476; James Scott, *Seeing Like a State: How Certain Schemes to Improve the Human Condition Have Failed* (New Haven: Yale University Press, 1998), p. 48; and Jeremy Black, *Maps and Politics* (Chicago: University of Chicago Press, 1997), pp. 9–18.

[52] Joel Ngugi, "Re-examining the role," pp. 471–476.

[53] James Scott, *Seeing Like a State*, p. 48; Daniel Branch, "Loyalists, Mau Mau, and elections in Kenya: the first triumph of the system, 1957–1958," *Africa Today* 53 (Winter 2006), p. 28; and Susanna Hecht and Alexander Cockburn, *The Fate of the Forest: Developers, Destroyers, and Defenders of the Amazon* (New York: Harper Collins, 1990), p. 168.

titles to vast tracts of land in their name, effectively transforming those originally owning such lands into squatters liable to eviction.[54]

FIELD RESEARCH

The author carried out 17 months of field research for this book in Botswana, Ghana, and Kenya between 2002 and 2005. The bulk of the research was done during 12 months of continuous research between September 2004 and August 2005. The author conducted approximately 215 formal, in-depth, semistructured interviews. Many informal discussions and a few group discussions were also held. Interviewees included upper-level state officials such as permanent secretaries and department heads. These were mostly based in national capitals. Interviewees also included lower-level state functionaries often based in outlying areas such as district commissioners, land control board and land dispute tribunal officials in Kenya, Office of the Administrator of Stool Lands (OASL) and Cocoa Swollen Shoot Virus Disease officials in Ghana, and land board officials in Botswana. Also interviewed were farmers, residential land users, real estate developers, traditional chiefs, civil society activists, land racketeers, and militia members – all involved in land markets.

Close observation of the functioning of various institutions provided information that placed the statements of interviewees in perspective. Observation often involved simply sitting in on the proceedings of various agencies such as the land tribunal in Gaborone, Botswana, land control boards in various parts of Kenya, and the OASL in various parts of Ghana. At other times it took the more involved form of participant observation where the author played various roles in the activities of these agencies. This included helping land board members measure, survey, and demarcate plots as well as entering applicant information into the database of a land board in Botswana.

In Kenya, this field research was concentrated in Nairobi and in Nyeri, Laikipia, Uasin Gishu, Taita Taveta and, to a lesser extent, Nakuru and Kiambu districts. In Botswana, most of the research was undertaken in Gaborone, and in Central, Kweneng, Kgatleng, and Northeast districts. In Ghana, research started in the Greater Accra Region and moved on to the Ashanti, Eastern, and Western regions of the country. Specific places visited included Kyebi, Asamankese, Akyem Oda, Nkawkaw and Mpraeso in the Eastern Region; Kumasi, Tepa, Offinso,

[54] James Scott, *Seeing Like a State*, p. 48.

Nkawie, Obuasi, and Asante Mampong in the Ashanti Region; and Enchi, Essem, Sekondi-Takoradi, Sefwi-Wiawso, Sefwi-Bekwai and Juaboso in the Western Region. The choice of areas was informed by various factors such as the presence of archives, location of land administration bodies, the presence of plantations, mines, and tourism concerns, and land distribution patterns.

Research was additionally conducted at the national archives in Accra, Gaborone, and Nairobi, and work also took place in the Akyem Abuakwa State Archive at the palace of the Okyenhene in Kyebi, Ghana.

In the appendix to this book, the author discusses in more detail the intricacies and politics of access during this field research.

2

Explaining Institutional Choice and Change

In November 2004, I visited the mining town of Obuasi, the main base of Anglogold-Ashanti (formerly Ashanti Goldfields) in Ghana's Ashanti Region, to conduct some interviews for this book. While there, I interviewed Nasiru Muntari,[1] a staff member of the state's Town and Country Planning Department, about land administration and property rights issues in the area. He patiently pointed out some of the problems: Chiefs disputed over land rights; one chief gave the same plot to two or three different people; two chiefs allocated the same land to different people; and so on.

It seemed as if these chiefs – who would otherwise prefer secure property rights – were suffering from distributive conflicts over land and a lack of information about their boundaries and the extent of allocations. Common sense seemed to dictate that if lands were dutifully surveyed, demarcated, and adjudicated, and chiefs were given registers in which they could record allocations, they would surely avoid infringing on each other's parcels and end these problems. So I asked Muntari what the state was doing to help chiefs solve these distributive conflicts and information problems.

Muntari's response was unsettling. He claimed that, after working with chiefs for seventeen years, he had come to the conclusion that chiefs did *not* want clear boundaries, functional property registers, and

---

[1] This is a fictitious name in line with Institutional Review Board confidentiality requirements.

an environment devoid of disputes. He argued that the chiefs would sabotage any effort to provide these features. According to Muntari, in the absence of such mechanisms, cash-strapped, land-hungry chiefs could conveniently "mistakenly" allocate the lands of neighboring chiefs or sell land that they or their ancestors had sold earlier. Further, where tenants engaged in subversive political behavior, chiefs could conveniently award their rights to more loyal subjects in the absence of clear documentary evidence of such rights. Simply put, chiefs did not want property rights security.[2]

Efficiency Theory and Its Revisionists

Muntari's explanation challenged the view that rising land values would create a universal preference for property rights security – an assumption that pervades much of the literature on the transformation of property rights. This limits the ability of the literature to explore the possible existence and implications of a preference for insecure property rights among certain land market participants.

Early *market efficiency* theories of property rights leaped from exploring the positive social effects of institutions to positing these positive social effects as the causes of the institutions. Scholars such as North and Thomas, and Demsetz,[3] argued that, as land values increase, the potential gains from land transactions grow, but an environment of insecure rights impedes the accrual of these gains. This is because such an environment raises transaction costs, including the cost of information on interests in land parcels and the cost of adjudicating disputes and enforcing rights in land.

Institutions that secure property rights reduce these costs. Further, the gains from rising land values can offset the costs of building these expensive institutions. For these reasons, efficiency theory came to the conclusion that, as land values increase, rational actors will try to create institutions that secure property rights.[4]

---

[2] Interview with a staff member of Town and Country Planning in Obuasi (Gh 38), November 11, 2004.

[3] Douglass Cecil North and Robert Paul Thomas, *The Rise of the Western World; A New Economic History* (Cambridge: Cambridge University Press, 1973); and Harold Demsetz, "Toward a theory of property rights," *American Economic Review*, 57 (May 1967).

[4] Demsetz, "Toward a theory," p. 350; and North and Thomas, *The Rise of the Western World*, pp. 19–23.

A *revisionist* view in the literature embraced the demand-side assumptions of efficiency theory – that rising land values will create an interest in property security among land market participants. But it pointed to efficiency theory's failure to consider problems with the *supply* of demanded institutions as its major flaw. Firmin-Sellers, Bates, Knight and Riker and Sened,[5] among others, pointed to the fact that demanded institutions are not always supplied as the cause for persisting insecurity in the face of rising land values in many places, which is contrary to the predictions of efficiency theory.

Revisionists can be divided into two broad categories. *Institutional revisionists* such as Joireman, Herbst, Grindle, and North[6] have paid close attention to corruption and the institutional capacity of ruling authorities to create and maintain property institutions to explain why institutions have been supplied in some cases but not in others. They also have examined the role of the path-dependent characteristics of institutions in hindering reforms.[7]

Political revisionists include scholars such as Knight, Riker and Sened, Firmin-Sellers, Moe, Olson, and Feeney.[8] They have focused on the causal salience of collective action problems, distributive conflicts, and the unwillingness of rulers to anger powerful constituents who benefit

---

[5] Firmin-Sellers, *The Transformation*, pp. 9–14; Robert Bates, "Contra Contractarianism: Some Reflections on the New Institutionalism," *Politics and Society*, 16 (June–September 1988), pp. 387–401; and Jack Knight, *Institutions and Social Conflict* (New York: Cambridge University Press, 1992), p. 42; William Riker and Itai Sened, "A Political Theory of the Origin of Property Rights: Airport Slots," *American Journal of Political Science* 35 (November 1991), pp. 953–955.

[6] Sandra Joireman, "Enforcing new property rights in Sub-Saharan Africa: the Ugandan constitution and the 1998 Land Act," *Comparative Politics* 39 (July 2007), p. 467; Jeffrey Herbst, *States and Power in Africa: Comparative Lessons in Authority and Control* (Princeton: Princeton University Press, 2000), p. 193; Merilee Serrill Grindle, *Challenging the State: Crisis and Innovation in Latin America and Africa* (New York: Cambridge University Press, 1996); and Douglas North, *Institutions, Institutional Change, and Economic Performance* (New York: Cambridge University Press, 1990).

[7] North, *Institutions, Institutional Change*, Ch. 11.

[8] Riker and Sened, "A political theory," pp. 953–955; Knight, *Institutions and Social Conflict*, p. 42; Firmin-Sellers, *The Transformation*, pp. 9–14; Terry Moe, "Power and political institutions," *Perspectives on Politics* 3 (February 2005), p. 1; Mancur Olson, *The Logic of Collective Action; Public Goods and the Theory of Groups* (Cambridge, MA: Harvard University Press, 1965); David Feeney, "The development of property rights in land: a comparative study," in R. Bates, ed. *Toward a Political Economy of Development: A Rational Choice Perspective* (Berkeley: University of California Press, 1988); Mancur Olson, "Dictatorship, democracy, and development," *American Political Science Review* 87 (September 1993); and Ben Ross Schneider, "Elusive synergy: business–government relations and development," *Comparative Politics* 31 (October 1998).

from old definitions of rights to explain the supply or lack thereof of stronger institutions.

These revisionists assume that everyone wants secure property rights and the lower transaction costs they bring, but that some leaders are not able to create these institutions for various reasons. Indeed, some of these scholars do not even tackle the question of *whether* rights are defined and enforced. They focus instead on *how* they are defined and enforced. For instance, in his exploration of economic transformation in history, North[9] argued that both Spain and France suffered economic backwardness in the medieval period because their monarchs allocated and enforced growth-inhibiting monopoly rights to powerful constituencies. English and Dutch leaders, however, defined and enforced rights in ways that fostered efficiency and competition, thus spurring growth. Rulers in all of these countries defined and enforced rights. The question North tackled is why some leaders defined and enforced them in more economically efficient ways than others. The question of whether some even wanted to define and enforce rights did not arise.

As I conducted my field research, I realized that, in line with Muntari's view – and contrary to the belief in a universal preference for security in much of the literature – there were many instances in which key actors seemed to embrace and benefit from weak institutions for governing rights as land values increased. In Kenya, Kihika Kimani, whose story is told in Chapter 1, was only one notable example of many politicians in the 1970s who undermined and exploited property institutions to extort money from peasants. They also held these peasants in captive audience meetings, got them to vote in certain ways, and even moved people to different areas to get their preferred blend of voters in specific constituencies.[10] In Ghana, colonial as well as postcolonial leaders exploited weak property rights institutions in much of the country to credibly threaten to punish errant traditional chiefs that opposed state leaders.[11] In the Ga Traditional Area of Ghana, chiefs dependent on revenues from land sales exploited an environment of insecurity to reallocate rights already allocated by their

---

[9] Douglas North, *Structure and Change in Economic History* (New York: Norton, 1981), pp. 150–157.

[10] "Kihika Kimani to face uphill battle," *Weekly Review* (Nairobi), April 27, 1979; "Bogus companies," *Weekly Review* (Nairobi), May 23, 1980.

[11] Kwamena Bentsi-Enchill, *Ghana Land Law: An Exposition, Analysis, and Critique* (Legon: African Universities Press, 1964), p. 19; and Richard Rathbone, *Nkrumah and the Chiefs: The Politics of Chieftaincy in Ghana, 1951–60* (Accra: F. Reimmer, 2000), p. 128.

predecessors.[12] The fact that many of these same leaders either neglected or deliberately undermined property rights institutions in the face of significant activism by security-seeking groups raises the possibility of a preference for an environment of insecurity among certain political leaders.

Elsewhere, scholars working on the post-Soviet Russian political economy have explored why powerful and wealthy oligarchs have been sometimes the most vociferous opponents of efforts at creating public institutions that secure property rights.[13] Rosenthal[14] explores the deliberate subversion of property rights in land by kings in Old Regime France to reallocate lands already allocated by their predecessors.

On account of these phenomena, this book departs from much of the literature on the transformation of property rights by taking an agnostic stance about the effect of rising land values on leaders' preference for security. The discussion begins with the assumption that rising land values do not necessarily spawn preferences for security among political leaders involved in land markets. We then investigate and explain why rising land values create an interest in the strengthening of institutions that govern land rights in some cases but not in others. In the following sections, we construct a theory of land exploitation that explains divergent preferences and integrates them into an explanation that accounts for how elites handle property rights institutions in various African societies.

Modes of Extracting Gains from Land

We must look at how leaders derive benefits from land in order to understand whether they prefer an environment of secure or insecure rights. Political leaders value land because of the various political and economic gains that they can acquire from it. These gains do not accrue simply from the ownership or control of land. They have to be extracted through various means.

---

[12] "Chiefs, plots, and lands department," *Ghanaian Chronicle* (Accra), December 10, 2001; and "Menace of land guards evokes fear in capital," *Africanews* 40–42, July 20, 1999, http://lists.peacelink.it/afrinews/msg00022.html. (Accessed April 18, 2007.)

[13] Konstantin Sonin, "Why the rich may favor poor protection of property rights," *Journal of Comparative Economics* 31 (December 2003), pp. 715–731; and Glaeser, Scheinkman, and Shleifer, "The injustice of inequality," pp. 199–222.

[14] Jean-Laurent Rosenthal, *The Fruits of Revolution: Property Rights, Litigation, and French Agriculture, 1700–1860* (New York: Cambridge University Press, 1992), pp. 137–141.

Different modes of exploiting land have diverse institutional requirements.[15] Institutions that facilitate one mode of drawing gains from land
might hinder another. It has been argued in a large body of literature that
secure titles facilitate the farming and real estate development activities of
landholders. They lower the private costs of protection that investors face
and reduce uncertainty over whether they will be able to keep the land
until they benefit from their investments. They also allow investors to use
land as collateral.[16] But secure titles may be less conducive for a politician
seeking to use threats to the rights of landholders to win their votes.
Landowners with secure title will scoff at the efforts of the politician.
What our politician needs is an environment with unclear boundaries,
ineffective titles, and poor enforcement of rights. Then he or she will be
able to credibly threaten the landowner with eviction for noncompliance.
As a result, whether leaders develop a preference for continuing insecurity
or security of rights in the face of rising land values will depend on how
they use land.

We can differentiate between two ways in which political leaders in
these countries extract value from land – through *direct* and *indirect*
means. The main distinguishing feature is whether the political and economic gains are mediated by the productive use of land. When the benefits that leaders draw from land are mediated by the use of land for
productive activities such as farming, mining, tourism operations, and
real estate development, we say that these profits from land are accrued
through indirect means.

These gains are indirect because they flow from the productive use of
land. Many ruling politicians and bureaucrats in Botswana were cattle
ranchers before going into government.[17] Traditional chiefs in the Akyem
Abuakwa Traditional Area of Ghana granted land to tenant cocoa farmers in exchange for a share of the seasonal crop, in addition to owning
farms.[18] Some of the resources that they acquired from these productive
activities were used to sustain their political positions, pursue litigation
over land and chieftaincy, etc. In Early Kenya, politicians such as Jomo

---

[15] North, *Institutions, Institutional Change*, pp. 47–48, 70.

[16] World Bank, *Building Institutions for Markets*, pp. 31–35; Goldstein and Udry, "The
profits of power"; Joireman, "Enforcing new property rights," p. 466; and de Soto, *The
Mystery of Capital*, pp. 6–7.

[17] J. Holm, "Botswana: a paternalistic democracy," in Larry Diamond, Juan Linz, and
Seymour Martin Lipset, eds. *Democracy in Developing Countries* (Boulder, CO: Lynne
Rienner, 1988), p. 201.

[18] Robert Addo-Fening, *Akyem Abuakwa, c. 1874–1943: A Study of the Impact of Mis-
sionary Activities and Colonial Rule on a Traditional State* (Ph.D. thesis, University of
Ghana, 1980), pp. 388–390.

Kenyatta, Jackson Angaine, and Kenneth Matiba owned large commercial farms, hotels, and residential buildings. A lot of the economic profits from these productive activities were transformed into political capital to fund campaigns, pay off allies, pay people to intimidate opponents, and so on.

Where leaders' gains are not mediated by the productive use of land, we say that they draw benefits from land directly. Their profits from land accrue directly because they are not dependent on the productive use of land. Examples include traditional chiefs who sell land parcels in the Ga Traditional Area of Ghana.

Generations of national leaders in Ghana, beginning with British colonial officials, have exchanged land for the political support of chiefs. They have allowed chiefs to control land in exchange for their allegiance.[19] In late postcolonial Kenya, officials at the Ministry of Lands in collaboration with KANU politicians issued land titles to reward political allies.[20] Some of these politicians also raided securities markets in land titles by using encumbered and fake titles to secure loans from banks.[21] President Mugabe has been accused of skillfully manipulating land reforms to garner political support by dishing out parcels to his allies and seizing the lands of opponents.[22] In all of these cases, the political and economic gains that leaders have derived from land have been divorced from productive activities such as the operation of tourism sites, cattle ranching, or real estate development on these lands.

This is a distinction about how leaders benefit from land and not one about the characteristics of pieces of land. People can profit from the same piece of land simultaneously in different ways that can become increasing abstracted from the land itself, as is demonstrated in the work of de Soto and Cronon,[23] among others. For instance, at the foothills of Mount Kilimanjaro on the Kenyan side of the border lies the massive Taveta Sisal Estate owned by farmer-cum-politician Basil Criticos, who

---

[19] Rathbone, *Nkrumah and the Chiefs*, p. 13; and Samuel K. B. Asante, *Property Law and Social Goals in Ghana, 1844–1966* (Accra: Ghana Universities Press, 1975), pp. 40–47.
[20] Kenya, *Report of the Commission of Inquiry into the Illegal/Irregular Allocation of Public Land* (Nairobi: Republic of Kenya, 2004), p. 76.
[21] Ibid., p. 66.
[22] Kenneth Good, "Dealing with despotism: the people and the presidents," in Henning Melber, ed. *Zimbabwe's Presidential Elections 2002* (Uppsala: Norkiska Afrikainstitutet, 2002), pp. 12–18; and Tonny Addison and Liisa Laakso, "The political economy of Zimbabwe's descent into conflict," *Journal of International Development* 15 (2003), p. 459.
[23] de Soto, *The Mystery of Capital*; and William Cronon, *Nature's Metropolis: Chicago and the Great West* (New York: W. W. Norton and Company, 1991), Ch. 3.

won the Taveta Parliamentary seat in 1997. Criticos has been accused of encouraging peasants to squat on parts of his estate in exchange for their votes.[24] These peasants use the land to grow various crops. Criticos also mortgaged 15,000 acres of his estate, on which politically supportive squatters were located, to the National Bank of Kenya and defaulted on the loan. The Bank then foreclosed on the property and sold it to the government of Kenya, which decided to settle squatters on it.[25]

On the one hand, the gains that squatting farmers received from these parcels were derived indirectly because they accrued them from their farming activities. The gains of Criticos, on the other hand, accrued directly in that he first "sold" the land to the squatters for their votes and then "sold" the land to the bank for money, in both cases deriving benefits that were divorced from the productive use of the land.

Leaders whose gains are drawn indirectly from land have a preference for strong property rights institutions. This is because the agricultural, real estate, tourism, and mining operations from which they draw economic and political gains are heavily dependent on these institutions. A significant literature exists on how secure land rights and titles facilitate and render more profitable these economic activities. Security encourages people to invest in these productive activities without fear of losing their farms, apartment buildings, or hotels before they profit from them. The low cost of private protection and litigation over land rights increases the amounts of funds available for investment and also increases the gains from such investment.

Titles allow people to use their properties as collateral for loans to invest in these productive activities. Further, security releases labor for productive activities by obviating the need to sit on and physically protect land rights. Uncertainty over rights, insecure titles, and the high costs of private protection make productive activities such as farming and real estate development more difficult and less profitable, even if possible.[26] Political leaders involved in indirect ways of using land thus

---

[24] Interviews with official of the Taita Taveta District Lands office (Ken 58), May 11, 2005; and a Taveta elder in Taveta (Ken 65), May 13, 2005.

[25] "Kivutha: Criticos owes the president an apology," *Kenya Broadcasting Corporation*, September 28, 2007. http://www.kbc.co.ke/story.asp?ID=45329. (Accessed January 23, 2008.)

[26] World Bank, *Building Institutions for Markets*, pp. 31–35; Goldstein and Udry, "The profits of power"; Joireman, "Enforcing new property rights," pp. 465–466; "The agenda of positive change," *Accra Mail*, February, 4 2002; "Land banks to attract investors," *Ghanaian Chronicle* (Accra), November 28, 2001; and "Reserve lands for investors," *Ghanaian Chronicle* (Accra), October 4, 1999.

seek to reinforce property rights institutions to maximize their gains from land.

Leaders whose gains are drawn directly and are not mediated by the productive use of the land have very different incentives. Since their gains are not drawn from the eventual productive uses to which land may be put, they have little incentive to undertake the costly task of establishing property rights institutions that facilitate these activities. The continuation of an environment of weak rights imposes little costs on them in this regard. Even more importantly, they often find that weak institutions and the foggy environment that they create make the direct means through which they draw gains from land easier and more profitable. Below are four micro-mechanisms through which this occurs.

1. Facilitating the Political Market in Land/Solving the Aflao Problem. When the people of Aflao in Ghana asked the Convention Peoples Party (CPP) to provide them with pipe-borne water during campaigns for pre-independence by-elections in 1956, CPP strongman Krobo Edusei gave them a disturbing but insightful answer: "You think I am a fool to give you water to drink and vote against me? After the election if you vote CPP, I will give you water to drink."[27] Both sides in this dispute were suffering from two common problems that can prevent the consummation of mutually desirable political exchanges: (i) the inability of politicians to credibly threaten to punish voters who accept gifts but fail to render support afterwards, and (ii) the inability of voters to credibly commit to render support once they receive the gifts.

These problems arose because, once Edusei had delivered a pipe-borne water system, it would have been difficult for him to take it back; the people of Aflao would have had secure rights to the system, just by virtue of its very nature. Given this, they would have been able to defy him and vote their conscience or for other vote buyers after they received the water without fear of the system being taken away by the CPP. The people of Aflao thus found it difficult to convince Krobo Edusei that they would not renege on their pledge once they received the water for the same reason. This acceptance of favors followed by a refusal to render services in return is a situation with which many politicians are all too familiar. Politicians routinely make extravagant promises before elections but do not always return to deliver on them once they get the

[27] Quoted in Rathbone, *Nkrumah and the Chiefs*, p. 133.

votes they need. As a politician, Krobo Edusei's suspicions were thus understandable.

Here we have what we can call the Aflao problem. Two parties that are mutually willing to consummate a political exchange cannot do so because of the secure rights that voters are likely to have over one of the main items to be exchanged: a market failure. These problems arise because the market for political support is a spot market only in very rare cases. Cases in which politicians hand out gifts in exchange for the immediate handover of voter cards or attendance of a rally are rare. Most of the time people receive gifts in exchange for a later vote or other political service. Scholars have reflected on the enforcement as well as the monitoring problems that arise in such vote-buying schemes.[28]

The Aflao problem also threatens the exchange of land for support where the institutions that govern land rights are robust and well-functioning. It becomes difficult for politicians offering land parcels to credibly commit to punish grantees that receive the land but later refuse to render political support. The security of rights means that politicians cannot repossess the land once the grant is made. Knowing this, the grantees are then able to sell their support to yet another politician or just act on their conscience. This is especially true where grantees lack other interests that can be harmed by political leaders. Thus, in an environment of secure property rights, politicians willing to offer land for political support, and voters willing to sell their support for land grants may still find it difficult to complete such transactions despite their mutual willingness.

Weak property rights institutions solve the Aflao problem and keep the political market in land operational. On the one hand, they allow politicians to credibly threaten to punish grantees by taking back these lands if they fail to deliver support once they receive land parcels. On the other hand, weak rights allow people looking to peddle their support for land to credibly commit to render support once they receive land. They can assure the politician of their intent to comply by pointing to their knowledge that their continued enjoyment of rights after the elections depends on the goodwill of the politician. As I show below,

---

[28] Valeria Brusco, Marcelo Nazareno, and Susan Stokes, "Vote buying in Argentina," *Latin American Research Review* 39 (June 2004); Chin-Shou Wang and Charles Kurzman, "The logistics: how to buy votes," in Frederic Schaffer, ed. *Elections for Sale: The Causes and Consequences of Vote Buying* (Boulder, CO: Lynne Reinner, 2007); and "What is vote buying," in Schaffer, ed. *Elections for Sale*, pp. 19–25.

an effort at obviating the Aflao problem is the main reason why generations of colonial and postcolonial officials in Ghana have refrained from reinforcing institutions that secure land rights in most of the country.

2. *Gerrymandering Without Redrawing Boundaries.* Political leaders facing competition during elections often feel the need to change the voting composition of certain constituencies to increase their support and reduce that of their opponents. One way to do this is to redraw constituency boundaries – a practice commonly known as gerrymandering. By changing the boundaries of the constituencies, politicians map out areas populated by opposition supporters and map in more loyal followers. Alternatively, they can change boundaries to inject the likely foes of opposing politicians into the constituencies of those politicians in order to limit their chances of winning elections. But politicians do not always have the power to redraw constituency boundaries. So, in the absence of this power, some resort to the clever practice of gerrymandering by reorganizing land ownership patterns. They expel opposition supporters and bring in friendly voters or undercut opponents by flooding their constituencies with voters that are known to oppose them.

Weak property rights are invaluable in enabling this practice. They allow one to evict hostile voters and bring in loyal ones without resorting to the very expensive and cumbersome mechanisms of the market and courts. Leaders in such an environment can increase their chances of winning elections in their constituency by mobilizing forces to throw out opponents and award their rights to supporters who are sometimes brought in from other areas. Politicians can also harm the chances of opponents by evicting their supporters and awarding their rights to new residents who are unlikely to vote for those opponents. In these situations, as per the logic of the Aflao problem described above, the precariousness of rights also gives newly settled people an incentive to obey political leaders since they risk losing their new rights otherwise. Such attempts at gerrymandering constituencies by KANU politicians in Kenya through the eviction and settlement of people led to over 1500 deaths and 300,000 displacements in the 1990s.[29]

3. *Enabling Fraudulent Emergency Fundraising for Political Action.*
When leaders face political crises that threaten their survival, they often

---

[29] IDMC, "'I am a refugee,'" p. 13.

require substantial amounts of resources on short notice to stave off opposition. These resources go into recruiting and arming militia, buying votes and other forms of political support, organizing rallies, etc. Where leaders profit from land through sales, weak property rights institutions such as faulty title registries and corrupt and ineffective judicial systems can allow them to multiply their gains from land over the short run.

Instead of selling each parcel once, they can sell the same rights to two or three different people. Also, they can deviously grant the same land parcel to two or three individuals or groups simultaneously in exchange for support. Similarly, they can sell land to which they have no rights. In the absence of functional title registries, buyers have a difficult time checking for encumbrances on land before they buy. Once they buy such plots, a weak judicial system makes it difficult for them to bring the politician to justice.

These fraudulent schemes by politicians are socially costly. They cause litigation between alternative grantees of the land and sometimes result in violent confrontations. They can also reduce the gains that politicians make from land over the long run. As people realize the uncertain nature of the land rights offered by politicians, they may reduce the amounts they offer for these plots, leading to declines in land sellers' profit margins. It is critical to note here that these potential long-term losses do not always dissuade politicians embroiled in crises from pursing this course of action. After all, without the help of these short-term resources, they might not survive to enjoy long-term gains.

Chapter 5 discusses how Kenyan KANU politicians in the 1990s engaged in the fraudulent multiple sales of land to build up their campaign chests in an effort to stave off competition from opposition parties after the return to multiparty democracy. But as Chapter 6 shows, the activities of these politicians were not new. In the 1970s, aspiring Kenyan politicians engaged in a decade of fraudulent sales of encumbered rights as they sought to gain power and prevent Vice President Daniel arap Moi from succeeding President Jomo Kenyatta.

4. *Allowing Land-Hungry Leaders to Reallocate Existing Grants.* Weak property rights institutions come in handy in enabling land-hungry leaders to renegotiate or reallocate already-sold land. This usually occurs in cases where political leaders are dependent on the sale of land for their revenues. In such a situation the amount of land available to leaders shrinks with each grant made. Given the incentive of present rulers to make as many sales as they can, the situation is soon reached where there is little or no land for them to sell, leaving them without revenues. In such a situation, weak property rights institutions allow leaders to reallocate existing grants and resell land that has already been sold. This activity takes various forms. Leaders sell lands that had been granted by their predecessors or that they themselves had already granted to new buyers. Alternatively, they threaten present holders to buy the land all over again or risk losing it. They also grant rights belonging to other sellers that they have no right to alienate.

These practices could, over time, lead buyers to reduce the amounts they offer for land in accordance with how many times they expect to pay for the land and how many other people they think might be sold the same land. But for these desperate leaders, the choice is between receiving a fraction of the price that they can get for one strong grant by abrogating existing grants and receiving nothing by upholding existing grants. The choice of making one strong, reputable grant that buyers will be willing to pay a prime price for is out of the question. Weak property rights are convenient here because they enable these leaders to essentially confiscate the whole or part of the property of landholders by forcing them to pay more for their property or risk losing the property altogether. Weak property institutions also allow leaders to allocated these properties to new buyers altogether. Chiefs in the Ga Traditional Area in Ghana are notorious for such allocation of already allocated land and for their efforts at undermining the judiciary and police force that could prevent their activities.[30]

These diverse benefits of an environment of weak property rights give political leaders who draw gains from land that are unmediated by productive activities an interest in preserving weak property rights as land values increase.

It should be clarified here that the distinction drawn between direct and indirect ways of using land is not a judgmental one between meaningful versus nonmeaningful, or good and bad, ways of using land. The categorization is only an analytic instrument to help us make sense of leaders' preference for secure or insecure rights. It distinguishes between direct modes of drawing gains from land that allow politicians to benefit from fraudulent and sometimes criminal activities facilitated by weak property rights and indirect modes that punish leaders who cultivate

---

[30] "Chiefs, plots, and lands department," *Ghanaian Chronicle* (Accra), December 10, 2001; "Menace of land guards evokes fear in capital," *Africanews* 40–42, July 20, 1999, http://lists.peacelink.it/afrinews/msg00022.html. (Accessed April 18, 2007.)

insecurity. Direct ways of drawing gains from land are not inherently less meaningful or less beneficial to society. The sale of land in itself does not constitute a criminal or socially unbeneficial activity, and most ordinary people who sell land do not engage in fraudulent sales. de Soto has cleverly demonstrated how secondary markets where securities like titles are traded can generate capital for various economic activities.[31] The point here is that these ways of using land often allow politicians to benefit from their fraudulent and violent exploitation through the subversion of property institutions in ways that the indirect extraction of gains from land does not permit.

Secondary markets in titles represent a good example here. KANU politicians and their allies, looking for cash to fund campaigns in the 1990s, set upon secondary markets in Kenya to very negative effects. Many of them took out loans from banks using problematic, illegal, and irregular land titles as collateral.[32] To achieve this, they had to tamper with Ministry of Lands records that banks could use to determine the validity of titles. They also had to get Ministry of Lands officials to vouch for the validity of what they knew were problematic titles[33] and connive with some bankers.

Loans were taken out with titles drawn up for public lands, state properties and state forests, among other properties, in the 1990s.[34] When the new National Rainbow Coalition government threatened to cancel up to 200,000 titles in 2004, the Kenya Bankers' Association, Law Society of Kenya, Kenya Institute of Planners, and Institution of Surveyors of Kenya all voiced deep concern over the damage to secondary markets and the general economy that would be wrought by the move.[35] Banks stood to lose USD 844,155 borrowed on forest lands in the Rift Valley Province alone.[36] Joseph Wanyela, the Chairperson of the Kenya Bankers Association, expressed bankers' concerns over these threats of cancellation

---

[31] de Soto, *The Mystery of Capital*.

[32] Kenya, *Report of the Commission of Inquiry into the Illegal/Irregular*, p. 68.

[33] An angry head of the Kenya Bankers Association pointed out that when the state threatened to revoke such problematic titles in 2004, banks always cleared titles with the state before accepting them as collateral. "How should the Ndung'u Report recommendations be implemented? What Kenyans say," *Land Update, Kenya Land Alliance* 3 (October–December 2004), p. 12.

[34] Kenya, *Report of the Commission of Inquiry into the Illegal/Irregular*, p. 68.

[35] "Kenya starts process to cancel 12,000 title deeds," *The East African* (Nairobi), February 28, 2005; "Ndung'u Report: Kimunya 'can't cancel' bad titles," *Daily Nation* (Nairobi), January 24, 2005; and "How should the Ndung'u Report," p. 11.

[36] "Kenyan ministers' row over 'grabbed' forest land deepens division in NARC," *The East African* (Nairobi), April 4, 2005.

succinctly. "What the threats have best achieved is that they have created a lot of confusion among traders.... Many transactions have stalled because of the uncertainty that surrounds title deeds. We do not know which ones the government will declare genuine."[37]

The Ndung'u Commission of Inquiry that recommended the revocation of these titles was quick to reject claims of victimization by banks, pointing out that some bankers were partly responsible for the problems. Banks had given out loans to private individuals offering collateral that included titles for plots on which state military barracks and high courts were located![38] By undermining various land administration institutions, politically connected individuals had fraudulently exploited secondary markets in securities that, if well functioning, should have had a positive impact on the Kenyan macro-economy.

The placement of gains from mining in the indirect category that gives leaders a preference for land rights security seems to fly in the face of literature on the resource curse. This literature includes the correlation between reliance on minerals and bad institutional outcomes[39] and wars. It also seems to belie the apparent skill of some African leaders in extracting natural resources in highly insecure environments.[40] Scholars have specifically emphasized the extent to which leaders deliberately avoid any efforts at constructing formal institutions in such spheres, thriving instead on an environment of informality.[41]

---

[37] "How should the Ndung'u Report," p. 13.

[38] Kenya, *Report of the Commission of Inquiry into the Illegal/Irregular*, p. 66.

[39] See Terry Karl, *The Paradox of Plenty: Oil Booms and Petro-States* (Berkeley: University of California Press, 1997); Paul Collier, *The Bottom Billion: Why the Poorest Countries Are Failing and What Can Be Done About It* (New York: Oxford University Press, 2007), Ch. 3; Michael Ross, "The political economy of the resource curse," *World Politics* 51 (January 1999); Indra de Soysa, "The resource curse: are civil wars driven by rapacity or paucity?" in Mats Berdal and David Malone, eds. *Greed and Grievance: Economic Agendas in Civil Wars* (Boulder, CO: Lynne Rienner, 2000); Paul Collier, "Doing well out of war: an economic perspective" in Mats Berdal and David Malone, eds. *Greed and Grievance*; and Paul Richards, *Fighting for the Rain Forest: War, Youth and Resources in Sierra Leone* (Oxford: James Currey, 1996).

[40] See Reno, *Warlord Politics*; Musifiky Mwanasali, "The view from below," in Mats Berdal and David Malone, eds. *Greed and Grievance: Economic Agendas in Civil Wars* (Boulder, CO: Lynne Rienner, 2000); William Reno, "Shadow states and the political economy of civil wars," in Mats Berdal and David Malone, eds. *Greed and Grievance: Economic Agendas in Civil Wars* (Boulder, CO: Lynne Rienner, 2000), pp. 56–60; and Stephen Ellis, *Mask of Anarchy: The Destruction of Liberia and the Religious Dimensions of an African Civil War* (New York: New York University Press, 1999), 164–180.

[41] Reno, *Warlord Politics*, p. 3; Reno, "Shadow states," p. 53; and Musifiky Mwanasali, "The view from below," p. 139.

However, my claim is not inconsistent with this literature. This is partly because I am not commenting on whether the possession of these resources will generate growth or lead to greater political order in countries. I am only making the limited claim that leaders would want strong property rights institutions that ensure enough security in such areas to facilitate the extraction of these minerals.

In the more stable African countries, the validity of this is clear. Leaders in these countries often make strenuous efforts to guarantee security in areas in which they extract key minerals by deploying various formal institutions, as suggested by my argument. These mining regions sometimes have the tightest security as a result, including the requirement of special permits for entry. This is the case with the mining town of Orapa in Botswana. But, as I point out in Chapter 3 of this work, even Ghanaian state leaders who have deliberately paid little attention to property security in much of the country have always done a lot to ensure security in the concessions of mining companies. They do so because they see these areas as the economic nerve center of the state and their governments.

There is evidence that even occurrences in more conflict-ridden countries do not undermine the claim that leaders have a preference for strong institutions that will guarantee security of rights in these areas. A first step in realizing this should be a move away from interpreting their informalization of institutions and dexterity at exploiting resources in these unstable environments as a preference for insecurity and informalization. As Reno, a key contributor to the literature on resource wars and warlord politics, points out, leaders resort to such thorough informalization only because formalization threatens to shift power to their opponents.[42] In other words, informalization and its skilled exploitation are responses to a certain strategic context, not necessarily evidence of the preference of leaders.

Indeed there is evidence that even these warlords and bandits invest a lot in ensuring security in mining areas. Often this takes place while they shirk any such responsibility in the rest of their realm or even deliberately spread insecurity elsewhere. This sometimes involves deploying elite forces from friendly states to these areas as happened in the Democratic Republic of Congo where Zimbabwean Defense Force members were involved in protecting mines for President Laurent Kabila and his allies.[43]

---

[42] Reno, *Warlord Politics*, pp. 1–7; and Chabal and Daloz, *Africa Works*, pp. 88–89.
[43] Reno, "Shadow states," p. 57.

At other times ensuring security in these areas has taken the form of hiring various mercenary private security firms. The South African firm Executive Outcomes, among others, was thus very active in counterinsurgency and protecting mining areas in Angola and Sierra Leone.[44] Sometimes mines are simply handed over to these mining/security firms in exchange for lump payments.[45] Like more stable countries that often try to restrict civilian activity in such areas, some of these leaders and rebels depopulate mining areas to better ensure security and monopolize benefits from mines.[46] Generally, since these mines often provide leaders of stable as well as unstable areas with key resources to perpetuate their rule, ensuring enough security to extract resources, as my argument predicts, makes a lot of sense and characterizes the approach of leaders in areas both stable and conflict-ridden.

Capacity: Translating Preferences into Institutions

As revisionists such as Feeney, Riker and Sened, Firmin-Sellers, Knight, and Joireman have noted, preferences do not automatically translate into actual institutions.[47] Considering the ability of elites to bring about their institutional preferences is critical for two reasons. First, as will be demonstrated in the empirical chapters, even within the same country or region there are always multiple forces with diverse interests concerning whether property institutions should be reinforced. It is thus very important to show why the preferences of certain groups are translated into institutional outcomes while those of others remain mere preferences. At an initial and very fundamental level, there is the conflict between supporters and opponents of an institutional structure that either enhances security or perpetuates insecurity of property rights. Disagreement exists at another level: within a group that supports either secure or insecure property rights. This is because, as Knight and Firmin-Sellers have noted, there are multiple ways of designing institutions to facilitate security, and each design has different distributional consequences.[48]

---

[44] Reno, *Warlord Politics*, pp. 129–131, Chabal and Daloz, *Africa Works*, pp. 88–89; Richards, *Fighting for the Rain Forest*, p. 17.

[45] Richards, *Fighting for the Rain Forest*, p. 17.

[46] Reno, "Shadow states," p. 57.

[47] Feeney, "The development," p. 273; and Riker and Sened, "A political theory," p. 953. Firmin-Sellers, *The Transformation*; Knight, *Institutions and Social Conflict*; Joireman, "Enforcing new property rights."

[48] Knight, *Institutions and Social Conflict*; Firmin-Sellers, *The Transformation*, pp. 11–12.

A system of individual freehold might benefit some while disadvantaging others who might prefer a system of communal tenure. Therefore, elites seeking to impose secure property rights, for instance, face the challenges of (1) collaborating within their group to (2) coerce societal members opposed to the security of rights.[49] This book pays a lot of attention to conflict between supporters and opponents of property rights security because it is a fundamental one that has been largely ignored in the literature on the emergence, transformation, and persistence of property rights institutions.

Second, most of the institutions that are the subject of this book are so costly that even in the absence of opponents, a high level of capacity is required for their creation and maintenance. Cadastral surveys to enable title registration are very costly. Once these surveys are carried out, hiring, training, and paying professionals with the technical ability to register and keep proper and easily accessible records on titles and deeds is also expensive. Creating tribunals to adjudicate land disputes and marshaling institutions to monitor and enforce rights across a country are also costly. Even where leaders face no opposition, it is not a foregone conclusion that they will be able to create and ensure the proper functioning of these institutions over time, as we will see in the empirical chapters. We, thus, need the capacity variable to link preferences to outcomes.

Four elements of capacity are focussed on – coercive capacity, control over policymaking, legitimacy, and revenues – to gauge elites' ability to bring about their institutional preferences. Coercive capacity includes police forces, private militias, and administrative organizations that can compel and monitor behavior. These institutions are most adept at the exercise of brute force. The strength of coercive institutions depends on their size, the extent of their logistical supplies, and the ability of elites to control ground officers. Principal-agent problems and the capture of lower-level officials by social groups can weaken the ability of senior officials and politicians.

Closely related to coercive capacity is legitimacy, the extent to which the populace regards the orders of leaders as "obligatory or exemplary."[50] Where considered legitimate, the urge to obey such authority

---

[49] Moe, "Power and political institutions," p. 215.
[50] Max Weber, *Economy and Society: An Outline of Interpretive Sociology* (Berkeley: University of California Press, 1978), p. 31.

comes from reasons that go beyond coercion and crass expediency calculations to involve reflections about the validity of such authority.[51] Legitimacy is significant because it reduces the costs of creating institutions by obviating the need to back up every project with raw coercion and material incentives.[52]

Revenues are also important because they can be transformed into political resources to create and fund property rights institutions. The consideration of revenues raises the danger of endogeneity because the amount of revenues rulers have might depend on the property rights institutions that exist in their realm. But we can uncouple the two because African leaders often accrue a great deal of their revenues from foreign aid and mineral revenues that have little to do with wider property rights arrangements in their country.[53] Further, a regime of secure property rights in land does not, in itself, guarantee high investment, healthy economic growth, or large revenue streams.[54]

Policymaking authority directs how coercive capacity is used. Elites' control over policymaking concerns the extent to which they concentrate decision-making power through control of legislative and various executive decision-making agencies.

Even though capacity has a significant effect on property rights institutions, it affects the various outcomes under study differently because subverting rights institutions is much less difficult than building and reinforcing them. For instance, creating title registries requires a high level of capacity, but these same registries can be destroyed easily by torching registry buildings.

It will be clear from the empirical analysis that the capacity of political leaders and their opponents depends on both state and nonstate sources. Many of the leaders discussed here preside over state machineries. Discussion of their capacity is thus often a commentary on the capacity of the state over which they preside. But some of these leaders, such as traditional chiefs, draw most of their capacity from nonstate sources such as private militia. Even state leaders sometimes have connections to, and make use of, such nonstate sources of capacity.

---

[51] Ibid.
[52] North, *Structure and Change*, p. 53.
[53] Robert Bates, *Prosperity and Violence: The Political Economy of Development* (London: W. W. Norton, 2001).
[54] Ngugi, "Re-examining the role."

Divergent Institutional Choices

We distinguish between four types of responses by political leaders. *Reinforcement* occurs when leaders create and strengthen institutions, make and implement laws and policies, and boost the manpower and logistical resources of these institutions. *Subversion* occurs when elites oppose the establishment of institutions, undermine the manpower and logistical supplies of institutions, and undercut professional standards and operating procedures. With *limited enhancement*, laws and policies that would strengthen institutions are made, but these are accompanied by little effort at implementation. Administrative structures that implement laws are not established or empowered to operate well. *Neglect* occurs when leaders do little to make policies that either strengthen or weaken institutions. While with limited enhancement insufficient efforts are made to implement policies, with neglect no effort is made to implement policies where they inadvertently extend to areas that elites wish to disregard.

The designation of each action within a category is partly an interpretive exercise that locates that action within a set of actions undertaken by leaders. For instance, the way in which we characterize the passage of national laws depends on whether and how elites seek to implement them. If they consistently concentrate implementation efforts in District A of a country that is overwhelmingly targeted for rule enforcement in other ways, then we might characterize their response in the rest of the country as neglect rather than limited enhancement. The national nature of the laws might be simply an artifact of the character of law-making instead of any effort to target property rights institutions in places outside of District A.

Many of the efforts aimed at creating and strengthening institutions that secure land rights discussed here predate the introduction of neoliberal reforms in African countries. But they have much in common with what have come to be termed "second-generation neoliberal reforms." These are efforts at creating market-friendly institutions such as property rights, the rule of law, and contract enforcement to help states realize the potential benefits of "first-generation" macroeconomic reforms.[55] In line

---

[55] Moises Naím, *Latin America's Journey to the Market: From Macroeconomic Shocks to Institutional Therapy, Occasional Papers; No. 62* (San Francisco: ICS Press, 1995); World Bank, *The State in a Changing World: World Development Report 1997* (New York: Oxford University Press, 1997), p. 152; and World Bank, *Building Institutions for Markets*, pp. 4–7.

with these reform recommendations, states such as Ghana, Uganda, and Tanzania are in the process of serious land administration reforms.

Explaining Institutional Choice in Botswana, Ghana, and Kenya

Rising land values have increased the potential economic and political gains to be derived from land. The accrual of these benefits has to be facilitated by the creation of suitable institutions. The kinds of institutional environments that various leaders have seen as suitable has depended on how they have extracted gains from land. Further, the extent to which leaders have been able to transform their preferences into actual institutional outcomes has depended on their capacity. Leaders who have exploited gains from land in indirect ways have developed a preference for strong institutions that secure rights in land. Leaders in three of the cases in this book fall into this category. In Botswana and Early Kenya (1963–1990), state leaders were heavily involved in the productive use of land, as were traditional chiefs in the Akyem Abuakwa Traditional Area of Ghana since the reign of Nana Ofori Atta (1930–1999).

Batswana and Kenyan leaders drew extensive gains from farming, real estate and tourism concerns.[56] The high capacity of these Kenyan and Batswana elites allowed them to create new institutions and reinforce old ones such as land tribunals, land title registries, land control boards, land adjudication and settlement departments, etc. Chiefs in post–Ofori Atta Akyem Abuakwa who were also heavily invested in farming had less capacity. While these leaders have succeeded in creating an environment of security,[57] their weak capacity has prevented them from creating

---

[56] Isaac Ncube Mazonde, *Ranching and Enterprise in Eastern Botswana: A Case Study of Black and White Farmers* (Edinburgh: Edinburgh University Press for the International African Institute London, 1994), p. 21; Richard Werbner, *Reasonable Radicals and Citizenship in Botswana: The Public Anthropology of Kalanga Elites* (Bloomington: Indiana University Press, 2004), pp. 80–81; Holm, "Botswana," p. 186; James Gatanyu Karuga, "Land transactions in Kiambu," *Institute for Development Studies University of Nairobi, No. 58, Working Paper 58* (1972), p. 15; Holmquist, Weaver and Ford, "The structural development," p. 79; Peter Anyang' Nyong'o, "State and society in Kenya: The disintegration of the nationalist coalitions and the rise of presidential authoritarianism, 1963–1978," *African Affairs* 88 (351–1989, p. 247; and Interview with an official of the Lands Commission in Accra (Gh 1), September 24, 2004; and Addo-Fening, *Akyem Abuakwa*

[57] Interview with an official of the Lands Commission in Accra (Gh 1), September 24, 2004; and Addo-Fening, *Akyem Abuakwa* and Polly Hill, *The Gold Coast Cocoa Farmer: A Preliminary Survey* (London: Oxford University Press, 1956), p. 13; Great Britain, *Report*

title and deed registries, undertaking surveys and setting up expensive adjudicative mechanisms that we see in Botswana and Early Kenya, restricting their response to one of limited enhancement.

Unlike the leaders above, Ghanaian state leaders, elites in Late Kenya (1991–2000), and chiefs in the Ga Traditional Area and Akyem Abuakwa before the reign of Nana Ofori Atta (mid-1800s–1920s) all drew significant gains from land in direct ways unmediated by the productive use of land. Ga and pre–Ofori Atta Akyem chiefs sold land rights and used land to reward supporters and punish opponents.[58] Colonial and postcolonial leaders in Ghana used land in most of the country to buy the compliance of traditional chiefs.[59] In Kenya, elites in the 1990s used land rights to gerrymander constituencies, sold land to muster funds for campaigns, and generally rewarded supporters and punished opponents with land rights.[60]

All of these leaders either neglected or actively undermined institutions that govern land rights to facilitate their activities. In Ghana state leaders lacking sufficient capacity simply neglected institutions in much of the country to create an environment of uncertainty over rights that allowed them to credibly threaten and expropriate the land rights of chiefs who refused to be cooperative. The effects of the weak capacity of the state were most evident in the few enclaves that state leaders saw as critical to the survival of the state. These hosted military barracks and government ministries, and housed vital sources of state revenues such as mines and industries. Efforts at creating these islands of security resulted at best in the limited enhancement of institutions because of the weak capacity of the state.[61] Without effective control over coercive forces and policymaking, and lacking sufficient revenues and legitimacy, state leaders struggled to enforce security even in those enclaves.[62]

---

of the Commission on the Marketing of West African Cocoa, Vol. 5845. [Parliamentary papers] Cmd. (London: H. M. Stationary Office, 1938), p. 19.

[58] R. J. H. Pogucki, *Land Tenure in Ga Customary Law* (Accra: Government Printer, 1955), p. 31.

[59] Bentsi-Enchill, *Ghana Land Law*, p. 19; Rathbone, *Nkrumah and the Chiefs*, p. 129; Administration of Lands Act 1962.

[60] Kenya, *Report of the Commission of Inquiry into the Illegal/Irregular*; and Kenya, *Report of the Judicial Commission Appointed to Inquire into Tribal Clashes*.

[61] Mahama and Dixon, "Acquisition and affordability," p. 37; and "Reserve land for investors," *Ghanaian Chronicle* (Accra), October 4, 1999.

[62] Ghana, *National Land Policy* (Accra: The Ministry of Lands and Forestry, 1999), pp. 3–4.

Highly capable elites in Late Kenya launched an outright assault on institutions that severely undermined the system that they had invested in creating earlier. The environment of uncertainty that resulted from these attacks facilitated their efforts at threatening the property rights of would-be opponents, rewarding supporters, throwing out opposition supporters from certain constituencies, etc. The forceful subversion of institutions was best captured in the bold declaration by the Minister of Local Government in the early 1990s that land titles are "mere pieces of paper."[63]

In pre–Ofori Atta Akyem Abuakwa and the Ga Traditional Area of Ghana, land-selling chiefs had little incentive to create autonomous institutions that would guarantee property rights in land. They were not involved in the productive use of land, which benefits tremendously from these institutions. Even more importantly, these chiefs soon developed a preference for weak property rights institutions to enable them to resell already-sold land. Assuming that the land possessed by each chief is fixed, every sale shrinks the land available for the existing and following chiefs to allocate. As land becomes scarce, chiefs develop more of an incentive to abrogate rights already allocated by their predecessors and to reallocate land. Such multiple sales of the same piece of land and sales of land to which chiefs have had no rights proliferated in the Ga and Akyem Abuakwa Traditional Areas during this period.[64]

Because such reallocation is difficult where autonomous institutions guarantee allocated rights, chiefs began to favor weak institutions. Such reallocation transformed rights sold by these chiefs into a good of uncertain quality akin to those written of by Akerlof.[65] Some buyers who were aware of the uncertain quality of the rights on sale tried to get more certain land from state agencies instead, when they could afford the higher prices. Others simply hedged their bets by lowering the price they paid for rights sold by chiefs.[66] But for chiefs, these lower prices did not constitute a tragedy. After all, the options they faced were to get nothing from these

[63] "The indigenous and the natives," *Weekly Review* (Nairobi), July 9, 1993.

[64] Anne Phillips, *The Enigma of Colonialism: British Policy in West Africa* (London: James Currey, 1989), pp. 64–65; Ilegbune, "Concessions scramble," pp. 17–23; and Firmin-Sellers, *The Transformation*, p. 52.

[65] George Akerlof, "The Market for 'Lemons': Quality Uncertainty and the Market Mechanism." *Quarterly Journal of Economics*, 84 (August 1970).

[66] Phillips, *The Enigma*, pp. 64–65; and Mahama and Dixon, "Acquisition and affordability," p. 24.

lands by respecting existing grants, or to get a fraction of the price by reallocating rights to lands already allocated by their predecessors.

However, the maintenance of an environment of insecurity led to further problems. Crafty con men recognized the opportunity to manipulate the paucity of institutions to sell land they did not own. Chiefs could not always keep these actors from cashing in on the racket. This led to further insecurity because rights to the same land were sold by multiple sellers, leading to the creation of many conflicting interests. Further, once buyers lowered how much they offered for parcels, chiefs began to see no harm in selling even lands that belonged to other chiefs, leading to the creation of even more conflicting interests. Efforts at seeking solutions to the conflicts spawned by these activities have led to a proliferation of litigation and the creation of private enforcers known as *landguards*, who are employed to defend and contest land rights in the Ga Traditional Area.[67]

Many chiefs in the Ga Traditional Area employed their limited capacity to maintain the weak institutions that facilitate activities such as the reallocation of already-allocated plots.[68] This took place in the face of opposition by many landlords and residents' associations formed to protect ordinary people from the predatory activities of various con men and chiefs. Beyond failing to establish documentation and credible adjudication systems, some chiefs have cultivated armed militia that violently suppress these residents' associations. Further, many chiefs have undermined state efforts at ensuring security in various enclaves in the Ga Traditional Area by bribing police, judicial officials, and land administrators.[69]

In Akyem Abuakwa, heightened conflict between the Okyenhene and lower chiefs transformed many traditional leaders into farmers and eliminated their interests in weak property rights by ensuring that they gained little from such multiple allocation and reallocation of land. No such transition occurred in the Ga Traditional Area.

---

[67] Center for Democracy and Development (Ghana), *Corruption and Other Constraints on the Land Market and Land Administration in Ghana: A Preliminary Investigation*, Vol. 4, *Cdd-Ghana Research Paper* (Legon: Center for Democracy and Development, 2000), p. 19.

[68] Interviews with an official of the Lands Commission, Accra (Gh 2), September 24, 2004; another official of the Lands Commission in Accra (Gh 1), September 24, 2004; a long-term employee of a real estate development agency in Accra (Gh iv), July 13, 2002; and the chairman of a landlords and residents association in the Ga Traditional Area (Gh ii), July 10, 2002.

[69] "Chiefs, plots, and lands department," *Ghanaian Chronicle* (Accra), December 10, 2001.

TABLE 2.1. *Use, Capacity, Outcomes, and Cases*

Capacity	Mode of Exploiting Land	
	Indirect	Direct
High	Reinforcement • Botswana • Early Kenya	Subversion • Late Kenya
Low	Limited enhancement • *Post–Ofori Atta Akyem Abuakwa* • Ghana (Enclaves)	Neglect • Ghana • *Ga* • Pre–Ofori Atta Akyem Abuakwa

Table 2.1 summarizes the location of various cases studied here in relation to the two explanatory variables.

This argument, which asserts that how political leaders use land impacts how they deal with property rights, complements a literature that has shown that existing institutional environments impact the ways in which people seek to use land.[70] Institutional environments do influence how people use land, and, because political leaders know this, they seek to create various institutional environments based on how they, their allies, and opponents extract political and economic gains from the land.

The temporal nature of much of the analysis in this book allows us to avoid the potential vicious cycle of arguing that institutions impact how people use land and how people use land impacts the institutions they create. What we have instead is a theoretical story about the positive feedback effect of property rights institutions in many of the settings discussed. In Ghana, colonial leaders seeking to establish the right environment to facilitate indirect rule adopted the dual strategy of neglecting property rights in most of the country and at the same time focusing efforts on institutional creation in various enclaves.

When postcolonial leaders such as Kwame Nkrumah took over, the existence of this dualistic approach to property rights institutions made the continued use of control over land as a bargaining chip in relations with chiefs attractive. Once these postcolonial leaders began to engage in these bargains with chiefs, they developed an interest in maintaining the dualistic approach. In Ghana, as in many of the other cases studied

---

[70] de Soto, *The Mystery of Capital*, pp. 6–7; and World Bank, *Building Institutions for Markets*, pp. 4–8.

here, we thus witness long-run institutional trajectories characterized by positive feedback effects.

The Relationship between Preferences and Capacity

It is important to address the question of the extent to which the capacity of leaders exerts an independent effect on their preferences. Does the capacity of a leader determine his or her preference for stronger or weaker institutions? Does the security of a leader's hold on power determine the preference that he or she has for stronger or weaker land adjudication tribunals, deeds and title registries, and enforcement mechanisms?

One answer to these questions, and an objection to the analysis in this book, is that the two explanatory variables are not sufficiently independent of each other. The idea here is that capacity exerts an independent effect on the preference of a leader. A leader with a more secure hold on power is more likely to have longer-term horizons, discount the future less, invest in the productive use of land, and create the institutions that will facilitate such use. A leader facing insecurity is more likely to have shorter-term horizons, eschew long-term productive investments in land, manipulate land to fight for political survival, and ensure the persistence of weak institutions that allow him or her to do so. As Levi notes, leaders facing insecurity are "worried less about what was most productive over time and more about how to survive in office (or at all) another year."[71] If this objection were valid, the focus on how leaders draw gains from land and its impact on their preferences would be redundant at best and diversionary at worst.[72]

It is argued in this book that the two variables are sufficiently independent of each other. The objection is flawed on both theoretical and empirical grounds. On theoretical grounds, it unjustifiably conflates efforts at ensuring political survival with the subversion of property rights. It assumes that the best way that all beleaguered politicians can ensure their survival in all contexts is by subverting property rights. But there is no basis for this claim. One can agree with the view expressed by Levi[73] that a leader with an insecure grip on power will scramble to secure his or her

---

[71] Margaret Levi, *Of Rule and Revenue* (Berkeley: University of California Press, 1988), p. 89.

[72] See John Gerring, *Social Science Methodology: A Criterial Framework* (New York: Cambridge University Press, 2001), pp. 142–143, for a discussion of the criterion of independence in causal analysis.

[73] Levi, *Of Rule and Revenue*, p. 89.

hold without agreeing that the best strategy for trying to keep power in all contexts is to undercut the protection of property rights.

The recent subversion of property rights by the Moi administration in Kenya in the 1990s is a good example of a politician undermining security in order to maintain power. The recent antics of Zimbabwe's President Mugabe present more evidence here. But those who wish to generalize from these observations to the broader claim give too little credence to the importance of political context. While the 1990s made subversion of rights a good strategy for President Moi to retain power, it is conceivable that, within other contexts, strengthening those institutions would have been the better strategy.

In fact, as is pointed out in Chapter 6,[74] we saw the working of this logic when the same President Moi tried to overcome early challenges to his rule, which included a military coup after he succeeded Jomo Kenyatta as president of Kenya in 1978. Land-buying company executives led the effort to prevent Moi from succeeding Kenyatta and presented a strong threat to his rule once he did so. The power of these executives was based on the exploitation of the land rights of hundreds of thousands of small landholders in the Central and Rift Valley provinces. President Moi rightly saw the imposition of stronger property institutions that would allow peasants to withdraw support from executives without threats to their land rights as a way of breaking the backs of company executives and ensuring his political survival. This strategy succeeded in spectacular fashion.

Another example is the response of British colonial officials to the vicissitudes of colonial rule in the three countries studied here. The officials did the most to create institutions that govern property rights in the country where their rule faced the most violent challenge – Kenya. Despite the plenitude and intensity of armed resistance, British administrator there meticulously created title registries, survey departments, etc. In fact, the introduction of title registration for blacks through the Swynnerton Plan has been rightly portrayed by some as a deliberate counterinsurgency device by the British.[75] Securing the land rights of black yeomen farmers in Kenya was an instrument for perpetuating power in the face of a bloody anticolonial insurgency. In Botswana, where the British were most secure, faced almost no challenge, and were actually begged by some

[74] See the section titled "'Vanity shares': the refinement and exportation of technologies."

[75] Daniel Branch, "Loyalists, Mau Mau, and elections," p. 28. Also see Ngugi, "Re-examining the role," p. 500; Atieno-Odhiambo, "Hegemonic enterprises," p. 238.

traditional leaders to undertake rule, they did almost nothing to create institutions that govern property. The British left Botswana as one of the poorest countries in the world in terms of institutions and infrastructure at independence. Ghana falls in the middle of this continuum both in terms of challenges to colonial rule and the institutions that leaders created to govern land rights.

The extent of leaders' power cannot predict their preference for secure or insecure rights because the specific strategy that they resort to in order to survive challenges depends on the context in which they are embroiled. Wilkinson makes a similar point in his recent work on political competition and ethnic violence when he points out that heightened competition and the threats it poses to leaders may or may not lead to ethnic violence, depending on contextual factors.[76] Here we can draw insight from Brenner's insistence on the need to consider the impact of contexts in the study of European economic transformation as different contexts led actors in pre-industrial Europe to respond in different ways to similar "demographic or commercial trends."[77]

Another theoretical failing of this view is that it takes steady, secure rule as a settled state of affairs without looking into the finer details of how rule is created, made secure, and maintained over time. Secure leaders are seen as those who face no serious challenges, not as those who are able to continually prevent any serious challenges from materializing or maturing. In these narratives, continued, secure rule becomes a passive end state rather than an active process and something that leaders often have to continuously work at constructing and maintaining in the face of ongoing challenges. Once we begin to understand this, we can begin to recognize that even secure leaders cannot simply forget about all political considerations related to their survival in their decision-making. They have to employ various strategies to buttress their power and suppress would-be challenges. The argument put forth in this book is that leaders do not all use the same strategy, and the method that each leader chooses depends heavily on the specific context in which he or she is located. The refusal to secure rights and so enforce support among various constituencies can be how a leader maintains security over a long period of time.

---

[76] Stephen Wilkinson, *Votes and Violence: Electoral Competition and Ethnic Riots in India* (New York: Cambridge University Press, 2004), pp. 236–239.

[77] Robert Brenner, "The agrarian roots of European capitalism," *Past and Present* 96 (August 1982), p. 16.

On an empirical level, it is tempting to point to Botswana as an example of how security of tenure gives leaders long time horizons and gets them to make and implement socially beneficial policies. The creation and reinforcement of secure land rights may be counted as one example. But those who make such arguments lack a comparative perspective and lose sight of the fact that many other long-lasting and secure leaders in postcolonial Africa have not benefited their countries as much. Among these leaders we can count the late Mobutu Sese Seko of Zaire, Gnassingbe Eyadema of Togo, and Omar Bongo of Gabon. We also have current leaders such as Paul Biya of Cameroon who clearly enjoys secure tenure. Meanwhile, in Rwanda, Paul Kagame's Rwandan Patriotic Front, which has been under constant threat, seems to be building market enhancing institutions that are attracting significant international praise.[78] The leaders of Rwanda probably see these reforms as a way of ensuring their survival in the face of severe challenges. They probably believe that these reforms might give them some legitimacy in the eyes of the international community as well as in some domestic constituencies. Such legitimacy could lead to material and ideological support to enable them to confront the persistent threat of insurgency, condemnation of their suppression of domestic opponents and military undertakings in neighbouring Democratic Republic of Congo.

PART II: WHY INSTITUTIONS EVOLVE: ENDOGENOUS CONTRIBUTIONS TO CHANGE

Why do the institutions that leaders invest so much in constructing sometimes change? While we see much continuity in the institutional choices of Batswana leaders, there was a drastic change in Kenya. In Ghana, there was stability in the choices of state leaders going back to the colonial period until signs of change appeared on the horizon with the election of the New Patriotic Party (NPP) in 2000. Also, while the structure of weak institutions persisted in the Ga Traditional Area, we witnessed a significant shift in the Akyem Abuakwa Traditional Area.

The dominant view in the literature on the new institutionalism is that exogenous shocks are the key causes of change in institutions (like those studied here) that display effects of strong positive

---

[78] "A pioneer with a mountain to climb," *The Economist*, September 25, 2008. http://www.economist.com/world/mideast-africa/displaystory.cfm?story_id=12304755. (Accessed March 2, 2009.)

feedback.[79] These shocks can result in a drastic change in the key actors or the environment within which they operate, thus resulting in institutional transformation.

There is clear evidence of this logic at work in the fomentation of institutional change in Ghana and Kenya. But, because these means of institutional change are already widely discussed in the literature, here we will focus on the less-studied area of endogenous contributions to institutional change. In Chapter 6, where we address this in more empirical detail, insights are drawn from how the institutional innovations of Kenyan con men and non–policymaking politicians contributed to the decline of the system of land documentation in that country.

While some scholars have focused on endogenous contributions to institutional change,[80] few examine specifically how endogenous factors contribute to change in institutions that display strong positive feedback effects.[81] The focus of most work on institutions generally limits the extent to which their insights can be extended to institutions that display positive feedback effects. This is because there are many plausible reasons that would lead us to expect that some institutions might actually contribute to their own downfall. As Mahoney[82] notes, some institutions influence later ones by producing reactions and backlashes that move things in directions that undermine and deviate from the existing institutions that unleashed these dynamics. Demonstrating endogenous contributions to change in institutions that display positive feedback

---

[79] James Mahoney, "Path dependence in historical sociology," *Theory and Society* 29 (April 2000), p. 42; and Ira Katznelson, "Periodization and preferences: reflections on purposive action in comparative historical social science," in James Mahoney and Dietrich Rueschemeyer, eds. *Comparative Historical Analysis in the Social Sciences* (New York: Cambridge University Press, 2003).

[80] Huseyin Leblebici et al, "Institutional change and the transformation of interorganizational fields: an organizational history of the U.S. radio broadcasting industry," *Administrative Science Quarterly* 36, No. 3 (September 1991), pp. 333–337; March Schneiberg, "Combining new institutionalisms: explaining institutional change in American property insurance," *Sociological Forum* 20, No. 1 (March 2005), pp. 106–111; and Paul DiMaggio, "Interest and agency in institutional theory," in Lynne Zucker, ed. *Institutional Patterns and Organizations: Culture and Environment* (Cambridge, MA: Ballinger Publishing Company, 1988), p. 13; Marc Schneiberg and Elisabeth Clemens, "The typical tools for the job: research strategies in institutional analysis," *Sociological Theory* 24, No. 3 (September 2006); and Elisabeth Clemens, "Organizational repertoires and institutional change: women's groups and the transformation of U.S. politics, 1890–1920," *The American Journal of Sociology* 98, No. 4 (January 1993).

[81] One example is Avner Greif and David Laitin, "A theory of endogenous institutional change," *American Political Science Review* 98 (November 2004).

[82] Mahoney, "Path dependence in historical sociology," pp. 526–527.

effects presents us with a tougher puzzle because we are told that, once established, "over time it becomes more and more difficult to transform the pattern or select previously available options."[83] How can these institutions then contribute to their own decline?

Punctuated Equilibrium and Exogenous Shocks

As Thelen and Streeck[84] point out, most of the work on change in institutions that demonstrate positive feedback effects emphasizes sudden discontinuous changes sparked by exogenous shocks. It is said that institutions are characterized by long periods of stability produced by their positive feedback effects.[85] These periods of stability are punctuated by disruptive moments of change–critical junctures – in which exogenous shocks break down institutions, creating periods of contingency that allow agents to choose between alternatives.[86] In many of the cases in this book, we see exogenous shocks sweeping away old policymakers and ushering in new ones or drastically altering the context in which policymakers operate, thus affecting their preferences.

In Ghana, the 2000 elections marked the defeat of National Democratic Congress (NDC) elites who had warmly embraced the long-standing commitment of colonial and postcolonial state leaders to ignoring institutions in most of the country and focusing on a few enclaves. The New Patriotic Party (NPP) politicians who were ushered into office were rooted in the economy in a different way. Having been locked out of national rule for about 20 years, many had resorted to agriculture, real estate development, and other business activities to survive and fund their political activities. They were enmeshed in indirect ways of exploiting land. Predictably, when they came into power, one of their first activities was to proclaim a "Golden Age of Business" and launch an ambitious, 15-year Land Administration Project that included the

---

[83] Mahoney, "Path dependence in historical sociology," p. 508.

[84] Wolfgang Streeck and Kathleen Thelen, "Introduction: institutional change in the advanced political economies," in Wolfgang Streeck and Kathleen Thelen, eds. *Beyond Continuity: Institutional Change in Advanced Political Economies* (New York: Oxford University Press, 2005), pp. 1–2.

[85] Mahoney, "Path dependence in historical sociology;" and Paul Pierson, "Not Just What, but When: Timing and Sequence in Political Processes," *Studies in American Political Development* 14 (Spring 2000).

[86] Paul Pierson, *Politics in Time: History, Institutions, and Political Analysis* (Princeton: Princeton University Press, 2004), p. 144.

establishment of title registries and land adjudication tribunals around the country.[87]

Change at the subnational level in rural Akyem Abuakwa similarly has given credence to the importance of exogenous shocks to instigating institutional change. The 1912 succession of Amoako Atta III by Nana Ofori Atta, who was intent on reining in lower chiefs who were siphoning off revenues from land sales, was the main exogenous shock here. As recounted in Chapter 4, while the aggressive efforts of Ofori Atta did not entirely succeed in forcing these chiefs to hand over revenues, it got them to shift away from the outright sale of land and toward investment in farming and sharecropping. This shift gave them a new preference for more secure property institutions that facilitated agriculture and the annual harvest from which they drew significant revenues.

In line with such emphasis on exogenous shocks, analysts have laid the blame for the erosion of land documentation in Kenya at the feet of the exogenous shock of redemocratization in the 1990s and its impact on the behavior of KANU state leaders during that period.[88] There is an element of truth to this claim. The exogenous shock of redemocratization drastically changed the environment in which key state leaders operated and transformed their preferences. It led to a weakening of their preference for robust institutions that govern land rights. Instead, they began to see weaker institutions that created clouds of uncertainty around land rights as being more preferable as they sought to manipulate property rights to ensure their survival. Chapter 5 discusses this in great detail.

But this account of institutional change in Kenya makes complete sense only if we identify the fate of land documentation exclusively with the preferences and actions of state policymakers. This assumption, however, is questionable because institutions are not merely what powerful policymakers want them to be. Extensive work by Hyden and Scott,[89] among others, has shown that social realities are not simply what

---

[87] Read more about the Land Administration Project at its website http://www.ghanalap
.gov.gh/index1.php?linkid=48. (Accessed September 30, 2008.)

[88] Jacqueline Klopp, 2000. "Pilfering the public: the problem of land grabbing in contemporary Kenya," *Africa Today* 47 (Winter 2000); Jacqueline Klopp, "Can Moral Ethnicity Trump Political Tribalism? The Struggle for Land and Nation in Kenya," *African Studies* 61 (December 2002), pp. 269–294; IDMC, "'I am a refugee'," pp. 13–20; interviews with an official of the Ministry of Lands in Nairobi (Ken 1), February 14, 2005, and a Land Control Board member in Nyeri District (Ken 18), March 3, 2005; Kenya, *Report of the Commission of Inquiry into the Illegal/Irregular*, pp. 8, 82.

[89] Goran Hyden, *Beyond Ujamaa in Tanzania* (London: Heinemann, 1980); and James Scott, *Domination and the Arts of Resistance: Hidden Transcripts* (New Haven, CT: Yale University Press, 1990).

leaders want them to be, and that less central actors contribute in significant ways to shaping such realities. Drawing insights from these scholars, we explore the activities of more marginal actors as a contribution to the literature on endogenous contributions to institutional change.

The Contradictory Potential of Institutions

The emphasis on exogenous sources of institutional change is grounded in an understanding of institutions with positive feedback effects as unambiguous entities that structure behavior in coherent and uniform ways.[90] They are said to exert what Schneiberg has called "isomorphic pressures"[91] on agents through incentives and distributional consequences. These incentives create and reinforce constituencies that become dedicated to the survival of these institutions, and they reduce and raise the costs of those that might be interested in institutional change.

A small but growing literature has offered alternative accounts of how these institutions change. It has raised the possibility of gradual instead of disruptive changes, and suggested that endogenous factors may play a significant role in generating institutional transformation.[92] These suggestions are akin to those offered by many other scholars who study institutional change generally without specific attention to institutions that display positive feedback effects.[93]

An understanding of the contradictory potential of institutions is grounded partly in a view of institutions as ambiguous entities, as has been suggested by various scholars.[94] One aspect of the ambiguity of

---

[90] Pierson, "Not Just What," pp. 76–77; Brian Arthur, *Increasing Returns and Path Dependence in the Economy* (Ann Arbor: University of Michigan Press, 1994); Douglas North, *Institutions, Institutional Change*, p. 94.

[91] Schneiberg, "Combining new institutionalisms," p. 103. Also see Leblebici et al., "Institutional change," p. 336; Kathleen Thelen, "Historical institutionalism in comparative politics," *Annual Review of Political Science* 2 (June 1999), pp. 392–396.

[92] Grief and Laitin, "A theory of endogenous institutional change," p. 634; and Kathleen Thelen, *How Institutions Evolve: The Political Economy of Skills in Germany, Britain, the United States, and Japan* (New York: Cambridge University Press, 2004), p. 30; Streeck and Thelen, "Introduction," p. 8; and Jacob Hacker, "Policy drift: the hidden politics of U.S. welfare state retrenchment," in Wolgang Streeck and Kathleen Thelen, eds. *Beyond Continuity: Institutional Change in Advanced Political Economies* (New York: Oxford University Press, 2005), p. 41.

[93] Schneiberg, "Combining new institutionalisms," p. 128; Schneiberg and Clemens, "The typical tools," p. 218; Leblebici et al., "Institutional change," p. 333; and DiMaggio, "Interest and agency," p. 13.

[94] John Comaroff, "Class and culture in a peasant economy: the transformation of land tenure in Barolong," *Journal of African Law* 1 (Spring 1980), p. 107; Ngugi, "Re-examining the role," p. 472; Gregory Jackson, "Contested boundaries: ambiguity,

institutions is that their forms do not necessarily dictate specific functions and render all other functions impossible.[95] Institutional structures can be used to do different things resulting in different practical effects that have different ethical implications. Thelen[96] has pointed out one implication of this ambiguity. The functions to which institutions are put can change over time as new interests come into power or the environment facing old interests changes.

In this book, I take this line of argument a step further by pointing out that institutions with positive feedback effects can display contradictory potential. They can engender and sustain dominant constituencies that support the continued existence of these institutions while *simultaneously* fostering subordinate groups that thrive on and are dedicated to their subversion. This view of institutions shifts from the "temporal segregation"[97] seen in works[98] that subscribe to what DiMaggio[99] has called the "internal logic of contradiction" inherent in the process of institutionalization. According to such a view, the factors that are responsible for the rise of an institution at time one then contribute to its decline at a later time.

My account of the contradictory potential of institutions draws insights from these works, but abandons the "temporal segregation" of the contradictory effects of institutions. Some of the very characteristics of these institutions that produce dominant coalitions invested in their perpetuation also simultaneously create subordinate groups that thrive on the subversion of these institutions. The coexistence of these forces makes

and creativity in the evolution of German codetermination," in Wolgang Streeck and Kathleen Thelen, eds. *Beyond Continuity: Institutional Change in Advanced Political Economies* (New York: Oxford University Press, 2005), p. 229; Kathleen Thelen, "Timing and Temporality in the Analysis of Institutional Evolution and Change," *Studies in American Political Development* 14 (Spring 2000), p. 105; Streeck and Thelen, "Introduction," pp. 17–18.

95 Thelen, "Timing and temporality," p. 105; and Streeck and Thelen, "Introduction," p. 19.
96 Thelen, "Timing and temporality," p. 105.
97 This term was used in Stephen Barley and Gideon Kunda in "Design and devotion: surges of rational and normative ideologies of control in managerial discourse," *Administrative Science Quarterly* 37, No. 3 (September 1992), p. 386; they borrow from David Maybury-Lewis, "The quest for harmony," in David Maybury-Lewis and Uri Almagor, eds. *The Attraction of Opposites: Thought and Society in the Dualistic Mode* (Ann Arbor, MI: University of Michigan Press, 1989).
98 DiMaggio, "Interest and agency," p. 13; and Schneiberg, "Combining new institutionalisms," p. 106; Barley and Kunda, "Design and devotion," p. 386.
99 DiMaggio, "Interest and agency," p. 13.

these institutions – even at the height of their dominance – subjects of intense contestation.

In this book, two broad mechanisms are laid out by which institutions that display positive feedback effects can have conflicting potential. These institutions may create mental frames that are exploitable by subversive groups in ways that undermine those institutions. They may also create material conditions that are exploitable by subversive groups. These two mechanisms are in addition to the ability of institutions to create grievances through the very exclusionary character that makes them popular to winners who become invested in perpetuating them.[100]

Property rights institutions such as land documentation that produce both winners and losers are particularly likely to create such grievances.[101] But the mechanism of grievance production is of limited analytic utility to the discipline of political science because the creation of grievances is consistent with a view of such institutions as having only positive feedback effects. This is because grievances do not automatically translate into the economic and political resources required by subversives to struggle against dominant institutions.[102]

The mechanisms identified in this book are political opportunities that create and sustain insurgent groups that subvert institutions. Further, the emphasis on grievance implies that when institutions change it is because those disadvantaged by them seek to transform them. As shown in this chapter, institutional changes can also be wrought by actors who bear no grievance towards institutions. They may even love these institutions, but their exploitation of such institutions can ultimately contribute to change.

Creating Exploitable Beliefs. Institutions that display positive feedback effects can create beliefs in a general population that are exploitable by groups that are dedicated to and thrive on the subversion of these institutions. Many institutions, such as property rights systems, work by creating certain expectations in the minds of agents about the meanings and implications of acts and symbols. The success of an institution then depends on and can be measured by the extent to which people hold on to the expectations that it creates.

---

[100] Clemens, "Organizational repertoires," p. 757; Schneiberg and Clemens, "The typical tools," p. 218; and Schneiberg, "Combining new institutionalisms," pp. 120–121.

[101] Ngugi, "Re-examining the role," pp. 471–478.

[102] Theda Skocpol, *States and Social Revolutions: A Comparative Analysis of France, Russia and China* (New York: Cambridge University Press, 1979), pp. 13–14.

For example, a system of title registration is successful to the extent that it leads parties to believe that documents represent certain rights to pieces of land that can be transacted in various ways. It is these beliefs and expectations that allow titling systems to facilitate market transactions and give real property that important "invisible, parallel life" as capital that de Soto[103] writes about. But, some of these expectations that institutions produce can also create opportunity structures that make it easier for agents bent on subverting these institutions to do so.

In Brazil, for example, con men exploited the belief of American and European environmentalists in the efficacy of titles, to sell "titles" to lands belonging to the Brazilian state in the Amazon, with one con man alone selling "title" to an area the size of Ireland.[104] Every fake title that goes into circulation contributes to a decline in public confidence in the system of land titling.

Creating Exploitable Material Conditions. The workings of institutions with positive feedback effects also create material conditions that can be exploited in ways that subvert the institutions that created them. Insurgent agents can latch on to such opportunities and thereby gain sustenance from the subversion of these institutions.

One such exploitable material condition, pointed out by Schneiberg,[105] is the market failure that some institutions with positive feedback effects can create by not effectively dealing with existing problems or creating new problems as they solve old ones. Dominant institutions that restrict the supply of needed goods may be kept in place by powerful actors who draw private benefits from them. The consequent scarcity of highly desired goods provides a niche for agents invested in alternative institutional forms to supply these goods in ways that further motivate and enable them to struggle for institutional change.

For example, in the Ga Traditional Area in Ghana, chiefs and state officials who had benefitted from weak property rights used their power to perpetuate these arrangements despite their significant social costs, which included the restriction of the housing supply. Paradoxically, some

---

[103] de Soto *Mystery of Capital*, p. 6.

[104] In Brazil, con men exploited the credulity of American and European environmentalists to sell "titles" to lands belonging to the Brazilian state in the Amazon with one con man alone selling "title" to an area the size of Ireland. "Brazil hunts Amazon land thief," *BBC News*, January 9, 2001. http://news.bbc.co.uk/2/hi/americas/1107272.stm. (Accessed June 12, 2007.)

[105] Schneiberg, "Combining new institutionalisms," p. 123.

of the biggest beneficiaries of this insecurity and subsequent shortage in the housing supply were burgeoning real estate development agencies that were some of the biggest advocates of reforms to ensure greater property rights *security*.

The insecurity of land rights provided a fertile ground for nascent real estate development agencies by forcing many wealthy Ghanaians to resort to buying houses from them instead of buying their own plots to build houses. These buyers calculated that these agents knew more about the land market and would have finished fighting rival claims to the land during the construction of houses. Because of this increasing patronage, real estate firms such as Manet, Regimanuel Gray, and Ayensu River Estates have thrived in the Greater Accra Region.

Given the costs that insecure property rights impose on these businesses, these agencies have become strident proponents of reforms aimed at securing property rights in Ghana.[106] These real estate agencies, which are the beneficiaries of the insecurity in the land market, have become key subversive agents bent on overthrowing the dominant arrangements of insecurity that is partly responsible for the rise of the real estate agencies in the first place.

In Botswana, constrictions in the supply of land resulted from secure property rights and ease of access to land. These constraints have created material conditions that nurture agents who thrive on activities that subvert the security of property. Secure rights and ease of access to land encourage many people who do not even need land to apply for parcels in as many areas of the country as they can, thus hampering the ability of the state to deliver land to those who are most in need of it.[107]

Further, because of the security of rights, they often do not even bother to fence or develop these lands once they receive them from land administration agencies.[108] These unmarked plots are then targeted by wily individuals who trick rural land boards lacking proper records to reallocate them to people by arguing that they are unallocated lands. These activities create conflicting claims and undermine state efforts at rationalizing land allocation and increasing land rights security. These subversive

---

[106] Interviews with an official of the Ghana Real Estate Developers' Association (GREDA) in Accra (Gh 4), September 27, 2004; another official of GREDA in Accra (Gh 9), October 6, 2004; and an employee of a real estate development agency in Accra (Gh 10), October 6, 2004.

[107] Kalabamu and Morolong, *Informal Land Delivery*, p. 71.

[108] Interview with a member of the subordinate land board in the Central District (Bots 33), February 12, 2004.

activities of entrepreneurs of double allocation[109] rest on the exploitable material conditions created by a system of relatively secure property rights as well as the ease of access to land in many areas in Botswana.

This account of the contradictory potential of institutions presents us with mechanisms that we can use to conceptualize endogenous contributions to change in institutions that display positive feedback effects. In addition to producing the positive feedback effect of creating and empowering supporting coalitions, such institutions can also generate and sustain marginal actors that thrive on their subversion.

Recognizing endogenous contributions to change allows us to explore ways in which endogenous and exogenous factors collaborate to engender and shape institutional change.[110] While institutions may foster subversive groups the capacity of these groups to cause serious institutional change might be limited. These subversive agents may be marginal actors innovating with institutional forms and operational logic on the periphery. Exogenous changes that impact the distribution of preferences and power in favor of subversive elements then aid in bringing formerly marginal forms and logics from the periphery to the mainstream.[111] These exogenous shocks can be changes in the political environment that encourage members of dominant groups to alter their preferences, aligning these preferences with those of subversive groups. These more powerful actors can then bring their power to bear against the institutional system. Alternatively, a shock such as a major defeat in an election, can erode the power of a dominant group, allowing existing subversive forces to take over and move institutions in a different direction.

In Kenya, the aggressive efforts of colonial and postcolonial state officials succeeded in popularizing land documents.[112] But by the late 1990s, the efficacy of land documents had dramatically declined.[113] In Chapter 6, we argue that the activities of subversive forces partly nurtured by the system of land documentation contributed in significant ways to the decline in the efficacy of land documents in Kenya. The promotion of land documentation in the Kenyan environment produced and empowered a

---

[109] "Double allocation" refers to situations where land administration agencies create conflicting interests by giving the same right to land to two different people.
[110] Streeck and Thelen, "Introduction," p. 22.
[111] Ibid.
[112] Meek, *Land, law, and custom*, pp. 93–94; Kenya, *Report of the Commission of Inquiry into The Illegal/Irregular.*
[113] Kenya, *Report of the Commission of Inquiry into the Illegal/Irregular*, p. 189.

dominant constituency of white settlers and new, black, landed elites who then tried to impose an "imprimatur of legal invincibility" on land documents such as titles.[114]

But documentation simultaneously fostered con men who thrived on its subversion. By aggressively promoting land documentation, the colonial and postcolonial states created the popular belief that various pieces of paper encapsulated certain rights to specific land parcels.[115] Given the general environment of relatively weak police and judicial structures, the increasing belief in the efficacy of land documentation among the Kenyan population made it easier for con men to defraud buyers by exchanging fake land documents for money and political favors.[116]

The issuance and circulation of these fake documents gradually undermined the efficacy of land documents. When senior state leaders embraced similar strategies after the exogenous shock of redemocratization in the 1990s, their actions only fostered a process that had already taken root. The argument here is that land documentation has contradictory potential. The actual effect it had in the Kenyan context depended partly on the wider environment of weak policing and land hunger in the country. However, in order to understand the activities of con men, we must take into account the ways in which the widespread trust in land documentation facilitated their activities.

Some Scope Conditions

The arguments in this work are not meant to apply to all of Africa or to land politics everywhere. They are bounded by various scope conditions. To begin with, the arguments made here work best in countries that function moderately well. Botswana, Ghana and Kenya have all escaped the civil wars and political instability that have plagued some other countries on the continent. In many of the most unstable countries, such as the Democratic Republic of Congo, Sierra Leone, and Somalia, there has been an obvious alternative explanation for the absence

---

[114] Ibid., p. 16.
[115] Ibid.
[116] "Vanity shares," *Weekly Review* (Nairobi), June 20, 1980; letter from the District Commissioner, Kwale, to the District Officer of Coast Division, Kwale, on April 4th, 1968. KNA CC/12/47; letter from J. M. Masesi of Garissa to Minister for Lands and Settlement on June 25, 1968. KNA CC/12/47; and letter from the managing director of the Kenya Express Land and Estate Agent to Mr. James Crispus on April 5, 1968. KNA CC/12/47.

of well-functioning institutions that govern property rights. Undertaking cadastral surveys, building and equipping title registries, and setting up land tribunals are impossible for leaders to do since their control over any part of their country is often very temporary or nonexistent. Leaders often cannot hold territory securely enough to allow for these activities.

Also, the argument mostly focuses on, and therefore applies to, the activities of national and subnational political leaders for two related reasons. First, they are the ones most concerned with the political calculations that are focussed on here. An ordinary farmer is unlikely to be concerned with using land to buy votes.

Second, it is political leaders that usually have or can create enough impunity to get away with some of the more fraudulent and violent ways of exploiting land described here with little consequence. They are the rule makers in society who can engineer the system to escape the law. In effect, part of this work is about political leaders' creation of an institutional environment of impunity, which enables them to manipulate property rights in various ways. The arguments here are mostly inapplicable to less powerful people who lack and cannot create impunity. Most land sellers would resist the temptation to resell land they have already sold even when they face severe financial difficulties. Apart from the police and judiciary who might crack down on them, the aggrieved parties might manhandle such con men on their own. Where ordinary con men are tempted to get involved in these activities, they take careful measures to hide their actions and are often pursued by the law.

The argument often focuses on the fraudulent activities of land sellers and politicians who exchange the same piece of land multiple times for votes or money. In this book, we show how this is often not the effect of innocent mistakes but a deliberate means of maximizing revenues and votes from properties over which they, in effect, have no rights. These activities do not occur everywhere. They are restricted to areas where land is extremely desirable because of various reasons that include population pressure that comes from rapid rural–urban migration.

Land scarcity can also be due to grossly unequal land distributions that allow large numbers of people access to a very limited area. The expropriation of some of the most fertile lands for white settler use and the takeover of many of these estates by black politicians after independence in Kenya had a similar effect: The creation of irrigation schemes; the concentration of social services such as roads, pipe-borne water, and electricity; and the discovery of minerals in an area could have a similar impact. However, it is important to note that in most regions in the three countries studied here and in the rest of Africa, it is impossible to engage in such fraud because land is not so valuable that people would be willing to pay for rights that they knew to be uncertain. In fact there are places where people will not even buy land once even if they knew the rights to be certain because land has not been commercialized up to now or still does not have significant monetary value.

Conclusion: Grounding the Rethinking of Preferences

The efforts that inform much of this work to better specify the preferences of political leaders towards property rights security should be seen as part of a long-standing effort to better understand the preferences of actors through more thorough examinations of the actual political economic environments in which they operate. The belief in a universal preference for security is based on a hasty leap from an observation of the effect of rising land values on the preferences of actors involved in *certain* ways of using land to a generalization about the effect of rising land values on *all* land users.

The early literature on the transition from feudalism to capitalism in Europe made a similar leap. From observing certain cases in which the spread of markets and money led to the shift from feudal socioeconomic structures of production to capitalist ones, scholars have claimed that the spread of markets and money necessarily gave feudal lords a preference for capitalist modes of production.[117] Lords were said to have realized that the most efficient way of producing enough to supply new markets was through the shift from feudal arrangements that were less efficient to capitalist production relations. Further, the money that serfs paid for the commutation of their serfdom was thought to be another incentive.[118]

By examining lords enmeshed in other sociopolitical environments, Brenner and Dobb[119] argued that the spread of markets and money did not necessarily give all lords a preference for capitalist modes of

---

[117] Adam Smith, *An Inquiry into the Nature and Causes of the Wealth Of Nations* (New York: Modern Library, 1937); Immanuel Wallerstein, *The Modern World-System, Studies in Social Discontinuity* (New York: Academic Press, 1974); and Paul Sweezy, *The Transition from Feudalism to Capitalism; A Symposium* (New York: Science and Society, 1954), pp. 44–45.

[118] Sweezy, *The Transition.*

[119] Robert Brenner, "The origins of capitalist development: a critique of neo-Smithian Marxism," *New Left Review* 104 (1977); and Maurice Dobb, *Studies in the Development of Capitalism* [2d (rev.)] (London: Routledge & Kegan Paul, 1963).

production. Akin to some political leaders who sought to perpetuate insecurity in the face of rising land values, the preference of some lords for feudal modes of production was only intensified by the spread of markets and money. This is because there was not necessarily one best way to extract the benefits offered by markets and the new money economy. Lords could resort to more efficient capitalist social relations or simply squeeze more labor and rent out of serfs.[120] The choices that different groups of lords made depended on wider sociopolitical factors that varied across Europe.[121] This explained the puzzling observation that the spread of markets actually led to the strengthening of feudal socioeconomic production relations in some regions of Europe where this was least expected to occur according to existing theories.[122]

Here in this book we similarly shed light on the anomaly of political leaders deliberately subverting institutions that govern property institutions by examining different ways of drawing benefits from the land. The fieldwork that exposed these alternative modes of exploiting land and their institutional needs was thus critical to this understanding of how and why capable and well-informed leaders subvert institutions that govern property rights in land. Fundamentally, the analysis here is a theoretical one akin to Foucault's reversal in his work on the perpetuation of the prison system despite its evident failures.[123] To borrow Foucault's words, this study sheds light on the politics of property rights partly by "revers[ing] the problem" to ask "what is served by the failure" of property rights institutions. "What is the use of these different phenomena that are continually being criticized" and maligned by development experts, economists, and political scientists alike as inefficient and extremely harmful to economic development and political order?[124] The following chapters discuss the handsome analytic dividends that this reversal pays through an exploration of politics in the land arena at both the national and subnational levels in Ghana, Botswana, and Kenya.

---

[120] Brenner, "The origins," p. 42; and Dobb, *Studies in the Development*, p. 41.
[121] Brenner, "The origins," p. 43; and Dobb, *Studies in the Development*, p. 43.
[122] Dobb, *Studies in the Development*, p. 39.
[123] Michel Foucault, *Discipline and Punish: The Birth of the Prison* (New York: Pantheon Books, 1977).
[124] Ibid., p. 272.

3

Varying Responses by Ghanaian and Batswana State Leaders

Residents of the prestigious Airport Residential Area in Accra, Ghana, woke up to a bewildering sight on April 12, 1999. With protection from well-armed members of the Ghana Armed Forces, the Accra Metropolitan Assembly (AMA) was using bulldozers to demolish a newly constructed, $3-million-dollar, 65-bedroom hotel. In the days that followed, Ghanaians were to learn that the Salaam Hotel was owned by a certain Alhaji Yusuf. The AMA made strenuous efforts to convince Ghanaians that the demolition was nothing out of the ordinary, and that it was carried out after Alhaji Yusuf failed to comply with an order to stop building in a water-logged area. Given the widespread practice of building with little attention to building codes in the capital, many Ghanaians refused to believe the story that it was a normal demolition. Besides, all the other buildings in close proximity to the Salaam Hotel, which were clearly sitting in waterlogged plots too, were left untouched by the AMA.[1]

Suspicion that the demolition was part of very high Ghanaian politics over control of the state was strengthened as the days unfolded. President Jerry Rawlings and his vociferous strongman, Tony Aidoo, both publicly defended the demolition. Their efforts at justifying the demolition took it out of the realm of ordinary AMA business. The use of well-armed soldiers instead of the police to provide protection for the demolition team also fueled suspicion that very senior government officials had a hand in the demolition.

---

[1] "Demolition of $3 million ultra-modern hotel," *The Independent* (Accra), April 27, 1999; "Reduced to rubble," *The Independent* (Accra), April 29, 1999; and AMA's madness: there are many illegal structures," *The Independent* (Accra), April 29, 1999.

It was later alleged that Alhaji Yusuf had been one of the big bank-rollers of the ruling National Democratic Congress (NDC) headed by President Jerry Rawlings. He was thought to have angered the NDC government by backing Goosie Tanoh's Reform Movement, which had broken away from the NDC and was perceived as a very dangerous threat to NDC reelection efforts in the approaching 2000 elections.[2] Indeed, the NDC's rabid fear of the damaging effects of the Reform Movement was shown to be grounded in reality during the 2000 elections, when its candidate, John Atta Mills, lost to the opposition New Patriotic Party's John Agyekum Kuffour. This "ad-hoc letting down of the axe" on the neck of Alhaji Yusuf, as the opposition People's National Convention (PNC) was to describe it, was thought to have been ordered by President Rawlings in an effort to teach Alhaji Yusuf a lesson.[3] During a visit to the site of the demolition, Dr. Edward Mahama of the PNC laid a wreath at the site with the following message: "Herein lies: Ghanaian initiative, Ghanaian entrepreneurship, Ghanaian self-reliance courtesy [of the] National Destruction Company."[4]

The ad hoc nature of the demolition of the Salaam Hotel provides an excellent example of how generations of colonial and postcolonial state leaders in Ghana have handled property rights institutions. They have avoided creating autonomous, well-functioning laws, administrative structures, and enforcement mechanisms that would guarantee rights in most of the country, trying to do so only in a few enclaves seen as key to the survival of the state. In the absence of these autonomous institutions, state leaders have become the grantees and guarantors of rights, wielding this power in highly capricious ways to generate and deploy power and guarantee their own control of the state apparatus, with little regard to the wider, harmful economic and political effects of their actions.

State leaders in Botswana have done the opposite, deliberately and con-sistently investing resources in creating institutions that govern property rights in land throughout their country. The state in Botswana also demol-ishes houses, and these demolitions often affect the poor and powerless who can least afford court action against demolition orders.[5] Residents of the peri-urban settlement of Mogoditshane, who occasionally bear

[2] "Demolition of $3 million ultra-modern hotel," *The Independent* (Accra), April 27, 1999.
[3] AMA's madness: there are many illegal structures," *The Independent* (Accra), April 29, 1999.
[4] "Reduced to rubble," *The Independent* (Accra), April 29, 1999.
[5] "Criticism mounts against demolitions," *Mmegi* (Gaborone), September 29, 2005.

the brunt of such demolitions by the "Yellow Monsters," as the state's bulldozers have come to be known, will readily attest to this.[6] However, unlike in Ghana, discussions of these demolitions often revolve around not high partisan politics and the personal decisions of politicians, but the workings of various laws and land administrations agencies such as land boards, the Lands Department, the Land Tribunal, and the courts, which leaders have sought at great expense to create and continuously reinforce.[7] What explains this variation?

In line with the argument laid out in Chapter 2, BDP leaders and their close allies – like their counterparts in Early Kenya – have significant cattle ranching and real estate interests and have sought to create strong property institutions to facilitate these interests. They have been deeply steeped in exploiting gains from land through indirect means, giving them a strong incentive to reinforce institutions that guarantee property rights across the country, including in those areas from which the state draws little revenue. Apart from allowing these BDP leaders to avoid wasteful private protection of their ranches and concentrate their resources on productive investments, the land documents issued by these land administration institutions enable them to use their properties as collateral to raise funds for investment. They have been able to translate this preference for security into institutional outcomes because of their strong capacity. The wealth thus created for politicians and bureaucrats has been used to entrench BDP control of the state. Further, the allies enriched have generously contributed to and vociferously supported BDP election efforts.

As private citizens, generations of Ghanaian state leaders have exploited land in direct ways unmediated by productive activities in most of the country. They have used land to buy the support of powerful traditional chiefs as they have sought to win and maintain their hold over the Ghanaian state. This is fundamentally similar to the use of land rights by elites in Late Kenya to buy and maintain support. An environment of insecurity has facilitated this exchange between chiefs and rulers by allowing leaders to credibly threaten to abuse the property rights of recalcitrant chiefs who fail to keep their side of the bargain. Thus, ruling elites have had a dominant preference for weak property rights institutions in most of the country and have neglected existing institutions. It is only in a few enclaves seen as critical to state revenues

---

[6] Interview with a residential land user in Mogoditshane (Bots 18), January 30, 2004.
[7] "Clergy joins demolitions fray," *Mmegi* (Gaborone), February 1, 2002.

that are drawn through the productive use of land that leaders have had a preference for security. But their ability to actually reinforce institutions has been compromised by their weak capacity.

BACKGROUND

About 80 percent of Botswana's 1.7 million people are concentrated along a narrow southeastern strip of the country.[8] This strip, along with the northern edges of the country, is relatively fertile and green. The rest of the country – about 70–80 percent – is arid and is part of the Kalahari Desert.[9] The British declared a protectorate over Botswana in March 1885, but they left Batswana chiefs with extensive powers over their territories up to 1936 under a system of "parallel rule."[10]

During the precolonial period, land was relatively abundant in these areas.[11] There was a "free right of avail" to land for all *male* members of various groups. Male adults were granted plots from land already held by their families, or they could access land from the community reserve by asking ward heads who represented chiefs. Women could only access land through male relatives.[12] Land was relatively abundant.[13] Cattle husbandry was the main agricultural activity, even though arable agriculture and hunting-gathering existed.[14]

The expropriation of extensive tracts of land by white settlers and concessionaries around Lobatse, the Tuli, Tati, and Ghanzi blocks, and Gaborone,[15] and the expansion of cattle herds had, by the late colonial period, limited the availability of arable and grazing land.[16] The rapid urbanization that followed independence in 1966 further reduced available residential land and led to burgeoning disputes over land rights

---

[8] Louis Picard, *Politics and Rural Development in Southern Africa: The Evolution of Modern Botswana* (London: Rex Collings, 1985), p. 4.

[9] Molosiwa, *Botswana*, p. 13.

[10] Ibid., *Botswana*, p. 40.

[11] Susan Wynne, "The land boards of Botswana: a problem in institutional design," (PhD dissertation, Indiana University, 1989), p. 9.

[12] Kalabamu and Morolong, *Informal Land Delivery*, pp. 14 and 41.

[13] Wynne, "The land boards," p. 9.

[14] Picard, *Politics and Rural Development*, p. 12; and Adrian Cullis and Cathy Watson, "Winners and losers: privatising the commons in Botswana," *Securing the Commons No. 9* (London: International Institute for Environment and Development, 2003), pp. 4–5.

[15] Thomas Tlou and Alec C. Campbell, *History of Botswana* (Gaborone: Macmillan Botswana, 1984), p. 157.

[16] Cullis and Watson, "Winners and losers," p. 6; and Wynne, "The land boards," p. 3.

around the city of Gaborone and in towns and urban villages such as Francistown and Palapye.[17]

Upon gaining independence in 1966, the BDP, led by Seretse Khama, made the thorough reform of the land sector a key goal of government.[18] The first National Development Plan released in August 1968 stated with regard to land that:

> The need for reform is recognized and detailed study of the possible changes which might be introduced is being made. In townships and large villages it is essential to grant a form of title which offers complete security and enables land to be regarded as a fully negotiable asset.... In tribal areas...progressive farmers must be encouraged to develop their holdings by offering more clearly defined security than that available under customary law.[19]

Ghanaian leaders made no such unambiguous commitments at their independence from Britain in 1957. Britain had formally established the Gold Coast colony in 1874.[20] Ghana's landscape ranges from a forested southern sector to a savannah northern area. As in Botswana, a "free right of avail" to land for all members of various groups existed in the areas that became Ghana. Land was abundant. Children inherited the plots of their relatives. People could acquire the right to use new plots by asking chiefs, lineage, and clan heads.[21] Land tenure was mostly communal. Chiefs, and lineage and clan heads, held the managerial interest in land on behalf of group members[22] who held beneficiary interests and had user rights that sometimes granted them exclusive rights to parcels of land.[23]

The advent of cocoa and oil palm production as major commercial activities, expansion of mining, and rapid population growth all sparked land scarcity, the commercialization of land, and increases in land values in many parts of the country beginning in the mid-1800s.[24] Rapid

---

[17] Kalabamu and Morolong, *Informal land delivery*, p. 68; and I. Mandaza, I. 1991. "Forward," in Mpho Molomo and B. Mokopakgosi, eds. *Multi-party Democracy in Botswana* (Harare, Zimbabwe: SAPES Books, 1991), p. x.

[18] Wynne, "The land boards," p. 1.

[19] Botswana, *National Development Plan, 1968–73* (Gaberones: Government Printer, 1968), p. 10.

[20] A. Adu Boahen, *African Perspectives on Colonialism, The Johns Hopkins Symposia in Comparative History; 15th* (Baltimore: Johns Hopkins University Press, 1987), p. 27.

[21] Asante, *Property Law*, pp. 4–5.

[22] Bentsi-Enchill, *Ghana Land Law*, pp. 14–16.

[23] Asante, *Property Law*, p. 5.

[24] Ilegbune, "Concessions scramble," pp. 18–20; Meek, *Land, Law and Custom*, p. 171; Katherine Gough and P. W. K. Yankson, "Land Markets in African Cities: The Case of Peri-urban Accra, Ghana," *Urban Studies* 37 (Part 13–2000), p. 2492; and Bentsi-Enchill, *Ghana Land Law*, p. 64.

urbanization during the colonial and postcolonial period resulted in the marked expansion of cities such as Accra, Kumasi, and Sekondi-Takoradi. Cities such as Accra expanded beyond their formal boundaries, spilling land users into adjoining peri-urban areas such as Gbawe, Oblogo, and Amasaman. Disputes over land rights proliferated, often degenerating into violence.[25]

In 1897, the Colonial administration attempted to convert lands belonging to various communities in the Gold Coast Colony into crown lands that would belong to the British Crown.[26] Traditional chiefs and western-educated elites united under the banner of the Aborigines Rights Protection Society forced the British to give up the idea in the south of Ghana, where I concentrate my analysis.[27] Since that unsuccessful attempt to expropriate chiefs' control over land, colonial and postcolonial leaders in Ghana have adopted the two-pronged response of neglecting property rights institutions in the vast majority of the country while trying to reinforce these institutions in a few enclaves in the country.

Below, I highlight the stark contrast between the ways in which leaders in these two countries have handled institutions that govern property rights in land. I begin first with the responses of Batswana leaders and then go on to those of Ghanaian rulers.

DIFFERENT RESPONSES TO RISING LAND VALUES

Rules Governing Transactions

In Botswana, a key goal of the Tribal Land Act of 1968 was to specify relatively easy and uniform rules on how to transact in the 70 percent of land that is under customary land tenure.[28] The state has continued to strengthen the newly created land boards that were established across the country to implement these rules. It has improved the human

---

[25] W. O. Larbi, "Spatial planning and urban fragmentation in Accra," *Third World Planning Review* 18, No. 2 (1996), p. 210; and Edwin Gyasi, "The adaptability of African communal land tenure to economic opportunity: the example of land acquisition for oil palm farming in Ghana," *Africa* 64, No. 3 (1994), p. 401.

[26] This was to be achieved through the Public Lands Bill (1897). Bentsi-Enchill, *Ghana Land Law*, p. 20.

[27] Boahen, *African Perspectives*, pp. 69–70; Bentsi-Enchill, *Ghana Land Law*, p. 20; and Lund, *Local Politics*, p. 13.

[28] Mathuba, "Land administration," p. 4.

and logistical resources of these entities.[29] The state has also tried to establish simple rules for transactions in state land, which constitutes another 24.9% of land in Botswana.[30] The Department of Lands as well as Self-Help Housing Agencies (SHHA) have been reformed to supply state land to people using increasingly simpler rules.[31] The state has set up various commissions to examine the operations of some of these institutions.[32]

In Ghana, state authorities have not established clear rules on how customary land – which represents around 80 percent of land in the country – can be transacted, despite making a series of laws that specify how they cannot be transacted.[33] Further, the state has not created decentralized structures similar to land boards in Botswana that enable land users to comply with even the broad rules it has set out.[34] State and vested lands under the management of the Lands Commission,[35] which constitute about 20 percent of the country's land mass, are not always exceptions to this neglect. In many state and vested land areas the state

[29] Botshelo Mathuba, "Opening address by Permanent Secretary, Ministry of Lands and Housing, Bothselo Mathuba, at a joint orientation workshop for new land board members, Ghanzi" (speech, Ghanzi, Botswana, January 26, 2004).

[30] Kalabamu and Morolong, *Informal Land Delivery*, pp. 61–63.

[31] Ibid.

[32] Notable examples of such commissions include the 2004 Judicial Commission of Inquiry into state land allocations in Gaborone, the 1992 Presidential Commission of Inquiry into the operations of the Botswana Housing Corporation, and the 1991 Presidential Commission of Inquiry into Land Problems in Mogoditshane and other Peri-urban villages.

[33] Interview with a regional land commissioner in Ghana, (Gh i), July 4, 2002; and Gough and Yankson, "Land markets," p. 2492. Various laws governing how not to transact in land include Republic of Ghana Constitution, 1992, art. 267 sec. 3; PNDC (establishment) proclamation (supplementary and consequential provision) Law (1982); Republic of Ghana Constitution, 1992, art. 267 sec. 5; and PNDC (establishment) proclamation (supplementary and consequential provision) Law (1982). This latter provision contradicts and overrides the Conveyancing Decree (1973), c. NRCD 175, which allowed for value consideration in cash or kind for transferring or altering title of land regardless of type of land.

[34] Osman Alhassan and Takyiwaa Manuh, *Land Registration in Eastern and Western Regions, Ghana*. Vol. 5, *Research Report* (London: Natural Resources Group International Institute for Environment and Development, 2005), p. 20.

[35] Republic of Ghana Constitution, 1992, art. 258, sec. 1, cl. A. Vested lands are customary land areas that have been vested in the President of the Republic of Ghana under the Administration of Lands Act (1962). The beneficiary interests in these lands remain with members of the traditional group that owns this land. However the managerial interest is transferred from the traditional chief of such a group to the president of the Republic of Ghana who exercises this managerial interest through the Lands Commission.

has not been able to ensure obedience of its procedures for transacting in land.[36]

Land Information Systems

In Botswana, one of the stated reasons for the passage of the Tribal Land Act (1968) was to generate written records of land interests.[37] To overcome initial barriers faced by land boards in performing this task the state improved the number and quality of their staff over time.[38] The state also introduced various means of documenting rights in customary land grants to allow for various income levels and demands for security.[39] SHHA and the Department of Lands also issued documents for state grants.[40] In a bid to further reinforce land information systems, the government introduced two web-based information systems – the State Lands Information Management System (SLIMS) and the Tribal Lands Information Management System (TLIMS) – to maintain information on state and tribal land.[41]

In colonial Ghana, Governor Guggisberg's suggestion that land title registration be introduced in 1927 was roundly dismissed by Sir Ransford Slater, who later became governor of the Gold Coast. His excuse was that no clear rights existed to be registered.[42] In contrast to those in Botswana, postcolonial Ghanaian governments have refrained from creating documentation systems in most of the country. The state has only tried to create such systems in a few urban areas, and what officials see as economic nerve centers used for mining.

Even though laws make documentation in principle possible throughout the country, state leaders have not built administrative structures

---

[36] Roth, Cochrane and Kasanga, *Land Markets And Legal Contradictions*, p. 1; and Gough and Yankson, "Land markets," pp. 2488–2489; and interview with an official of the Lands Commission in Accra (Gh 1), September 24, 2004.

[37] B. Machacha, "Botswana's land tenure: institutional reform and policy formulation," in J. W. Arntzen, W. L. D. Ngcongco, and S. D. Turner, eds. *Land Policy and Agriculture in Eastern and Southern Africa: Selected Papers Presented at a Workshop Held in Gaborone, Botswana, 14–19 February, 1982* (Tokyo: United Nations University, 1986).

[38] Mathuba, "Opening address;" Mathuba, "Land administration," p. 8; and Kalabamu and Morolong, *Informal Land Delivery*, p. 49.

[39] Kalabamu and Morolong, *Informal Land Delivery*, pp. 49–55.

[40] Ibid., pp. 62–63.

[41] Interview with an official of the Department of Lands, Gaborone (Bots 9), January 21, 2004; and another official of the Department of Lands, Gaborone (Bots 12), January 22, 2004.

[42] Meek, *Land, Law, and Custom*, pp. 172–173.

similar to the land boards in Botswana that would enable documentation of interests by the vast majority of those outside of these enclaves.[43] For instance, the Land Registry Act (1962) and the Conveyancing Decree (1973)[44] allow for the registration of deeds in various land transactions. The state did not set up administrative structures in most areas of the country to facilitate registration.[45] Even in those areas where the Lands Commission has carried out some documentation, records are faulty due to low staff skills and deliberate tampering.[46] The Compulsory Land Title Registration Law (1986)[47] has suffered a similar fate. By 1996, registration districts had been declared only in some areas of the capital, Accra and Kumasi.[48]

Adjudication

The Batswana state has sought to set up various means of adjudicating land disputes. Subordinate land boards play a major role in dispute resolution in the customary land areas that they govern.[49] People can appeal their decisions to main land boards.[50] Those dissatisfied with the rulings of main land boards could appeal to the Minister of Lands and Housing.

Because of issues of partiality and the workload of the ministers,[51] the government created a land tribunal in 1997[52] that deals specifically with appeals from land boards. Appeals from the tribunal are heard by the high court. Due to its success, a new tribunal was created in Palapye in

---

[43] Alhassan and Manuh, *Land Registration*, p. 20.

[44] Land Registry Act (1962), c. 122; and Conveyancing Decree (1973), c. NRCD 175.

[45] Roth, Cochrane and Kasanga, *Land Markets*, p. 7.

[46] Kasim Kasanga and Nii Ashie Kotey, *Land Management in Ghana: Building on Tradition and Modernity* (London: International Institute for Environment and Development, 2001), p. iv.

[47] Compulsory Land Title Registration Law (1986), c. PNDCL 152. This law fulfilled the 1924 dream of the Surveyor General of the Gold Coast, Colonel Rowe, who had called for the title registration of all land interests in Ghana. Meek, *Land, Law, and Custom*, 188.

[48] Roth, Cochrane and Kasanga, *Land Markets* p. 7.

[49] Mathuba, "Land Administration," p. 6; and interview with official of a subordinate land board in Kgatleng District (Bots 20) February 4, 2004.

[50] Mathuba, "Land administration," p. 5.

[51] Interviews with a staff member of the Lands Tribunal in Gaborone (Bots 2), January 13, 2004 (Bots 2), January 13, 2004; and another staff member of the Land Tribunal, Gaborone (Bots 7), January 20, 2004.

[52] The Land Tribunal was legally established by the Tribal Land (Establishment of Land Tribunals) Order, Statutory Instrument No. 59 of 1995. Published on September 22, 1995.

2004, with suggestions that it cover not only customary but also state land cases.[53] Appeals of the decisions of the Lands Department are still heard by the Minister and can be appealed to the President of Botswana.[54] The bias of both officials was revealed at a commission of inquiry in 2004, underscoring the need to transfer their adjudication responsibilities to the land tribunal.[55]

In Ghana, by contrast, the situation that Ormsby Gore, then Under-secretary for the Colonies, noted about the country in 1926 persists: "land litigation is the curse of the country."[56] Given the problems of the Ghanaian judicial system, many have long advocated the establishment of land tribunals like those in Botswana. Governor Guggisberg's appeal for such tribunals in 1927 was rejected by his successor Sir Ransford Slater.[57] Postcolonial Ghanaian rulers have similarly not established such tribunals. Instead, they have let the normal judicial system handle them. This, predictably, has congested the court system with land cases that often last for decades and brings little security to parties involved in disputes. Because of this, many involved in land disputes hire private militia for protection of their properties.[58] Provisions for the creation of specialized adjudicatory mechanisms under the State Land Act (1962) and the Administration of Lands Act (1962),[59] to deal with disputes, have not been implemented. Similarly, the Stool Lands Boundary Commission, which was supposed to adjudicate disputes over the boundaries of lands under the control of various chiefs, mostly existed on paper and lacked personnel and logistics.[60]

Enforcement

The Botswana police force and the local police serve as the ultimate enforcers of decisions on land matters in the country. All main and

---

[53] Interviews with a staff member of the Lands Tribunal in Gaborone (Bots 2), January 13, 2004; and another staff member of the Land Tribunal, Gaborone (Bots 7), January 20, 2004.

[54] Interviews with an official at the Ministry of Lands and Housing, Gaborone (Bots 44), March 2, 2004; and a staff member of the Department of Water Affairs, Mahalapye, Botswana (Bots 28), February 17, 2004.

[55] Botswana, *Report of the Judicial Commission of Inquiry into State Land Allocations in Gaborone* (Gaborone: Government Printer, 2004).

[56] Cited in Meek, *Land, Law, and Custom,* p. 172.

[57] Meek, *Land, Law, and Custom,* p. 172.

[58] Kasanga and Kotey, *Land Management,* p. 12; and Center for Democracy and Development, *Corruption and other constraints,* p. 19.

[59] State Lands Act (1962), c. 125; and Administration of Lands Act (1962), c. 123.

[60] Kasanga and Kotey, *Land Management,* p. 12.

subordinate land boards also act as monitoring groups during field visits.[61] A key challenge that initially plagued enforcement in Botswana was the fact that land boards and the Land Tribunal had no power to compel the police to enforce their decisions.[62] They had to seek the assistance of the courts to get the police to enforce their decisions. Legislation was introduced in 2003 to enable the Land Tribunal to sanction parties and allow these sanctions to be enforced by the police force.[63]

Once again, Ghana's widespread failure to enforce property rights in most of the country contrasts with serious efforts at enforcing rights in Botswana.[64] The police have exercised their enforcement powers very selectively in most of Ghana, including the cocoa-growing areas that fuel the country's economy[65] as well as peri-urban areas around Accra and Kumasi.[66] This is why many seek the help of *landguards*, who are groups of armed young men who act as private enforcers in the land market in the Greater Accra Region of Ghana. They are in some ways similar to Volkov's "violence entrepreneurs" and Gambetta's Sicilian mafia.[67] It is only in enclaves such as the city of Accra and some mining concessions that the government has occasionally made serious efforts to enforce property rights and deploy police officers to counter the activities of land encroachers and con men.

In Botswana, evidence of the continuous effort of BDP elites to reinforce institutions is apparent in how they have developed the land boards over time. Main land boards were established in 1970.[68] To make their operations easier and their services more accessible, subordinate land

---

[61] Interview with an official of a subordinate land board in Kweneng District, (Bots 13), January 27, 2004.

[62] Interview with staff of the Land Tribunal, Gaborone, (Bots 2), January 13, 2004.

[63] Tribal Land (Establishment of Land Tribunals) (Amendment) Order. Statutory Instrument No. 62 of 2003. Published November 28, 2003.

[64] Kasanga and Kotey, *Land Management*, p. iv.

[65] *Report of the Committee on Tenant/Settler Farmers on a Study of Problems of Landlords and Tenant/Settler Farmers in Sefwi-Wiawso and Juabaeso-Bia Districts Western Region* (May 1999).

[66] Interview with the chairman of a landlords and residents association in the Ga Traditional Area (Gh ii), July 10, 2002; Center for Democracy and Development (Ghana), *Corruption and Other Constraints*, 19.

[67] Center for Democracy and Development (Ghana), *Corruption and Other Constraints*. Mahama and Dixon, "Acquisition and affordability," p. 24; Diego Gambetta, *The Sicilian Mafia: The Business of Private Protection* (Cambridge: Harvard University Press, 1993); and Vadim Volkov, "The political economy of protection rackets in the past and the present," *Social Research*, 67 (Fall 2000). Also see Anton Block, *The Mafia of a Sicilian Village, 1860–1960* (New York: Harper Torchbooks, 1974) for an interesting discussion of protection rackets run by the mafia.

[68] Mathuba, "Land administration," p. 4.

boards were established in 1973.[69] Over time, subordinate land boards have also been established in areas identified as particularly problematic such as Mogoditshane in the Kweneng District.[70] The state created a Land Board Training Unit to train board members and staff.[71] Concerned with the performance of land boards, the government formed an Interministerial Committee to study them in 1977.[72] The government also formed a Lands Division in the Ministry of Local Government and Lands "to support the Lands Boards by providing them with professional, technical and administrative advice."[73] BDP governments have continuously reformed the staff and membership of the land boards to make them more skilled and representative.[74] Further, there has been an effort to provide boards with the logistics needed to perform their functions. Many land boards have gone from pacing out parcels by foot to the use of global positioning systems to demarcate plots.[75]

There is no evidence of such an effort by generations of postcolonial leaders in Ghana.[76] Generations of state leaders there have abdicated their regulatory role in the vast majority of the country. They have localized the effects of laws aimed at securing property rights with a national reach by limiting administrative apparatus to only a few areas of the nation.[77] But even in these enclaves, state efforts at reinforcing institutions have often been largely ineffective.

CATTLE BARONS AND REAL ESTATE MAGNATES IN BOTSWANA

BDP ruling elites have had a strong preference for reinforcing institutions that secure property rights in land because party and government officials, career bureaucrats, and leading BDP supporters all draw extensive economic and political gains from cattle ranching and real estate

---

[69] Wynne, "The land boards," p. 1.

[70] Interviews with a deputy land board secretary in Kweneng District (Bots 13), January 27, 2004; and a staff member of the Department of Surveys and Mapping, Gaborone (Bots 4), January 15, 2004.

[71] Mathuba, "Land administration," p. 8.

[72] Ibid.

[73] Ibid.

[74] Mathuba, "Opening address."

[75] Interview with a Deputy Subordinate Land board Clerk in Kweneng District (Bots 53), March 17, 2004.

[76] Ghana, *National Land Policy*; Roth, Cochrane and Kasanga, *Land Markets*; and Kasanga and Kotey, *Land Management*.

[77] Alhassan and Manu, p. 20.

concerns that benefit tremendously from these institutions. Large-scale cattle ranchers have played key roles in the leadership of the BDP and the various governments that they have formed since independence in 1966.[78]

Cattle ranching remains one of the few widely pursued private economic activities in Botswana, providing a livelihood for "80% of rural inhabitants and 46% of the national population."[79] Large herd owners, many of whom are also BDP government officials, dominate the cattle sector.[80] In 1985, Picard[81] reported that 5 percent of the country's population owned 45 percent of its estimated 3 million head of cattle, while 45 percent of the population owned no cattle at all. A study conducted in 1988 indicated that "almost all cabinet members" owned 200 or more head of cattle.[82] This has prompted some to call the BDP "a government of cattlemen"[83] and "a power bloc of cattle interests."[84]

Below these national party and state officials, local party officials and important government functionaries such as district commissioners and land board executives directly responsible for implementing land policy have been active in cattle ranching. They have eagerly bought into the national leaders' project of modernizing the agricultural sector through the reinforcement of institutions that secure property rights in land.[85]

When the Tribal Grazing Land Policy (TGLP) was proposed in the early 1970s, many cattle-owning district commissioners and land board members warmly embraced the proposed demarcation of large exclusive

---

[78] Charles Harvey and Stephen R. Lewis, *Policy Choice and Development Performance in Botswana* (Houndmills, Basingstoke, Hampshire: Macmillan, in association with the OECD Development Centre, 1990), pp. 9–10; Kenneth Good, "Corruption and mismanagement in Botswana," *Journal of Modern African Studies* 32 (September 1994), pp. 516–517; and Mazonde, *Ranching and Enterprise*, p. 20.

[79] Picard, *Politics and Rural Development*, p. 23; and Cullis and Watson, *Winners and Losers*, p. 4.

[80] Kenneth Good, "Interpreting the exceptionality of Botswana," *The Journal of Modern African Studies* 30 (1–1992), pp. 77–78; J. Holm, "Botswana," p. 192; and Cullis and Watson, *Winners and Losers*, p. 13.

[81] Picard, *Politics and Rural Development*, p. 23.

[82] Holm, "Botswana," p. 201.

[83] Harvey and Lewis, *Policy Choice*, pp. 9–10.

[84] Balefi Tsie, *The Political Economy of Botswana in SADCC* (Harare: SAPES Books, 1995), p. 261.

[85] Robert Hitchcock, *Kalahari Cattle Posts: A Regional Study of Hunter-Gatherers, Pastoralists, and Agriculturalists in the Western Sandveld Region, Central District, Botswana* (Gaborone: Ministry of Local Government and Lands Republic of Botswana, 1978), p. 32; and Louis Picard, "Bureaucrats, cattle and public policy: land tenure changes in Botswana," *Comparative Political Studies* 13 (3–1980), p. 315.

ranches for cattle owners.[86] This enthusiastic acceptance sometimes took disturbing proportions as the example below shows. Hunter-gatherer Basarwa populations lived on some of the lands chosen for these ranches. Some activists and scholars reminded state officials to proceed in line with Botswana's democratic tenets in appeals for the protection of hunter-gatherer rights against cattle ranchers eager to fence them out of their lands. With an attitude characteristic of many cattle-owning lower-level state officials eager for secure, cheap rights, one district commissioner is known to have responded to these pleas with the snide comment that even "democracy has its limits."[87]

The phenomenon of cattle ranching among ruling elites is partly a legacy of Botswana's past. Chiefs played a significant role in the cattle sector historically, and some of the most influential postcolonial BDP elites came from families of chiefs. Raising cattle was the most important means of wealth and power accumulation and demonstration in these societies.[88] Before independence, chiefs had became the largest cattle owners through ranching, the exaction of some penalties in the form of cattle and control over *matimela* (stray cattle).[89]

Seretse Khama, the first president of Botswana was a key member of the western-educated group of young men who formed the BDP. He was heir apparent of the Bamangwato and inherited the herd of his father.[90] "He [Khama] owned large herds of cattle and, as a substantial owner, was concerned that the right steps should be taken both locally and nationally to develop and improve the livestock industry."[91]

These cattle interests were of political importance in that some of the revenues from them were channeled into entrenching BDP political supremacy. Further, the BDP received strong financial support for its electoral activities from big ranchers in the Tuli and Tati blocks as well as

---

[86] Wily, *Land Allocation*, 81.

[87] Wily, *Land Allocation*, p. 38.

[88] Isaac Schapera, *A Handbook of Tswana Law, and Custom* (New York: Pub. for the International Institute of African Languages and Cultures, Oxford University Press, 1938); and Isaac Schapera, *Native Land Tenure in the Bechuanaland Protectorate* (Lovedale, South Africa, The Lovedale Press, 1943).

[89] Holm, "Botswana," p. 182.

[90] Peter Fawcus and Alan Tilbury, *Botswana: The Road to Independence* (Gaborone, Botswana: Pula Press: The Botswana Society, 2000), *Botswana*, p. 89.

[91] Fawcus and Tilbury, *Botswana*, p. 87. Also see Neil Parsons, Willie Henderson, and Thomas Tlou, *Seretse Khama, 1921–1980* (Gaborone: The Botswana Society, 1995), pp. 187–88, comment on his involvement in the cattle sector and advocacy on behalf of cattle owners even before he became prime minister and president.

Ghanzi.[92] This was partly because of their personal ties to Khama, who was about to go into commercial cattle ranching in collaboration with some of them just before he formed the BDP in 1962. These farmers also preferred the pro-capitalist BDP to the socialist and radical Botswana People's Party.[93]

It is important to note, therefore, that the facilitation of these cattle interests through the reinforcement of property institutions was not the result of a lack of political calculations. It was due to the presence of certain types of political calculations aimed at entrenching BDP rule. This is worth emphasizing because of the temptation to regard leaders who make economically sound policies as those who are able to set aside political considerations in favor of economic ones. As we will see in our discussion of elites in Early Kenya[94] who similarly sought to facilitate such productive interests by reinforcing institutions that govern land rights, political calculations aimed at entrenching power were at the heart of these moves.

The cattle interests of BDP elites and their allies had a serious influence on their land policies. Interestingly, some of these policies exclusively sought to facilitate the activities of big cattle ranchers, whose ranks were dominated by BDP elites. The Tribal Land Act (1968) required land boards to issue common law leases for grants of commercial grazing plots to individuals and syndicates.[95] These leases ensured greater security than the certificates of customary land grants that were issued for grants of rural residential land plots and for small-scale farming and grazing allocations. They could be used to secure loans from banks, unlike certificates of customary land grants. The Tribal Grazing Land Policy (1975) was specifically fashioned to provide large cattle owners with exclusive grazing rights to large tracts of secured and highly subsidized plots. It even allowed them to graze their cattle in the commons when overgrazing occurred within their fenced units.[96]

Further evidence of the causal significance of the cattle interests of BDP elites and their allies is seen in how these interests affected policymaking beyond the land sector. Large cattle owners received very generous state subsidies not available to small cattle owners and other actors in

[92] Fawcus and Tilbury, *Botswana*, p. 90; and Holm, "Botswana," p. 186.
[93] Fawcus and Tilbury, *Botswana*, p. 90; and Holm, "Botswana," pp. 185–186.
[94] See Chapter 5.
[95] Machacha, "Botswana's land tenure."
[96] Cullis and Watson, *Winners and Losers*, pp. 7–8.

the economy.[97] The state established the Botswana Vaccine Institute[98] in 1980 to provide highly subsidized vaccines to cattle owners.[99] The state distributed the operational surpluses of the Botswana Meat Commission as bonuses and rebates to farmers and instead used state revenues to partially fund the expansionary activities of the Botswana Meat Commission.[100] The government also sunk around 7000 boreholes by 1974 for drought relief. All of these boreholes were promptly claimed by large cattle owners for their own exclusive use.[101] Further, in addition to demarcating huge ranches at the Nojane Farms and allocating them to cattle ranchers at artificially low rents, the state even trained ranch assistants at Ramathlabama for these farms.[102]

The Presidential Commission on Economic Opportunities in 1982 pointed out the disturbing fact that, while the government spent 12.1 million pula on the cattle sector, it received only 7.5 million pula from that sector. The commission concluded that "the cattle industry thus made no contribution to government revenue, although it was a major industry and was dominated by the richest people in the country."[103]

The government declined to impose the new taxes the commission had suggested for the cattle sector.[104] Even if the cattle sector did not contribute to government revenue, it contributed immensely to the private economic and political fortunes of BDP members and their allies. As Mazonde[105] noted, in Botswana "cattle barons have influenced the livestock development policy in their favor," and "this has been made easier by the fact that the top policymakers at the national level are cattle barons."

The BDP elite's extraction of economic and political gains from land through productive activities went beyond the cattle sector to include the urban real estate sector where they played key roles as developers and

---

[97] Ibid., p. 13.

[98] The website of the Botswana Vaccine Institute is http://www.bvi.co.bw/PGContent. php?UID=1. (Accessed May 4, 2007.)

[99] Tsie, *The Political Economy*, p. 259; and Cullis and Watson, *Winners and Losers*, p. 13.

[100] Tsie, *The Political Economy*, p. 261.

[101] Ibid., p. 264.

[102] Mazonde, Ranching and Enterprise, p. 86.

[103] Harvey and Lewis, *Policy Choice*, p. 89.

[104] Ibid.

[105] Mazonde, *Ranching and Enterprise*, p. 21. Cullis and Watson, *Winners and Losers*, p. 13, make a similar comment.

managers rather than as mere sellers of land. They have been very similar to elites in Early Kenya in this respect. There have been indicators of the involvement of BDP stalwarts in the real estate sector despite the tendency of political leaders to conceal their economic interests.

One obvious indicator is Phakalane Estates, which is located close to Gaborone. It manages one of the most attractive pieces of real estate in Botswana.[106] David N. Magang, a former Minister of Works, Transport, and Communication, acquired this large tract of freehold land from its former owner.[107] His son Lesang Magang, who was a BDP youth wing chairman, now runs Phakalane Estates,[108] which leases and sells residential and commercial properties and operates a resort and golf course, among other things.[109]

The attorney general in 2004 and long-time bureaucrat, Ian Kirby, similarly owns and manages a vast tract of freehold land in Mokolodi. Minister of Minerals, Energy, and Water Resources, Charles Tibone, is involved in real estate management in Mokolodi on freehold land he acquired from Ian Kirby.[110]

An even more revealing indicator of the involvement of BDP stalwarts in the real estate sector appeared in the Leno Affair of 1986 when two groups shrouded in secrecy – GM Five and Leno Real Estates – acquired a piece of strategically located state land from the Lands Department at very low rates. The Assistant Minister of Local Government and Lands later indicated that the shareholders in Leno included many influential senior civil servants, cabinet ministers, and parliamentarians.[111] Mr. Tshipinare pointed out that they included President Ketumile Masire and his wife (directors of GM Five), P. Molosi (Permanent Secretary, Ministry of Local Government and Lands), P. Mmusi (Vice President and Minister of Finance and Development Planning), Ponatshego Kedikilwe (Minister for Presidential Affairs and Public Administration), M. Lekaukau (Permanent Secretary, Ministry of

---

[106] Interviews with a private real estate agent in Gaborone (Bots 55), May 23, 2005; and a private real estate agent in Gaborone (Bots 58), May 28, 2005.

[107] Interview with private real estate agent in Gaborone (Bots 8), May 28, 2005.

[108] "I won't stand, says Lesang Magang," *Daily News* (Gaborone), May 16, 2000.

[109] See the website of Phakalane Estates, http://www.phakalane.com/property/intro.asp. (Accessed May 1, 2007.)

[110] Interview with a keen and informed observer of the real estate market in Botswana, Gaborone (Bots 60), June 12, 2005.

[111] "Leno: the deafening silence," *Mmegi* (Gaborone), February 18, 1986; and Werbner, *Reasonable Radicals*, pp. 80–81.

Works and Communication), P. Matsetse (Permanent Secretary, Commerce and Industry), Festus Mogae (Permanent Secretary to the President and soon to-be President of Botswana) and the heads of the army and police.[112]

They acquired the land with the intention of building a high-rise with rental commercial space.[113] Apart from providing elites with money that could partly be used to further their political ends, such joint real estate development projects also served the political function of facilitating contact and increasing the levels of social capital among elites. Various commissions of inquiry since the early 1990s have further revealed the involvement of both politicians and bureaucrats in real estate development and management in Botswana.[114]

These politicians and senior bureaucrats are the same people who make land sector policies in Botswana, and their real estate interests have benefited greatly from their reinforcement of institutions.[115] The documentation of rights has allowed people to use land documents to generate capital through government and private sector loans, which they invest in real estate development, cattle ranching, and other sectors of the economy.[116]

The security provided by property rights institutions has removed the need for people to use capital and manpower to protect their holdings from rival claimants. This has freed up capital for investment in agriculture and real estate sectors. Unlike in Ghana, where private real estate developers cited insecure land rights as their biggest issue,[117] sector participants interviewed in Botswana said they had no such problem. Their

---

[112] "Masire I'm not in Leno," *Guardian* (Gaborone), March 7, 1986; and "Mystery company remains silent," *Daily Gazette* (Gaborone), January 22, 1986; "Lenogate: 'Mothibamele intervened for Leno'," *Guardian* (Gaborone), February 28, 1986; and "Minister talks on land purchase offer," *Gazette* (Gaborone), February 4, 1986.

[113] Werbner, *Reasonable Radicals*, p. 80.

[114] Botswana, *Report of the Judicial Commission of Inquiry into State Land Allocations*; Botswana, *Report of the Presidential Commission of Inquiry into Land Problems in Mogoditshane and Other Peri-Urban Villages* (Gaborone: Government Printer, 1991); and Botswana, *Report of the Presidential Commission of Inquiry into the Operations of the Botswana Housing Corporation* (Gaborone: Government Printer, 1992).

[115] Interview with a private real estate agent in Gaborone (Bots 58), May 28, 2005.

[116] Interview with private real estate agent in Gaborone (Bots 55), May 23, 2005.

[117] Interviews with an official of the Ghana Real Estate Developers' Association (GREDA) in Accra (Gh 4), September 27, 2004; another official of GREDA in Accra (Gh 9), October 6, 2004; and employee of a real estate development agency (Gh 10), June 10, 2004.

concerns lay instead with access to land.[118] As one estate agent who was a trained surveyor with experience in other African countries, told me:

Botswana is not perfect, but once you get land you enjoy the rights that you acquire. You can verify ownership by checking the deeds register. This is important because it allows you to ascertain the veracity of claims on land. Because of scientific surveys for many plots, boundaries are secure. The big problem is with access to land. Tribal land cannot be sold, which leads to artificially high prices for land and devalues the rights of those whose lands are repossessed by the state. Also, citizenship considerations in land allocation make it difficult for noncitizens to get land.[119]

The frequent movement of bureaucrats from state land agencies to the private real estate sector has also facilitated the percolation of the institutional preferences of private real estate agents into the state sector.[120]

These moves from the public to the private sector are akin to the "descent from heaven" (*amakudari*) among Japanese bureaucrats in the now-famous Ministry of International Trade and Industry described by Evans.[121] Two of the three owners of well-established private real estate agencies that I talked to were formerly staff members in the Ministry of Lands and Housing. They had then resigned their positions and formed separate, private companies.[122] They informed me that this was a common trend. They knew many of the officials in state land agencies and had maintained contacts with them.[123]

Further, because many state bureaucrats working in land administration agencies picture themselves working in the private real estate sector in the future, they tend to make policy decisions with these future roles in mind.[124] The Lesetedi Land Commission in 2004 found "evidence of

---

[118] Interviews with private real estate agent in Gaborone (Bots 58), May 28, 2005; another real estate agent in Gaborone (Bots 8), January 21, 2004; and a third real estate agent in Gaborone (Bots 55), May 24, 2005.

[119] Interview with a real estate agent in Gaborone (Bots 8), January 21, 2004.

[120] Interviews with a private real estate agent in Gaborone (Bots 54), May 24, 2005; and another private real estate agent in Gaborone (Bots 57), May 28, 2005. Interestingly, both agents previously worked in state land administration agencies. They then resigned and formed separate private companies. They know many of the officials in state land agencies and maintain contacts with some of them.

[121] Peter Evans, *Embedded Autonomy: States and Industrial Transformation* (Princeton: Princeton University Press, 1995), p. 50.

[122] Interviews with a real estate agent in Gaborone (Bots 8), January 21, 2004; and another real estate agent in Gaborone (Bots 55), May 23, 2005.

[123] Ibid.

[124] The proceedings of the Judicial Commission of Inquiry into State Land Allocations in Gaborone gave evidence of the thick link between public land administration officials

officials who left the department and later found employment or had
some sort of business relationships with entities who benefitted or were
closely associated with beneficiaries" of their decisions.[125] Two of the
officials in the Ministry of Lands and Housing embroiled in allegations
of maladministration had such histories. Hendrick Banda left his position in the Ministry to work for Luc Vandecasteele, the director of Busy
Five, which was entangled in suspect real estate dealings with the Ministry. Banda later established his own real estate company. Deusdedit
Rugaiganisa also left the Ministry to create his own real estate company,
which operated out of the premises of Seyed Abosadzl Jamali, the owner
of Universal Builders. Jamali had also been heavily implicated in shady
land dealings with Ministry officials including Deusdedit Rugaiganisa.[126]

Overall, the story of Botswana demonstrates Kang's[127] point that
cronyism is not necessarily an obstacle to economic growth. The BDP
elite is an entrenched network of tightly interrelated actors using their
control over the state to create a property rights system that facilitates
their extraction of vast economic gains from the cattle and real estate
sectors. Parts of these economic gains are then converted into political
resources to further entrench the BDP. As demonstrated above, the rules
in Botswana often disproportionately benefit the rich and powerful, and
some transactions are frequently mediated and governed more by extra-
legal private networks and relationships than legal market rules. However, on the whole, this informality and cronyism has not been detrimental
to the country's economic growth, even though it has mostly benefited
the rich and powerful. Ongoing property rights reforms made to facilitate these particularistic interests have benefited the country's mineral
extraction, cattle, wild life tourism, and real estate sectors.

THE ORIENTATION AGAINST INDIGENOUS PRIVATE
CAPITAL IN GHANA

In Ghana, state leaders were not heavily invested in productive activities
like their Batswana counterparts or the elites in Early Kenya. Ghanaian

---

and private real estate agencies. Botswana, *Report of the Commission of Inquiry into State Land Allocations.*

[125] Botswana, *Report of the Commission of Inquiry into State Land Allocations,* p. 148.

[126] "How civil servants fared in the Lesetedi Commission report," *Mmegi* (Gaborone), August 16, 2004.

[127] David Kang, *Crony Capitalism: Corruption and Development in South Korea and the Philippines* (New York: Cambridge University Press, 2002).

leaders' neglect of property rights institutions in most of the country was the effect of the direct ways in which they drew gains from land in their private capacity. Like elites in Late Kenya who similarly used land to purchase and ensure political support, Ghanaian leaders allowed chiefs the right to control land in exchange for cooperation (or nonopposition).

Weak property institutions facilitated these transactions by solving the Aflao problem. The uncertainty that surrounded rights enabled politicians to credibly threaten to punish chiefs who had reneged on the political bargain. Further, uncertain rights granted obedient chiefs the reward of land they could use as they pleased without the encumbrance of secure property rights.

Ghanaian leaders were not heavily involved in leading agricultural sectors such as cocoa and oil palm or the urban real estate sector. In this they differed drastically from Batswana and Kenyan leaders. Also, agricultural and nascent real estate interests that preferred secure property rights did not have significant influence on national rulers similar to that of big cattle ranchers on BDP governments in Botswana.

Small parcel owners with fewer than ten acres of cocoa trees dominate the cocoa sector, which is the most important agricultural sector in the country.[128] Big cocoa producers are rare, and most of them do not have more than 500 acres of cocoa.[129] For instance, the winner of the 2004 National Best Farmer Award, Madam Afua Frimpongmaa, had only 154 acres under cultivation.[130] There is a similar pattern in the cultivation of other crops such as oil palm, coffee, cassava, and maize.[131] Most of the

---

[128] Interviews with a Cocobod official in Kumasi (Gh 15), October 18, 2004; and an official of the Cocoa Swollen Shoot virus Disease (CSSVD) Unit in Kumasi (Gh 16), October 18, 2004; Alhassan and Manuh, *Land Registration*; Hill, *The Gold Coast Cocoa Farmer*; and Great Britain, *Report of the Commission*. This report stated that "remarkable enough in bare figures, [the amount of cocoa produced by Gold Coast farmers] may well be described as phenomenal when it is explained to be the sum of the production of small native farmers mostly of one to five acres," p. 16.

[129] Interview with a CSSVD Control Unit officer in Kumasi (Gh 16), October 18, 2004. He informed me that around 80 percent of farms in the Ashanti Region are small farms and that the few large farms are often subdivided once the original farmer passes away.

[130] "The women who made history on Farmers Day," *Daily Graphic* (Accra), November 11, 2004.

[131] Interviews with a District Chief Farmer in the Western Region (Gh 47), November 26, 2004; and a CSSVD official in a little town in the Western Region (Gh 48), November 26, 2004; and Kojo Amanor, and Maxwell Kude Diderutuah, *Share Contracts in the Oil Palm and Citrus Belt of Ghana* (London: International Institute for Environment and Development Drylands Programme, 2001).

few large-scale farmers are not national politicians or bureaucrats but
members of traditional chiefly families.[132]

In the Provisional National Defense Council/National Democratic
Congress (PNDC/NDC) governments that ruled Ghana from 1981 to
2000, Kwamena Ahoi and Ato Ahoi stood out as high-ranking government members who owned significant cocoa farms in the Western Region
of Ghana.[133] The dominant role of members of chiefly families in agriculture in Ghana is understandable. Chiefs are custodians of land in many
areas of southern Ghana, where the bulk of cocoa and oil palm production is done. Enterprising chiefs and royal family members used parts of
such land to enter into sharecropping arrangements with tenant farmers
in which the landowners ended up acquiring at least half of the farms
established.[134]

National leaders in Ghana were also far less involved in the private
real estate sector than Batswana or Kenyan elites. Public corporations
such as the State Housing Corporation, Tema Development Corporation, and Social Security and National Insurance Trust dominated the
real estate sector in Ghana until 1988, when the decision was made
to nurture a private real estate sector as part of the country's move to
a neoliberal market economy.[135] The ruling PNDC government helped
create the Ghana Real Estate Developers' Association (GREDA) in 1988.
It was formed as an umbrella organization to organize and facilitate the
activities of private real estate developers and agents in Ghana by eas-
ing access to secure land and finance.[136] GREDA had over 100 members
by 2005.

Interestingly, only two members of the NDC,[137] which ruled Ghana
between 1992 and 2000, were ever involved in GREDA as real estate

---

[132] Hill, *Gold Coast Cocoa Farmer*, pp. 13–14; Gareth Austin, "Capitalists and chiefs in
the cocoa hold-ups in south Asante, 1927–1938," *The International Journal of African
Historical Studies* 21 (1–1988), pp. 74–77; Great Britain, *Report of the Commission*;
interviews with a senior officer at Cocobod, Kumasi (Gh 15), October 18, 2004; and a
CSSVD officer in Kumasi (Gh 16), October 18, 2004.

[133] Interview with a CSSVD officer in the Western Region (Gh 46), November 25, 2004.

[134] Hill, *Gold Coast Cocoa Farmer*, pp. 8–14; interviews with a senior officer at Cocobod,
Kumasi (Gh 15), October 18, 2004; and a CSSVD officer in Kumasi (Gh 16), October
18, 2004.

[135] Interview with an official of GREDA in Accra (Gh 4), September 27, 2004.

[136] Ibid.

[137] The NDC was the party formed by President Rawlings' military PNDC to contest
democratic elections in 1992. They won parliamentary and presidential elections in
1992 and 1996 before they were ousted by the opposition New Patriotic Party (NPP)
led by John Kuffour in 2000.

developers. Victor Selormey, the Deputy Minister of Finance who owned a real estate company, was one of them.[138] Also, John Kuffour, who was PNDC Secretary for Local Government for six months in 1982 and later became President of Ghana from 2000 to 2008, owned a company involved in the supply of real estate inputs.[139]

The relative noninvolvement of national leaders in the agricultural and real estate sectors in Ghana was due to the dominance in Ghanaian politics of interests antithetical to the development of an indigenous capitalist class. These interests portrayed indigenous private capital as unpatriotic and greedy, demonized politicians involved in business, and valorized efforts at undercutting private indigenous business.[140] At critical times in the country's history, Kwame Nkrumah's Convention Peoples Party (CPP) and Jerry Rawlings' PNDC each subscribed to and reinforced this orientation.

The triumph of Nkrumah's CPP over the United Gold Coast Convention (UGCC) in pre-independence elections marked the initial triumph of this orientation against an indigenous private business class. Unlike the pro-capitalist and elitist UGCC, which drew heavy support from traditional chiefs and western-educated business people and professionals, Nkrumah was a radical nationalist with strong socialist leanings, and his party drew support from the urban and rural poor.[141] Nkrumah's antipathy towards indigenous capital was evident in his 1964 statement in Parliament that "we would be hampering our advance to socialism if we were to encourage the growth of Ghanaian private capitalism in our midst. This would, of course, be in antipathy to our economic and social objectives."[142]

---

[138] Interview with an official of GREDA in Accra (Gh 9), October 6, 2004.

[139] Informal discussion with two employees of GREDA in Accra (Gh 5), September 27, 2004.

[140] Dan-Bright Dzorgbo, *Ghana in Search of Development: The Challenge of Governance, Economic Management and Institution Building* (Uppsala: Distributor Dept. of Sociology Uppsala University, 1998), pp. 134–141; Kwame Ninsin, "Strategies of mobilization under the PNDC government," in E. Gyimah-Boadi, ed., *Ghana Under PNDC Rule* (Dakar: Codesria, 1993), p. 103; Gyimah-Boadi, "The search for economic development and democracy in Ghana: from Limann to Rawlings," in E. Gyimah-Boadi, ed., *Ghana Under PNDC Rule* (Dakar: Codesria, 1993), pp. 6–7; and Roger Tangri, "The politics of government–business relations in Ghana. *Journal of Modern African Studies* 30 (January 1992), p. 99.

[141] Dzorgbo, *Ghana in Search of Development*, pp. 37 and 122; Rathbone, *Nkrumah and the Chiefs*, pp. 22–23; and Kwame Nkrumah, *Autobiography* (London: T. Nelson, 1957).

[142] Cited in Dzorgbo, *Ghana in Search of Development*, p. 139.

He used import licenses, foreign exchange controls, and laws to disadvantage indigenous private capital and expressly forbade politicians in Parliament from participating in business.[143] Nkrumah was trying to prevent the rise of what he saw as a comprador indigenous business class that would challenge his Pan-African and personal ambitions.[144]

During his short reign as prime minister after Nkrumah's overthrow in the late 1960s, Kofi Busia hastily passed the Ghanaian Business Promotion Act in 1970 to foster indigenous capital.[145] This was a short-lived effort at promoting indigenous businesses that went so far as to take the drastic step of expelling many alien business people. But Jerry Rawlings' two military coups went far in reversing the gains under Busia and reinforcing the anti-indigenous capital culture. His Armed Forces Revolutionary Council (AFRC) (1979) and PNDC (1981–1992) were both supported by "workers, the urban unemployed, students, and the radical intelligentsia."[146] They accused business people of "economic sabotage," with punishments including public flogging, imprisonment, and destruction and confiscation of merchandise. AFRC soldiers even burnt down markets in Accra, Kumasi, and Koforidua to punish traders suspected of hoarding goods and evading price controls.[147]

The antibusiness fervor among Ghanaian state leaders contrasts with an entrenched pro-business attitude among state leaders in Botswana and Early Kenya. In Botswana, the Leno Affair of 1986 sparked a debate over the propriety of politicians entering into business. President Masire and Vice President Mmusi indicated that Botswana had a free market economy and that politicians should be *encouraged* to participate in business.[148] This legitimization of a fusion of politics and business in Botswana was similar to the Ndegwa Commission's 1970 approval of the participation of public officials in business in Kenya.[149] After the aborted

---

[143] Dzorgbo, *Ghana in Search of Development*, pp. 138–139; and Irving Markovitz, *Power and class in Africa: An Introduction to Change and Conflict in African Politics* (Englewood Cliffs, NJ: Prentice-Hall, 1977), p. 256.

[144] Dzorgbo, *Ghana in Search of Development*, pp. 139–140.

[145] Markovitz, *Power and Class*, p. 258.

[146] Dzorgbo, *Ghana in Search of Development*, pp. 212–222.

[147] Dzorgbo, *Ghana in Search of Development*, pp. 212–213; and Tangri, "The politics," p. 99.

[148] "Leno Real Estates is clean-Mmusi," *Daily News* (Gaborone), February 25, 1986; and "Masire: I'm not in Leno," *Guardian* (Gaborone), March 7, 1986; and "Mmusi on the land issue," *Guardian* (Gaborone), February 28, 1986; and "Masire: I'm not in Leno,"' *Guardian* (Gaborone), March 7, 1986.

[149] Nyong'o, "State and society in Kenya," p. 246.

effort in the form of President Busia's Ghanaian Business Promotion Act, Ghana only reached this stage attained by Kenya and Botswana when President Kuffour 's New Patriotic Party (NPP) gained power in 2000. The NPP is the ideological heir of the Danquah/Busia faction of Ghanaian politics, which had been locked out of power for most of Ghana's postindependence existence by governments that claimed allegiance to Nkrumah's socialist and nationalist politics. The NPP is full of erstwhile business people and farmers and one of President Kuffour's first actions was to declare a "Golden Age of Business." It is unsurprising that they launched an ambitious, 15-year Land Administration Project intended to reform land administration in the country.

One of the more controversial proposals of the NPP government was the allocation of a 100-acre land parcel to each minister and MP for large-scale agriculture. Announced by Kwamena Bartels, Minister of Private Sector Development and the President's Special Initiatives in September 2005, these land parcels were supposed to go along with "support in the form of seedlings, clearing of the land, planting, and maintenance of the farms over the next four years."[150] Widespread condemnation from various sections of the Ghanaian population led to the rapid withdrawal of the proposal by Kwamena Bartels that same month.[151]

This failed proposal for a massive land grab was eerily similar to the Government of Botswana's issuance of cheap, secure ranches through the Tribal Grazing Land Policy (1975) and other benefits to big cattle owners in Botswana described above. As indicated in Chapter 5, Early Kenya also witnessed a similar land grab through the Z-Scheme policy, which dished out 100-acre parcels with a farmhouse to politicians and senior bureaucrats under the pretence that they were master farmers who would act as models to peasants located around their farm.

Unlike their Batswana counterparts, generations of Ghanaian leaders have extracted political gains from land in ways divorced from the productive use of land by allowing chiefs to control land in exchange for their support or nonopposition. Before independence, control over land

---

[150] "Free farming land for ministers and MPs," Ghanaweb.com, September 21, 2005. http://www.ghanaweb.com/GhanaHomePage/NewsArchive/artikel.php?ID=90582. (Accessed January 2, 2008.); and "Bartels retracts statements on ministers and PSI," Ghanaweb.com, September 26, 2007. http://www.ghanaweb.com/GhanaHomePage/NewsArchive/artikel.php?ID=90965/. (Accessed January 2, 2008.)

[151] "Bartels retracts statements on ministers and PSI," Ghanaweb.com, September 26, 2007. http://www.ghanaweb.com/GhanaHomePage/NewsArchive/artikel.php?ID=90965. (Accessed January 2, 2008.)

oiled the machine of colonial indirect rule. Noninterference with "native" forms of land tenure was one of the main benefits that colonial authorities offered chiefs in exchange for their loyal service as instruments for controlling local populations.[152] As Mamdani[153] and Asante[154] note, this guarantee of "native" land tenure traditions often spilled over into the invention of traditions that quashed all challenges to the management of land by chiefs in exchange for their collaboration with the British.

As in Late Kenya, this exchange of land for political support was facilitated by a lack of strong, autonomous institutions that could guarantee property right. The absence of such institutions allowed the British to credibly threaten to expropriate the land rights of chiefs that proved troublesome. Rebellious chiefs learned over time that they could not find protection under autonomous public institutions that guaranteed their property rights. They needed to stay in the good books of colonial administrators on whom their continued enjoyment of rights now depended.

Chiefs did not realize this at first, and the British were quick to make an example of the mighty Asantehene (King of Asante) early on to drive home their point that only cooperative chiefs would have their land rights guaranteed. After many wars, in one of which the British Governor McCarthy was beheaded, the British finally crushed Asante's resistance in 1896 and sent the Asantehene into exile.[155] One of the more telling punishments for the Asante resistance was the vesting in the colonial government of all lands in a one-mile radius around the government fort in the heart of the Asante capital Kumasi. This transferred the custodial rights over those lands from the Asantehene to the colonial authorities and effectively deprived the Asantehene of the lands over which he had rights as the chief of Kumasi. These rights were only given back to the Asantehene in 1943 after years of cooperation with the colonial authorities.[156]

Chiefs have sometimes used land in ways that have threatened law and order and hindered the production of cash crops. This has frequently led newly arrived colonial officials, unaware of political arrangements, to lambaste chiefs. They have devised reforms that would create autonomous institutions such as title registries and land adjudication tribunals that would regulate chiefs' control of land and further promote commercial agriculture.

[152] Rathbone, *Nkrumah and the Chiefs*, p. 13; and Asante, *Property Law*, pp. 40–47.
[153] Mamdani, *Citizen and Subject*, pp. 21–23.
[154] Asante, *Property Law*, pp. 40–47.
[155] Rathbone, *Nkrumah and the Chiefs*, p. 10.
[156] Bentsi-Enchill, *Ghana Land Law*, p. 19.

In the end, the imperatives of political accommodation arrangements always won out and these reforms were not pursued.[157] Veteran officials saw the danger in transferring the guarantee of property rights from colonial officials to such autonomous institutions. Such a transfer would rob the colonial administration of the ability to use control over land to reward and punish chiefs, and it would similarly deprive chiefs of the ability to use land to manage their subjects on their own behalf and that of the British.

The colonial officer and anthropologist R. S. Rattray, who vociferously opposed some of these institutional reforms, was clear in pointing out that "it was the responsibility of the colonial states to prevent them [ordinary Africans] from escaping from the control of tribal authorities."[158] At a higher level, this lack of institutional reforms also prevented chiefs from evading the control of colonial officials.

In 1927, Governor Guggisberg recommended the establishment of separate land courts and title registration, and he established a Lands Department and Survey Department to effect these changes. The seasoned Governor Slater, who succeeded him, set aside those plans.[159] In 1931, another suggestion for the creation of a land court was dismissed by Slater, because it "would encourage litigation and also encourage subordinate chiefs to try to cut adrift from their paramount chiefs."[160]

In 1924, Colonel Rowe, the surveyor general of the Gold Coast, recommended title registration, but the proposal was turned down by the attorney general and acting governor general.[161] In the early 1900s, Governor Clifford rejected similar recommendations of the West African Lands Committee.[162] Seasoned British colonial officials knew that arbitrary power over land rights was central to both their control over chiefs and the chiefs' control over their subjects. Eradicating the arbitrary power of colonial officials and chiefs over land rights through the creation of autonomous title registries and land tribunals would have struck the very core of indirect rule. It was a step that they were not willing to take.

Postcolonial leaders embraced this environment of weak institutions and the leeway for arbitrary action that it gave them and their chiefly

---

[157] Berry, *Chiefs Know Their Boundaries*, pp. 10–20; and Meek, *Land, Law, and Custom*, pp. 172–173.

[158] Phillips, *The Enigma*, p. 122.

[159] Meek, *Land, Law, and Custom*, p. 172; and Phillips, *The Enigma*, p. 127.

[160] Meek, *Land, Law, and Custom*, pp. 172–173.

[161] Meek, *Land, Law, and Custom*, p. 188; and Phillips, *The Enigma*, p. 120.

[162] Cited in Ilegbune, "Concessions scramble," p. 27.

proxies. Even leaders like Nkrumah and Rawlings who are seen as opponents of the chieftaincy institution adhered to this system and only moved against chiefs that broke political arrangements.[163] Nkrumah stated his intention to follow this path in the *Accra Evening News* of January 5, 1950, even before he assumed power from the British when he warmed chiefs who were in league with "imperialists" that he will force them out of power.[164]

It is important to note that, for Nkrumah, "imperialist" could well describe any actor opposed to his leadership and vision. His subsequent expropriation of the custodial rights over land of the Asantehene and the Okyenhene, who were outspoken supporters of the opposition UGCC and National Liberation Movement (NLM), was a very good example of this use of land to punish chiefs who opposed the CPP.[165]

In the 1950s, the Okyenhene, king of Akyem Abuakwa, was vociferous in his support of the UGCC and then the NLM, which was formed after the collapse of the UGCC. He cracked down on CPP members in Akyem Abuakwa, campaigned for the opposition at polling stations during the 1951 elections,[166] and chaired NLM meetings in Kyebi as well as in areas outside of Akyem Abuakwa.[167] The Asantehene, king of Asante, followed a similar path. He aggressively suppressed CPP members in his area and openly supported the NLM.[168]

Nkrumah rightly perceived these chiefs to be important threats to his ambitions. A key facet of his attack on these chiefs was land legislation that effectively robbed them of their control over land. The Akyem Abuakwa (Stool Revenue) Act (1958) and the Ashanti Stool Act (1958) stripped the Okyenhene and the Asantehene of control rights over their lands. The laws shocked the two chiefs and many others that were involved in opposition politics into "loyal co-operation with the [CPP] government," as Nkrumah's powerful Minister of Information Kofi Baako was to put it in October 1958.[169]

The exchange of land for political support gave colonial and postcolonial national leaders a preference for weak institutions that govern land

---

[163] Rathbone, *Nkrumah and the Chiefs*, pp. 41, 113–141; and Catherine Boone, *Political Topographies*, Ch. 4.

[164] Quoted in Rathbone, *Nkrumah and the Chiefs*, pp. 22–23.

[165] Rathbone, *Nkrumah and the Chiefs*, pp. 113–141.

[166] Ibid., p. 40.

[167] Ibid., p. 91.

[168] Ibid., p. 84.

[169] Quoted in Rathbone, *Nkrumah and the Chiefs*, p. 141.

rights. Making the enjoyment of rights dependent on the goodwill of colonial and postcolonial state leaders instead of the dictates of autonomous institutions, allowed politicians to credibly threaten and abuse the rights of rebellious chiefs. The existence of an environment of secure property rights would potentially cause the market for such arrangements to fail. If chiefs knew that robust property institutions existed, they would feel free to oppose leaders, knowing that leaders could not retaliate by endangering their land rights. Knowing this, national leaders would have been weary of granting chiefs special privileges. Also, an environment of insecure property rights in local domains was the reward that chiefs received for their "loyal cooperation"[170] with state leaders. It avoided restraining chiefs with the straitjacket of strong property rights institutions that they might have found inconvenient.

The claim that both colonial and postcolonial state leaders in Ghana have had a dominant preference for weak property rights institutions to facilitate their power transactions with chiefs is disturbing. But Boone, studying Senegal, similarly noted how political arrangements between state leaders and key societal actors

> constrained rulers' willingness and capacity to accelerate processes of rural transformation that promised to enhance productivity, maximize marketed output, increase investment in agriculture, and concentrate rural surpluses in the hands of capitalist producers.... In colonial Africa the state's interest in promoting the exploitation of African land and labor could not be fully reconciled with its interest in political domination.[171]

The willingness of Ghanaian leaders to allow chiefs rights over lands unencumbered by strong property rights institutions was certainly made easier by the fact that leaders did not have significant real estate and agricultural interests that would have been harmed by the insecurity that some chiefs caused. Further evidence of the causal significance of state leaders' noninvolvement in agriculture can be seen in their treatment of cocoa farmers. Unlike big cattle ranchers in Botswana who are pampered by the state, cocoa farmers in Ghana have suffered at the hands of state

---

[170] Kofi Baako, Nkrumah's Minister of Information used this phrase in October 1958 to describe the new attitude of chiefs towards the government. This was after Nkrumah decisively crushed opposition from kings of Asante and Akyem Abuakwa in the late 1950s. Rathbone, *Nkrumah and the Chiefs*, p. 141.

[171] Catherine Boone, "States and ruling classes in postcolonial Africa: the enduring contradictions of power," in Joel Migdal, Atul Kohli, and Vivienne Shue, eds., *State Power and Social Forces* (New York: Cambridge University Press, 1994), p. 109.

leaders.[172] The state monopsony, Cocobod, has paid cocoa farmers well below the international market value for cocoa. This was as low as "36% of the border price" between 1978 and 1980.[173]

The readiness of Ghanaian leaders to tolerate and maintain uncertainty concerning land rights in most of the country has gone along with a desire to ensure security in a few enclaves in the country that have been seen as key to the survival of the state. This enclave approach is reflected in incessant calls for the establishment of so-called "land banks" by state officials, policymakers, and academics.[174] Land banks are supposed to be specially identified areas demarcated and shielded by the state from the rest of the land market. Here land would be surveyed and demarcated, and rights would be properly documented and enforced. These lands would then be made available to investors and those undertaking important state projects to shield them from the vagaries of the problematic land market that exists in the rest of the country.

In the words of Mahama and Dixon,[175] land banks are supposed to offer "a one-stop land acquisition service for potential investors similar to the free zones concept." This is in reference to the export processing zones created by some developing countries to attract foreign investment in their export sectors.

In 2002, the state budget included funds to create land banks in Dunkonah, Berekusu, and Manchie.[176] But this idea is far from new.

---

[172] Robert Bates, "Governments and agricultural markets in Africa," *Toward a Political Economy of Development* (Berkeley: University of California Press, 1988), pp. 331–335; and Jeffry Herbst, *Economic Reform in Africa: The Lessons of Ghana* (Indianapolis: Universities Field Staff International, 1990), p. 3.

[173] Herbst, *Economic Reform*, p. 3.

[174] Mahama and Dixon, "Acquisition and affordability," p. 37; "BUDGET: $52.3 million spent on Keta Sea Defense Project," *Ghanaweb*, February 23, 2002, http://ghanaweb. net/GhanaHomePage/NewsArchive/artikel.php?ID=21958&comment=0 (Accessed July 19, 2006.); "Land banks to attract investors," *Ghanaian Chronicle* (Accra), November 28, 2001; "District assemblies must set up land banks–Varsity Don," *Ghanaian Chronicle* (Accra), May 7, 2001; and "Reserve land for investors," *Ghanaian Chronicle* (Accra), October 4, 1999; See the statement by Minister for Lands, Forestry, and Mines, Dominic Fobih at http://www.ghanadistricts.com/home/?_=46& PHPSESSID=ab3bbd27799c43d1abaao5e52b9e5b04 (Accessed May 2, 2007.); and "Ghana: putting land litigation to rest," *Accra Mail* (April 3, 2007), http://allafrica.com/ stories/200704040731.html. (Accessed May 2, 2007.)

[175] Mahama and Dixon, "Acquisition and affordability," p. 37.

[176] "BUDGET: $52.3 million spent on Keta Sea Defense Project," *Ghanaweb*, February 23, 2002, http://ghanaweb.net/GhanaHomePage/NewsArchive/artikel.php?ID=21958& comment=0, (accessed July 19, 2006).

It is the very same idea that informed the acquisition of the 63-square-mile Tema Development Corporation lands by the colonial government in 1952.[177] Subsequent governments have compulsorily acquired about a third of all land in the Greater Accra area.[178] While the discourse on the creation of land banks sounds progressive, it is deeply discriminatory in quietly ignoring the responsibility of the state to secure the rights of all. It instead promotes a biased concentration of state efforts on securing the rights of private investors who supposedly contribute more to state revenues. Other countries transitioning to neoliberal economic systems have also experimented with land banks. The Tanzanian Investment Center has established a land bank covering more than 2.5 million hectares.[179]

The enclaves on which the state focuses contain the mining sector, which contributes a significant share towards GDP and government revenues.[180] They also host key industries that are seen as significant for state revenues and the reduction of unemployment. Important government installations and residential areas in the heart of the capital that contain foreign missions, NGOs, etc., are also in these enclaves. Often, as was the case with the Tema Development Corporation, these areas are compulsorily acquired by the state. But sometimes, as in the many mining areas, the state just imposes security on those areas without formally acquiring them. Their interest in ensuring security in these areas is seen in the incessant debates over the need to ensure security for investors.[181]

The cocoa sector is a particularly interesting case. Here leaders' political manipulation of land in their private capacity clashes with the state's extraction of scarce foreign exchange from cocoa production. The lands used for cocoa production are almost exclusively customary lands that

---

[177] See the website of the Tema Development Corporation. http://www.tdctema.com/Details.cfm?EmpID=36. (Accessed May 2, 2007.)

[178] Roth, Cochrane and Kasanga, *Land Markets*, p. 11.

[179] Issa Shivji, "Lawyers in neoliberalism: authority's professional supplicants or society's amateurish conscience," *Codesria Bulletin*, Nos. 3&4 (2006), p. 20.

[180] Nancy Clark, "The economy," in L. B. Berry ed., *Ghana: A Country Study* (Washington, DC: Federal Research Division Library of Congress, 1995), pp. 168–173.

[181] "BUDGET: $52.3 million spent on Keta Sea Defense Project," *Ghanaweb*, February 23, 2002, http://ghanaweb.net/GhanaHomePage/NewsArchive/artikel.php?ID=21958&comment=0 (accessed July 19, 2006); "Land banks to attract investors," *Ghanaian Chronicle* (Accra), November 28, 2001; "District assemblies must set up land banks–Varsity Don," *Ghanaian Chronicle* (Accra), May 7, 2001; and "Reserve land for investors," *Ghanaian Chronicle* (Accra), October 4, 1999.

government officials concede to chiefs in their arrangements of political accommodation. This coincidence gives leaders dual preferences concerning institutions that secure property rights in such areas. More autonomous institutions to govern rights would enhance cocoa production. But the flexibility that comes with the absence of these autonomous property institutions make possible the exchange of land rights for the collaboration of chiefs. Like their Senegalese[182] and British colonial counterparts,[183] postcolonial Ghanaian rulers have always prioritized the institutional needs of their private direct exploitation of land for political gain over the formal demands of their position as state leaders.

POWER AND THE DELIVERY OF INSTITUTIONAL FORMS

Batswana elites started out rather weak and gradually amassed more power over time, enabling them to actualize their preference for security by reinforcing property rights institutions. With such strong capacity, BDP elites best resembled their Kenyan counterparts, but they differed from Ghanaian state leaders. Ghanaian leaders started out in a strong position as heads of one of the most promising postcolonial states in Africa. But the power of these elites gradually declined because of a decline in the capacity of the state that they controlled.[184]

The weak capacity of Ghanaian elites raises the issue of whether insecure property rights in much of Ghana are not simply due to the inability of state leaders to protect rights instead of any deliberate effort at creating an institutional environment that facilitates the exchange of land for political support. The selectively protected enclaves in Ghana give us a critical case that shows the independent effect of the two explanatory variables discussed in this work. State leaders have made immense efforts to ensure security in many of these enclaves unlike in the rest of the country. This clearly shows divergent attitudes towards property rights security in the two areas, and this book argues that this divergence in institutional preferences is due to different ways of drawing gains from land inside and outside of those enclaves. But leaders' weak capacity has limited their efforts at securing rights inside the enclaves to the limited enhancement of institutions. This is unlike the situation in the rest of the country, where leaders simply neglect property rights institutions.

---

[182] Boone, "States and ruling classes," p. 109.
[183] Berry, *Chiefs Know Their Boundaries*, pp. 10–20.
[184] Dzorgbo, Ghana in Search of Development, Ch. 6.

The Effects of Growing Capacity in Botswana

The struggle to reinforce property rights in Botswana was part of an effort to construct the state in a way that facilitated modes of power and wealth accumulation disproportionally beneficial to BDP elites and their allies. The strong capacity of BDP leaders helped them to overcome stiff opposition from traditional chiefs who wanted to continue to control land allocation. In the struggle between the ruling BDP elites and chiefs, the BDP had an overwhelming advantage in its control over legislation and policymaking in the country. The BDP translated into consistent electoral success its support among the British colonial administration, wealthy cattle ranchers, western-educated professionals, and even some chiefs who feared antichieftaincy leftist parties.[185] It won all local and parliamentary elections and formed all governments since independence.[186] It used this stranglehold on policymaking to pass a series of laws that reinforced property rights and that eroded chiefs' powers to resist these lawmaking and implementation efforts.

The Tribal Land Act (1968) transferred all powers of chiefs over customary land to land boards.[187] The BDP preempted chiefs' efforts at resisting this law by drastically undercutting their powers. The House of Chiefs (Powers and Privileges) Act (1965) limited the House of Chiefs to an advisory role alongside the BDP-dominated National Assembly, which had real legislative powers.[188] The Chieftainship Act (1965) gave the President the power to recognize chiefs and to introduce proceedings leading to the removal of chiefs.[189] It also limited the exercise of chiefly power to traditional matters and required chiefs to take instructions from

---

[185] Holm, "Botswana," pp. 185–86; Good, "Interpreting the exceptionality," p. 72; and O. Molutsi, "Political parties and democracy in Botswana," in Mpho Molomo and B. Mokopakgosi, eds., *Multiparty Democracy in Botswana* (Harare, Zimbabwe: SAPES Books, 1991), pp. 6–8.

[186] Good, "Interpreting the exceptionality," p. 87. The BDP won 80.4% in 1965; 68.3% in 1969; 76.6% in 1974; 75.2% in 1979; 68% in 1984; 64.8% in 1989; 54.7% in 1994; 82.5% in 1999; and 77.2% in 2004. See Dieter Nohlen, Michael Krennerich, and Bernhard Thibaut, *Elections in Africa: a data handbook* (Oxford; New York: Oxford University Press, 1999); Botswana, *Report to His Honour the Vice President and Minister of Presidential Affairs and Public Administration on the General Elections, 1999* (Gaborone: Independent Electoral Commission, 1999); Botswana, *Report to the Minister of Presidential Affairs and Public Administration on the 2004 General Elections* (Gaborone Botswana: Independent Electoral Commission, 2004).

[187] Kalabamu and Morolong, *Informal Land Delivery*, pp. 48–49.

[188] J. H. Proctor, 1968. "The house of chiefs and the political development of Botswana," *Journal of Modern African Studies* 6 (May 1968), p. 59.

[189] Chieftainship Act (1965) c. 41:01.

the minister responsible for chieftaincy.[190] The Local Government (District Councils) Act (1965) transferred the administrative and taxation powers of chiefs to District Councils.[191]

The BDP 's monopolization of coercive force in the country bolstered its policymaking capacity. It maintained effective civilian control over the military and obviated coup threats against its rule partly by co-opting influential members of the military such as Mompati Merafhe and Ian Khama, who went from being senior officers in the military to BDP party members and leading cabinet officials.[192] Ian Khama eventually became President of Botswana in 2008. Control of the military and police gave the BDP the coercive capacity to achieve its ends in a country where there are no subnational armed groups. Apart from ensuring the stability of BDP power, this coercive capacity was occasionally employed to enforce rules concerning the acquisition and use of land through forcible evictions and demolition of houses to curb what is portrayed as the illegal acquisition of plots.[193]

The rising financial capacity of BDP elites played an even bigger role in their drive to build institutions that govern land rights. The country's finances improved dramatically after the discovery of the diamonds that have made Botswana the largest producer of gem-quality diamonds in the world.[194] These resources allowed the BDP to create and equip land boards and other land agencies.[195] They also enabled the state to offer competitive wages and allowances to land sector bureaucrats that have attracted some of the most talented Batswana and bureaucrats and professionals from other countries, including Ghana and Kenya.[196] The government similarly used some of these resources to train public and civil servants in Botswana and abroad. For instance, the inauguration of each

---

[190] Kalabamu and Morolong, *Informal Land Delivery*, p. 25.

[191] Ibid.

[192] Mpho Molomo, "Civil–military relations in Botswana's developmental state," *African Studies Quarterly* 5 (February 2001).

[193] Kalabamu and Morolong, *Informal Land Delivery*, p. 148; and "Criticism mounts against demolitions," *Mmegi* (Gaborone), September 29, 2005.

[194] Picard, *Politics and Rural Development*, p. 22; and Kalabamu and Morolong, *Informal Land Delivery*, p. 32; and See the Government of Botswana site, http://www.gov.bw/. (Accessed June 27, 2007.)

[195] Interview with a subordinate land board clerk in Kgatleng District (Bots 20), February 4, 2004.

[196] Interviews with an official of the Department of Surveys and Mapping, Gaborone (Bots 4), January 15, 2004; and a private real estate agent in Gaborone (Bots 54), May 24, 2004.

batch of land board members included training sessions, and occasional training sessions are held throughout their tenure.[197]

Beyond these tangible resources, the traditional legitimacy of early BDP leaders aided them greatly in their initial confrontation with chiefs over the Tribal Land Act. Traditional leaders with deep roots in Tswana culture loudly opposed the Tribal Land Act and land boards because these boards took over powers earlier exercised by chiefs. Seretse Khama's traditional legitimacy was crucial in counterbalancing this legitimacy of chiefs.[198] Khama, the leader of the BDP and the first president who oversaw many of the radical reforms that curbed the powers of chiefs, was the heir apparent to the Ngwato throne, which governed the Bangwato, the largest Tswana group.[199] Most Bamangwato regarded him with the respect that would befit their chief even after he rejected the throne for party politics.[200] The BDP was thus able to usurp the land administration powers of chiefs without much reprisal from the general populace. The confrontation became a case of the most powerful traditional chief undermining the institution of chieftaincy, instead of mere commoners taking on venerable chiefs.

The passage of national laws limiting the national and local power of chiefs did not totally eliminate the challenge posed by chiefs to the reform project of BDP leaders. BDP leaders used their policymaking and revenue advantage to some success in this struggle. Lacking coercive instruments like those possessed by some chiefs in Ghana, chiefs in Botswana used their local knowledge as instruments of resistance. Hayek emphasized the importance of knowledge of "the particular circumstances of time and place," as opposed to "scientific knowledge" possessed by central state officials and their land board agents, in the process of social transformation and governance.[201]

State leaders' success in remaking social realities depends on their ability to integrate local knowledge into broader plans that will direct the exercise of state power.[202] Where state officials lack sufficient knowledge of local realities, they will be unable to direct state power in ways that will bring about the targeted transformation. Worse still, local actors

[197] Mathuba, "Opening address."
[198] Good, "Interpreting the exceptionality.'
[199] Holm, "Botswana," p. 185.
[200] Parsons, Henderson and Tlou, *Seretse Khama*, pp. 165–169.
[201] Friedrich A. Hayek, "The use of knowledge in society," *American Economic Review* 35 (Sept. 1945), p. 521.
[202] James Scott, *Seeing Like a State*, p. 3.

unsupportive of these projects may use their local knowledge to divert state power in ways that are contrary to state goals.

In addition to creating new land interests, the Tribal Land Act required land boards to document land interests allocated by traditional chiefs before land boards came into existence.[203] Land boards needed to know the extent and locations of prior allocations by chiefs to document interests, resolve disputes, and avoid creating conflicting claims by reallocating lands that had already been allocated. Chiefs and their land overseers had a wealth of such knowledge. The newly created land boards did not.[204]

The government sought to harness chiefs' knowledge by initially allowing them to sit on land boards in 1970.[205] Many chiefs exploited this position to continue exercising their land administration roles, to the chagrin of senior state bureaucrats and land board members. Successive governments in Botswana used their firm control over the state to experiment with institutional forms that would eliminate the continuing influence of chiefs while seeking to exploit their local knowledge.

Pursuant to the recommendations of The Interministerial Committee on Land Boards in 1977, chiefs were removed completely from land boards in 1984.[206] Chiefs could still nominate land overseers to serve as conduits of local knowledge to land boards.[207] These land overseers were supposed to vet applications for land, visit plots, and sign applications guaranteeing that there were no encumbrances on such parcels before the land boards accepted applications.[208] Land overseers were also supposed to travel with land board members to show them where plots were located during allocation and dispute resolution trips.[209]

Many land overseers exploited their position to engage in subtle but telling acts of resistance to the state's transformative project by signing applications for land without visiting or investigating the applied-for plots.[210] The fact that the state did not provide land overseers with

---

[203] Mathuba, "Land administration."

[204] Wynne, "The land boards," p. 194.

[205] Response by the attorney general to a question in the House of Chiefs, *Official Report of the Proceedings of the Thirteenth Meeting of the House of Chief Sittings from 5th–7th August 1968* (Gaborone: Government Printer, 1968), p. 30.

[206] Mathuba, "Land administration."

[207] Interview with a subordinate land board clerk in Kweneng District (Bots 20), February 4, 2004; interview with a land board official in Central (Bots 22), February 11, 2004.

[208] Interview with a subordinate land board clerk in Central District (Bots 22), February 11, 2004.

[209] Ibid.

[210] Interview with land board member in Central District (Bots 33), February 21, 2004; interview with a former subordinate land board clerk in Kweneng District (Bots 48), March 4, 2004.

vehicles or allowances to facilitate these visits absolves them of much blame. But such behaviour often led to the double allocation of the same piece of land, in which previously allocated but undeveloped plots were legally allocated to new users. The two grantees would then clash once one of them tried to develop the plot. Land boards were always embarrassed when they caused such double allocations and gave another plot to one of the holders. Realizing this, some ingenious land overseers indirectly allocated land by deliberately causing land boards to allocate land that already belonged to someone else. Upon their realization of the mistake, embarrassed land board officials often quickly and quietly allocated a new plot to one of the users to cover their apparent blunder.[211]

BDP elites rightly recognized that local knowledge was a prime weapon in this struggle with chiefs. Government officials used their growing revenues to reduce the dependence of land boards on the knowledge of chiefs by investing in geodetic instruments that enable land boards to survey and demarcate large parcels of land.[212] Where it was known that no prior allocations were made, these demarcation exercises enabled land boards to function without the advice of traditional authorities without much consequence when allocating plots and resolving disputes. Subordinate land boards at Molepolole, Mochudi, and Lentsweletau fired their land overseers when these boards started allocating predemarcated plots.[213]

The Effects of Declining Capacity in Ghana's Enclaves

Ghanaian leaders have had far less policymaking and legislative capability, and this has impeded their ability to pass and implement laws that reinforce property rights institution in the enclaves they have focused on. Ghanaian politics have been highly divisive and competitive, leaving no faction with anything approximating the secure control of BDP elites in Botswana.[214] There have been a host of civilian and military factions that have sought, with considerable success, to control the state. By 1998, when Botswana had still been ruled by the same party since independence, Ghana had (mostly) endured a total of nine separate governments and

---

[211] Interview with a land board member in Central District (Bots 33), February 21, 2004.

[212] Interview with a subordinate land board clerk in Kgatleng District (Bots 20), February 4, 2004.

[213] Interview with a subordinate land board clerk in Kweneng District (Bots 48), March 4, 2004; interview with a subordinate land board clerk in Kgatleng District (Bots 20), February 4, 2004; and interview with a subordinate land board clerk in Kweneng District (Bots 53), March 17, 2004.

[214] Nohlen, Krennerich, and Thibaut, *Elections in Africa*, pp. 434–435.

had already experienced four successful coups.[215] This instability limited the ability of governments to pass and implement laws to reinforce property rights in those enclaves where they preferred security. Coup plotters eager to justify their illegal takeover of power often repealed or failed to implement laws passed by governments that they had overthrown.

The unstable nature of Ghanaian national politics was also seen in leaders' inability to monopolize coercive force in the country, as evidenced by multiple successful and unsuccessful military coups plotted by various factions of the military.[216] Further, private militias existed over whom national leaders had little control. *Landguards*, as these militias are known in popular parlance, acted as enforcers and racketeers in the land market in the Greater Accra area. They played the roles of foot soldiers in battles over land and chieftaincy, challenged state appropriation of stool[217] land, and operated protection rackets in the land market. In performing these activities, they sometimes even confronted and killed police officers.[218]

This weak policymaking and coercive capacity was compounded by the declining financial capacity of the Ghanaian state and the elites who controlled it. Oil crises, political instability, and flawed economic policies led to the near collapse of the economy by 1980.[219] Real GDP growth rates were negative for most of the late 1970s, and inflation soared to a

---

[215] Eboe Hutchful and Abdoulaye Bathily, *The Military and Militarism in Africa* (Dakar: Codesria, 1998), p. 212; and Dennis Austin and Robin Luckham, *Politicians and Soldiers in Ghana, 1966–1972* (London: Cass, 1975), p. 2.

[216] Hutchful and Bathily, *The Military and Militarism*; and Simon Baynham, *The Military and Politics in Nkrumah's Ghana* (Boulder: Westview Press, 1988); and Dzorgbo, *Ghana in Search of Development*, Ch. 6.

[217] According to Rathbone, a stool "refers firstly to a real stool or throne, upon which a chief sits. It also serves as a synonym for a chief's office and the state or section of state over which he and more occasionally she ruled," *Nkrumah and the Chiefs*, p. 13.

[218] "Ablekuma! Land guards massing again, Dansoman Police inactive," *Ghanaian Chronicle* (Accra), June 21, 2001; "Trouble looms in Oblogo over chieftaincy, land sales," *Ghanaian Chronicle* (Accra), February 15, 2001; "Another landguard attack at Ablekuma," *The Independent* (Accra), December 15, 1999; "Ablekuma saga continues, landguards still terrorizing Bortianor locals," *Ghanaian Chronicle* (Accra), May 18, 2001; and "Cop shot dead: 3 landguards in custody," *Daily Graphic* (Accra), December 18, 2004.

[219] J. H. Frimpong-Ansah, *The Vampire State in Africa: The Political Economy of Decline in Ghana* (London: J. Currey, 1991), p. 73; and Dzorgbo, *Ghana in Search of Development*, pp. 1–3; Kwasi Anyemedu, "The economic policies of the PNDC," in E. Gyimah-Boadi, ed. *Ghana Under PNDC Rule* (Dakar: Codesria, 1993), p. 15; and Jeffrey Herbst, *The Politics of Reform in Ghana, 1982–1991* (Berkeley: University of California Press, 1993), p. 14.

peak of 128 percent in 1983.[220] Widespread hoarding, smuggling, and illegal currency markets, as well as the withholding of Western aid, wreaked havoc on state revenues and jeopardized the state's ability to perform basic administrative duties.[221] Average real civil service wages dropped by more than 10 percent annually between the early 1970s and early 1980s.[222] These extremely low wages translated into "absenteeism, moonlighting, poor morale ...," and the migration of professionals to more lucrative countries such as Botswana.[223] It became easy for societal actors to capture state land administration officials by offering them bribes in cash and kind.[224]

To make matters worse, these weak Ghanaian leaders could not even draw on the traditional legitimacy that aided the BDP in its confrontation with traditional chiefs. Unlike Seretse Khama, Nkrumah, and Rawlings, two of the longest-serving rulers in Ghana were of common descent, a characteristic that endeared them to hordes of urban youth and discontented rural commoners.[225] But it also denied them the traditional legitimacy that chiefs enjoyed, a fact that shrewd leaders such as Nkrumah and Rawlings recognized.[226] Chiefs cleverly manipulated their traditional

---

[220] Ernest Aryeetey and Jane Harrigan, "Macroeconomic and sectoral developments since 1990," in E. Aryeetey, J. Harrigan, and M. Nissanke, eds. *Economic Reforms in Ghana: The Miracle and the Mirage* (Trenton, NJ: Africa World Press, 2000), p. 9.

[221] Naomi Chazan, *An Anatomy of Ghanaian Politics: Managing Political Recession, 1969–1982* (Boulder, CO: Westview Press, 1983), pp. 194–195; and Frimpong-Ansah, *The Vampire State*, pp. 94–114; Anyemedu, "The economic policies, p. 14; and Herbst, *Economic Reform*, p. 4; and Agbosu, "Towards a workable system," p. 64.

[222] P. Gregory, "Dealing with redundancies in government employment in Ghana," in D. Lindauer and B. Nunberg, eds. *Rehabilitating Government: Pay and Employment Reform in Africa*, World Bank Regional, and Sectoral Studies (Washington DC: World Bank, 1994), p. 196; and L. De Merode and C. Thomas, "Implementing civil service and employment reform in Africa: experiences of Ghana, Gambia, and Guinea," in D. Lindauer and B. Nunberg, eds. *Rehabilitating Government: Pay and Employment Reform in Africa*, World Bank Regional, and Sectoral Studies (Washington DC: World Bank, 1994), p. 161.

[223] Gregory, "Dealing with redundancies," p. 196; and Chazan, *An Anatomy of Ghanaian Politics*, p. 194.

[224] Gregory, "Dealing with redundancies," p. 96; Kasanga and Kotey, *Land Management*, p. iv; Center for Democracy and Development, *Corruption and Other Constraints*, p. 19; interviews with the chairman of a landlords and residents association in the Ga Traditional Area (Gh ii), July 10, 2002; and an employee of a real estate agency in Accra (Gh iii), July 3, 2002.

[225] Ninsin, "Strategies of mobilization," 101; and Rathbone, *Nkrumah and the Chiefs*, pp. 21–23.

[226] George Hagan, "Nkrumah's cultural policy," in Kwame Arhin ed. *The Life and Work of Kwame Nkrumah: Papers of a Symposium* (Accra: Sedco, 1991), p. 9; and "Don't subvert the state–Jerry," *Daily Graphic* (Accra), February 1, 1985.

legitimacy to resist state efforts at implementing land administration rules in the enclaves. When chiefs ran afoul of the law, as they often did in the administration of land, state officials and citizens found it harder to hold them accountable because of the aura of traditional legitimacy surrounding them.[227]

An enclave such as Accra, the nation's capital, where state leaders made efforts to strengthen property institutions, presents us with evidence of the debilitating impact of state incapacity. Over time the state compulsorily acquired about a third of all land in the Greater Accra area to locate state ministries and agencies, Burma camp, a vast military installation, the Kotoka International Airport, the 63-square-mile Tema Development Corporation industrial enclave, etc.[228] But it struggled to deploy the administrative and coercive machinery necessary to ensure an environment of security. Low-level land administration officials were corrupt and lacked adequate training and equipment to perform their duties.[229] The Lands Commission kept very poor records that were often deliberately manipulated by staff on low wages.[230] Under the very noses of the state, many chiefs, family heads, and con men fraudulently sold off huge parcels of state land, causing conflicting claims once the government had allocated these lands to others.[231] Where lands allocated by the state were still vacant, grantees often could not use them until they paid "digging fees" charged by *landguards*. Where people could not pay, their construction equipment was confiscated. Resistance led to beatings that sometimes left protesters hospitalized.[232]

The passage of the Compulsory Land Title Registration Law in 1986 was supposed to be a watershed in the effort to secure property rights in Ghana. The memorandum to the law rightly noted the pervasion of problems resulting from

[227] Interviews with a regional lands commissioner in Ghana (Gh x), July 24, 2002; and an official of the Office of the Administrator of Stool Lands in Ghana (Gh vii), July vi, 2002.

[228] Roth, Cochrane and Kasanga, *Land Markets*, pp. 10–11.

[229] Agbosu, "Towards a workable system," pp. 64–65; J. K. Dey, "The Problem of land registration in Ghana through the eyes of a surveyor or map maker," in A. K. Mensah-Brown, ed., *Land Ownership and Registration in Ghana: A Collection of Studies* (Kumasi, Ghana: Land Administration Research Centre University of Science and Technology, 1978), p. 92; and Mahama and Dixon, "Acquisition and affordability," p. 17.

[230] Interview with an employee of real estate agency in Accra (Gh iii), July 3, 2002.

[231] Interview with a senior official of the Lands Commission, Accra (Gh 1), September 24, 2004.

[232] "Another landguard attack at Ablekuma," *The Independent* (Accra), December 15, 1999.

...the absence of documentary proof that a man in occupation of land has certain rights in respect of it; the absence of maps and plans of scientific accuracy to enable the identification of parcels and ascertainment of boundaries; and the lack of prescribed forms to be followed in case of dealings affecting interests in land.[233]

To solve these problems, it introduced a "system of compulsory land title registration throughout Ghana."[234] However, in line with its enclave approach, the state tried to set up administrative structures to implement the law only in the enclaves of Accra and Kumasi. Fourteen years after the passage of the law, only a few areas of the capital had been declared registration districts because of the state's inability to meet the high costs of surveys and the administrative and technical structures to facilitate title registration.[235] Twenty-three years later, in 1999, the Ministry of Lands and Forestry conceded that the land market was plagued with "land encroachments, multiple sales of residential parcels...land racketeering, slow disposal of land cases by the courts, and a weak land administration system."[236]

In line with the argument in this book, outside the enclaves, there was a marked absence of efforts by Ghanaian leaders to establish strong, functioning institutions that guarantee rights. Where laws passed were national in character, leaders curtailed the spatial reach effects of these laws by refusing to set up any of the administrative structures that would allow these laws to be implemented in most of the country.[237]

The Compulsory Land Title Registration Law of 1986 mentioned above is one example in which implementation efforts have been limited to the cities of Accra and Kumasi. The Administration of Lands Act (1962) and the State Lands Act (1962) are laws, that if adhered to, would have provided rules on compulsory land acquisitions, curbed arbitrary action by the state, and provided chiefs and lineage heads with greater property rights security. State leaders refused to work within these rules, preferring instead an uncertain environment that allowed them to selectively reward and punish traditional authorities depending on their political activities. Chiefs who did not hold up their side of the bargain

---

[233] Land Title Registration Law, 1986, "Memorandum."
[234] Ibid.
[235] Roth, Cochrane and Kasanga, *Land Markets*, p. 7; and Mahama and Dixon, "Acquisition and affordability," p. 6.
[236] Ghana, *National Land Policy*, p. 3.
[237] Roth, Cochrane and Kasanga, *Land Markets*, p. 7; Alhassan and Manuh, *Land Registration*, p. 20l; and Mahama and Dixon, "Acquisition and affordability," p. 16.

often felt the retaliation of state elites. The Akyem Abuakwa (Stool Revenue) Act (1958) and the Ashanti Stool Act (1958) passed by Kwame Nkrumah's CPP were direct retaliation against the Okyenhene and Asantehene for their support of the NLM.[238] Instead of reinforcing property rights institutions in these areas, these laws allowed lower chiefs loyal to Nkrumah's CPP to assert more control over land to the detriment of their senior chiefs who were supportive of the opposition NLM.

State leaders ignored the efforts of weak, pro-security constituencies such as the many tenant and landlords associations formed by city residents to defend themselves against the predation of racketeers.[239] These voluntary organizations lacked the necessary cohesion and resources to influence state leaders to dispense with their accommodation arrangements with chiefs.[240]

Rural farmers did not have a stronger effect on the state. In the late 1980s, simmering tensions between tenant farmers and chiefs in Sefwi-Wiawso and Juaboso-Bia erupted after tenant farmers resisted attempts by chiefs to extract higher tributes and repossess lands from tenants.[241] The heavy reliance of the PNDC government on the cocoa sector for state revenues gave the state a good reason to protect tenant farmers clamoring for greater security.[242] For a while it seemed as if the government would break with long-standing norms and prioritize the institutional requirements of state revenues over those of the age-old bargain between chiefs and national leaders. It formed the Asare Committee to investigate farmer grievances in Sefwi-Wiawso, accepted recommendations of the committee, sent a surveyor to demarcate farms in the area and asked chiefs to issue farmers with deeds.[243] These efforts promptly stopped just as did similar earlier efforts of the zealous colonial officer Francis Fuller who

---

[238] Roth, Cochrane and Kasanga, *Land Markets*, pp. 10–11; Kwame Boafo-Arthur, "Chieftaincy and politics in Ghana since 1982," *West African Review* 3, No. 1 (2001); and Rathbone, *Nkrumah and the Chiefs*, p. 128.

[239] Katherine Gough, "The changing nature of urban governance in peri-urban Accra, Ghana," *Third World Planning Review* 21 (April 1999): pp. 393–410.

[240] Interviews with chairman of a landlords and residents' association in the Ga Traditional Area (Gh ii), July 10, 2002; and a residential land user who is a member of a landlords and residents association in the Ga Traditional Area (Gh 12), October 6, 2004.

[241] "Tenant farmer narrates his ordeal to committee," *Daily Graphic* (Accra), July 18, 1987; and "Ban on landlords, tenant farmers in Western Region still in force," *Daily Graphic* (Accra), March 12, 1987.

[242] "Six chiefs to pay back 84,450.50 cedis," *Daily Graphic* (Accra), May 5, 1983.

[243] "Committee on tenant farmers sits," *Daily Graphic* (Accra), May 22, 1986. The recommendations of the report can be found in *Report of the Committee on Tenant/Settler Farmers.* An interview with an official of the Office of the Administrator of Stool Lands

had tried to document stool land boundaries in the first decade of the 1900s.[244]

The institutional requirements of the age-old bargain had won once again! Sefwi-Wiawso royalty became friendlier towards the PNDC and helped transform the area into a stronghold of the NDC, the party formed by PNDC members upon the reintroduction of democracy in 1992. The state noticed the change and continued to allow chiefs unfettered control over land. The government ceased the surveying and documentation of land interests in the area.[245]

CONCLUSION

Property rights institutions are a key part of the structures that constitute the state. This chapter should be read then, at least partly, as a study of the motivations behind Batswana and Ghanaian leaders' choices of different ways of institutionalizing the state. In explaining their divergent institutional preferences, it is tempting to ascribe causal significance to the supposed economic exploitation of land by Batswana elite as against the political exploitation of land by Ghanaian elites. But we cannot simply portray political exploitation as problematic and economic exploitation as good.

Batswana leaders had serious political motivations for their creation of secure property rights institutions. They were providing favorable institutions to political allies – big cattle ranchers – who made handsome financial contributions to BDP electoral efforts. Further, parts of the gains that BDP leaders received from their cattle ranching and real estate activities were used for political action aimed at entrenching individual party members and the party as a whole. A characteristic of the direct/indirect typology developed here is that each of these ways of exploiting land can be used to extract both political and economic gains.

It is also tempting to ascribe the secure rights in Botswana solely to the long reign of the BDP. The persistence of weak property institutions in Ghana would then be ascribed to the tenuous and brief control of the state by various groups of leaders. The argument would be that unlike their Ghanaian counterparts, Batswana leaders can afford to secure rights

in the Sefwi-Wiawso traditional area (Gh 49), November 26, 2004, indicated the initial steps the PNDC took to implement some of these recommendations.

[244] Berry, *Chiefs Know Their Boundaries*, pp. 10–20.

[245] Interview with an official of the Office of the Administrator of Stool Lands in the Sefwi-Wiawso Traditional Area (Gh 49), November 26, 2004.

because they have held power with little threats to their authority. As I point out in my response to this objection in Chapter 2, this is informed by a lack of a comparative perspective. Other long-lasting and secure leaders, such as Paul Biya of Cameroon and the late Omar Bongo of Gabon are not known to have consistently engaged in reforms that have boosted markets.

Further, undermining the security of land rights is not always the best way for leaders facing challenges to their authority to ensure their survival. For these reasons, we cannot simply point to the long and relatively secure reign of the BDP as an explanation of their efforts at reinforcing institutions. We need to explore why they saw such institutional reforms as an effective means of gaining and maintaining their secure hold on the state. This book argues that their willingness to create strong property institutions depended on the specific contextual factors of how BDP politicians, bureaucrats, and their allies have drawn gains from land that they used to ensure their political dominance.

4

Traditional Leaders Take Charge in Akyem Abuakwa and Ga

When Kofi Bediako, a Ghanaian engineer who had worked and resided in the United States for many years, decided to return home to retire, he bought a plot of land from a traditional chief for the handsome sum of $2400 to construct a house in a peri-urban area of the Ghanaian capital Accra. However, like many who try to buy land in this area, Mr. Bediako's experiences were soon to become a nightmare.

As he was building his house, another Ghanaian who had recently returned from a sojourn in Britain claimed the same land and issued Mr. Bediako with court papers, requesting that he stop development of the plot. But while they were in court contesting ownership of the land, a third party, also claiming the land, brought in *landguards* armed with a bulldozer to tear down Kofi's development and keep all intruders off the land. Further investigation revealed that all three claimants had been sold the same piece of land by a chief who remained free even as the buyers fought over possession of the land.

The venality of some government officials and the generally low capacity of the Land Title Registry and the Lands Commission made searches of the register for ownership information not a particularly useful way of finding who owned parcels of land. *Landguards* thus took a leading role in protecting and contesting land rights in the Ga Traditional Area in which the capital city Accra is located.[1]

This story captures some of the ways in which Ga traditional leaders have subverted institutions that govern property rights and have created

---

[1] "Menace of land guards evokes fear in capital," *Africanews* 40–42, July 20, 1999, http://lists.peacelink.it/afrinews/msg00022.html. (Accessed April 18, 2007.)

an environment of confusion and violence in which they have reaped significant economic and political gains from the increasingly valuable land around Accra.[2]

In the late nineteenth century, chiefs in the neighboring area of Akyem Abuakwa handled property rights institutions in very similar ways.[3] However, unlike Ga leaders who have continued on this path, Akyem leaders since the mid-1900s have tried with some success to reinforce property institutions, thus creating levels of security that have attracted the attention of many.[4]

The analysis in this book shows how and why chiefs and lineage heads have dealt with property rights in different ways given that, as discussed in Chapter 3, generations of state leaders in Ghana have allowed chiefs in both areas great freedom in how they deal with land. The similarity of the bargain between state leaders and chiefs, discussed in Chapter 3, allows us to control for the similar impact of the state by holding it constant across these two traditional areas in Ghana. This is not an effort to exclude the state and those who control it from an exploration of subnational property rights dynamics. It is rather an explanation of why local land institutions nested within the larger macro-political institutional context of the same state vary. We can only understand the story told here within the wider context of the analysis of Ghanaian state leaders in Chapter 3.

The ways in which traditional leaders in these two areas have derived economic and political value from land explains how they have handled property rights institutions. Like the state leaders in Ghana discussed earlier, traditional leaders in both the Ga and Akyem Abuakwa traditional areas drew gains from land in direct ways unmediated by the productive use of land. They commercialized and sold land parcels as land prices rose steeply during the late 1800s and early 1900s.[5] Some of these revenues

---

[2] "Chiefs, plots, and lands department," *Ghanaian Chronicle* (Accra), December 10, 2001; interviews with the chairman of a landlords and residents association in the Ga Traditional Area (Gh ii), July 10, 2002; an employee of a real estate development agency in Accra (Gh iii), July 3, 2002; "Menace of landguards evokes fear in capital," *Africanews* 40–42, July 20, 1999, http://lists.peacelink.it/afrinews/msg00022.html (accessed April 18, 2007); "Chiefs, plots, and lands department," *Ghanaian Chronicle* (Accra), December 10, 2001; Mahama and Dixon, "Acquisition and affordability," p. 23.

[3] Ilegbune, "Concessions scramble," pp. 19–24.

[4] Addo-Fening, *Akyem Abuakwa*, p. 431; Firmin-Sellers, *The Transformation*, Ch. 4; Hill, *Gold Coast Cocoa Farmer*, p. 12; and interview with an official of the customary land secretariat of Okyeman, in Kyebi (Gh 55), December 13, 2004.

[5] Ilegbune, "Concessions scramble," pp. 19–24; and Robertson, *Sharing the Same Bowl*, p. 62.

were then used to fight political battles over chieftaincy. This sale of land led chiefs in both areas to undermine property institutions in their areas. Predatory leaders exploited buyers' trust to engage in the fraudulent multiple sales of land or sales of land to which they had no right – practices that were possible only in an environment in which property rights institutions were weak. The environment of insecurity and uncertainty that facilitated these activities was socially costly. Because chiefs drew little gains from the eventual productive use to which land was put, they could externalize much of this cost.

But the paths of leaders in these two areas diverged in the mid-1900s. Ga traditional leaders continued with the sale of land and so maintained weak institutions that allowed them to reallocate lands and allocate lands in which they had no interests. In Akyem Abuakwa, heightened conflicts between the paramount chief Nana Ofori Atta and lower chiefs between 1912 and 1943 led many chiefs and family heads to adopt agriculture and sharecropping arrangements as they sought to maximize gains from land that they could then use to protect their rule.

This shift to the productive use of land led traditional leaders to reinforce property rights institutions, just as state leaders in Botswana and Early Kenya had done. They now depended heavily on the seasonal harvest, for their revenues, but there would have been no crops to harvest in the disruptive environment that weak property institutions allowed for. They could no longer benefit from, or externalize, the high social costs of the insecurity and uncertainty associated with weak property rights institutions.

TRADITIONAL LEADERS RESPOND TO RISING LAND VALUES

The Ga people inhabit the Accra Plains close to the central part of Ghana's Atlantic coastline. The Ga are part of the larger Ga-Adamgbe group. After migrating to the area, they settled on the western side of the Accra Plains and they include the Ga Mashie of the central Accra as well as the neighboring peoples of Tema, Osu, Alata, Teshi, Nungua, and La. They formed a centralized political organization before 1600 that was destroyed when they were defeated in 1677 by the neighboring Akan state of Akwamu.[6] After that defeat, leaders of seven Ga communities – Asere,

---

[6] S. Quarcoopome, "The Decline of Traditional Authority: The Case of the Ga Mashie State of Accra.' Paper presented at International Conference on Chieftaincy in Africa, International Conference Center, Accra, January 6–10, 2003.

Abola, Gbese, Otublohum, Alata, Sempe, and Akanmaje – agreed to create an overlord (*mantse*) that would serve the ceremonial function of uniting different communities that were under the firm control of divisional chiefs and their underlings.[7]

Unlike the Ga political entity that is on the coast, the state of Akyem Abuakwa is located in Ghana's southern forest belt. The Akyem are part of the broader Akan group that inhabits most of southern Ghana and part of Cote d'Ivoire. Akyem Abuakwa, which was already established by 1692, was fashioned out of repeated military wars with neighboring Akwamu and Asante in the seventheenth, eighteenth, and nineteenth centuries. The exigencies of warfare probably influenced the centralized political organization of the Akyem compared to that of Ga.[8] The Okyenhene, King of Akyem Abuakwa, held substantive power over lesser chiefs and ordinary members of the state. Below the Okyenhene in descending order were senior divisional chiefs, divisional chiefs, chiefs, and headmen.[9]

The location of the Ga Traditional Area has made it a vital trade site for Africans and Europeans from as far back as the fifteenth century. The flourishing trade in the area led to the commercialization of land.[10] Increasing trade with Europeans along the coast made control of Ga lands and their trade routes very important. This trade brought new residents into the area. The construction of the James Fort and Christiansborg trading and slaving forts by Europeans in the late 1600s made this area even more attractive as a trading site.[11] The movement of the nation's capital to Accra in 1877 made it the leading industrial and service sector area as well as the most valuable commercial and residential real estate in the country.[12]

In Akyem Abuakwa, rich soil, dense rain forests, and mineral reserves made farming, gathering of wild crops like kola nut and rubber, exploitation of timber, and the traditional mining of minerals such as gold dominant economic activities before the mid-1800s.[13] The pivotal event in the

---

[7] Firmin-Sellers, *The Transformation*, p. 37.

[8] Addo-Fening, *Akyem Abuakwa*, pp. 6–12.

[9] Joseph Boakye Danquah, *The Akim Abuakwa Handbook* (London: F. Groom, 1928), p. 62.

[10] Claire Robertson, "Social and economic change in twentieth-century Accra: Ga women," (PhD dissertation, University of Wisconsin, Madison, 1974), p. 23.

[11] Daniel McFarland, *Historical Dictionary of Ghana*, African Historical Dictionaries, No. 39 (Metuchen, NJ: Scarecrow Press, 1985), p. xxii.

[12] Robertson, *Sharing the Same Bowl*, pp. 27–28; and Mahama and Dixon, "Acquisition and affordability," pp. 15, 20.

[13] Danquah, *The Akim Abuakwa Handbook*, pp. 40–44.

commercialization of land here was the arrival of many mineral and timber concessionaires and farmers looking for virgin forest land on which to farm oil palm and cocoa in the 1800s.[14]

One of the effects of the commercialization of land in these two areas has been the proliferation of enduring distributive conflicts over land ownership, control, and use. Parties in these conflicts have included the Ghanaian state, various levels of traditional chiefs, family heads, ordinary citizens originating from that area, and Ghanaians and foreigners seeking to make a fortune in the area. As pointed out in Chapter 3, the Ghanaian state has refrained from creating strong property rights institutions in most of these areas under the control of traditional chiefs. As I show below, in the absence of the state, chiefs in these two areas have handled property institutions in divergent ways.

Rules on Allocations and Transactions

Ga traditional leaders have made previously established rules on how to allocate land more murky and complex, thus creating a level of confusion that has made it hard even for Ghanaian residents in the Ga Traditional Area to know the proper way to acquire land.[15] This is similar to what chiefs in Akyem Abuakwa did before the reign of Nana Ofori Atta I in the early 1900s.[16] Since his reign, Akyem chiefs and elders have attempted to establish and clarify rules regulating land allocation and transfer that reduce confusion and conflict.[17]

Land Information Systems

Most leaders in the Ga Traditional Area have not created record systems that would keep information on the geographic properties of, and interests in, land parcels.[18] Sometimes chiefs have even refused to issue

---

[14] Ilegbune, "Concessions scramble," p. 17; Phillips, *The Enigma*, p. 63; and Addo-Fening, *Akyem Abuakwa*, p. 332.

[15] Mahama and Dixon, "Acquisition and affordability," p. 18; interviews with a residential land user in Accra (Gh vii), October 6, 2004; an employee of a real estate agency in Accra (Gh iii), July 3, 2002; a *landguard* in the Ga Traditional Area (Gh v), July 20, 2002; and another employee of a real estate development agency in Accra (Gh 8), October 6, 2004.

[16] Addo-Fening, *Akyem Abuakwa*, p. 333; and Ilegbune, "Concessions scramble," p. 23.

[17] Interview with an official of the customary land secretariat of Okyeman, Kyebi (Gh 55), December 13, 2004; and Addo-Fening, *Akyem Abuakwa*, p. 431.

[18] Interviews with official of the Lands Commission, Accra (Gh 2), September 24, 2004; and another official of the Lands Commission in Accra (Gh 1), September 24, 2004.

receipts for monies received when they have allocated land.[19] Surveyors and draftsmen who sometimes have issued indentures have operated as instruments of chiefs and not as professional bodies exerting
standards.[20] The absence of proper records has made it more difficult for
land buyers to cross-check before they have entered into land transactions.

Akyem chiefs before Ofori Atta behaved in very similar ways.[21] However, beginning with Ofori Atta's establishment of a lands office that
issued "native leases" in Kyebi, many lesser chiefs in Akyem Abuakwa
created smaller entities in their palaces to make and maintain records on
land transactions in the mid-1900s.[22] The native leases issued by Okyenhene's lands office, which included survey diagrams, were considered
legal by the colonial government and were only denied recognition by the
independent government of Ghana in 1962 through the Administration
of Lands Act.[23]

Adjudication Mechanisms

Like chiefs elsewhere in Ghana, leaders in the Ga Traditional Area have
courts that adjudicate a wide range of disputes.[24] In the Ga Traditional
Area, many of these courts lack integrity and credibility in land cases
because traditional chiefs and elders who have caused many land disputes
have also presided over them. In addition to these courts, the Ga *mantse*'s
palace has adjudicated disputes between chiefs over land rights. Many
chiefs, however, have refused to submit themselves to these courts or
have openly flouted decisions reached by them.[25]

Traditional chiefs in Akyem Abuakwa similarly have courts that have
sought to resolve land disputes.[26] The minimal involvement of chiefs and
elders in Akyem Abuakwa in causing land disputes after the mid-1900s
has given their courts more credibility.

[19] Gough and Yankson, "Land markets," p. 2493.
[20] Ibid., p. 2492.
[21] Ilegbune, "Concessions scramble," p. 23.
[22] Interview with an official of the Okyenhene's land secretariat, Kyebi (GH 55), December
17, 2004 (Gh 55); and Addo-Fening, *Akyem Abuakwa*, p. 431.
[23] Ibid.
[24] Interview with senior subject and close ally of a divisional stool in the Ga Traditional
Area (Gh 14), October 10, 2004.
[25] Interview with an official of the Ga Traditional Council (Gh 71), May 1, 2005.
[26] Interviews with an official of the customary land secretariat of Okyeman, in Kyebi
(Gh 55), December 13, 2004; and an official of the Okyeman Traditional Council in
Kyebi (Gh 62), December 16, 2004.

Beyond these courts the Okyenhene also has had two dispute resolution mechanisms. The arbitration court at Ofori Panin Fie is presided over by the Okyenhene or the Kyebihene and makes decisions that are regarded as final. Though not recognized officially by the state, most chiefs have subjected themselves to the proceedings of this court.[27] There is also the judicial committee of the Akyem Abuakwa Traditional Council which is recognized by the state and has resolved disputes between chiefs. This judicial committee has played a leading role in the settlement of interchief disputes over land in the absence of the state's Stool Lands Boundary Commission, which has existed mostly on paper.[28]

Enforcement

Ga traditional leaders have employed their enforcement powers in highly selective and disruptive ways through the cultivation and deployment of armed groups that have exacerbated violence and disruptions in the Ga Traditional Area.[29] *Landguards* have been the main enforcement arm of these chiefs and have been used to selectively settle and evict people regardless of the land rights that they had acquired.[30] *Landguards* also have extorted further payments from people who already have paid for their land by compelling them to pay "digging fees" before development. Those who have resisted have suffered physical assaults and the demolition of their physical structures.[31]

Akyem chiefs similarly enforced arbitrary decisions against land holders, including their citizens, in a disruptive and selective way before the reign of Ofori Atta I.[32] Since the mid-1900s, even though *asafo*[33] exist in Akyem Abuakwa, chiefs have not used them to evict and settle people

---

[27] Interview with an official of the Okyeman Traditional Council in Kyebi (Gh 62), December 16, 2004.

[28] Ibid.

[29] Interviews with a long-term employee of a real estate development agency in Accra (Gh iv), July 13, 2002; and the chairman of a landlords and residents association in the Ga Traditional Area (Gh ii), July 10, 2002.

[30] Interview with a long-term employee of a real estate development agency in Accra (Gh iv), July 13, 2002.

[31] Interview with an employee of a real estate development agency in Accra (Gh iii), July 3, 2002.

[32] Addo-Fening, *Akyem Abuakwa*, 333; and Ilegbune, "Concessions scramble," p. 23.

[33] *Asafo* companies were youth that constituted the main fighting force of these communities. See Dominic Fortescue, "The Accra crowd: the Asafo, and the opposition to the Municipal Corporations Ordinance, 1924–25," *Canadian Journal of African Studies* 24 (1990) 3, 348–375.

and engage in extortion and protection rackets like many Ga leaders use *landguards* in the Ga Traditional Area.

To understand this divergence in the ways in which chiefs have dealt with property institutions we need to focus on the different ways in which they have drawn gains from land.

THE ERA OF LAND SALES IN GA AND AKYEM ABUAKWA

Many Ga chiefs and lineage heads embraced the outright sale of land as land values rose in the mid-1800s.[34] The appearance of hordes of people willing to offer money up front for pieces of land proved tempting to Ga traditional leaders. Those who controlled land stood to make vast amounts of money from alienating lands that they had earlier granted free-of-charge to land users. Writing in 1955, Assistant Commissioner of Lands Pogucki noted that the "sale of land is a dealing long established in Ga customary law."[35] Firmin-Sellers similarly recognized the prevalence of outright land sales in the Ga Traditional Area before 1944.[36]

These sales quickly came to involve very large sums of money. Robertson noted that "land sales became a large source of income for Ga lineages, *mantsemei*, priests, and other individuals, mainly men.... Land value per acre went from about £800 in 1903 to £30,000 in 1954 in Central Accra."[37] The gains that traditional leaders received from these sales accrued up front and were not drawn from the productive residential and commercial uses to which these lands were later put.

Like their Ga counterparts, many Akyem chiefs enthusiastically embraced the opportunity for land sales presented by the commercialization of land in the mid-1800s.[38] Many neighboring Krobo and Akwapim farmers and flocks of mineral and timber concessionaires coming from as far away as Europe were willing to offer chiefs money up front for land. This contrasted with the chiefs' earlier need to levy tributes on agricultural, mineral, and gathering activities.[39]

---

[34] Robertson, *Sharing the Same Bowl*, p. 62; and Ilegbune, "Concessions scramble," p. 17; and Addo-Fening, *Akyem Abuakwa*, pp. 49, 329.

[35] R. J. H. Pogucki, *Land Tenure in Ga customary law* (Accra: Government Printer, 1955), p. 31.

[36] Firmin-Sellers, *The Transformation*, pp. 31, 52.

[37] Robertson, *Sharing the Same Bowl*, p. 49.

[38] Hill, *Gold Coast Cocoa Farmer*, 13; Great Britain, *Report of the Commission*, p. 19; and Amanor and Diderutuah, *Share Contracts*, pp. 1–2; and Phillip, *The Enigma*, p. 70.

[39] Addo-Fening, *Akyem Abuakwa*; and Hill, *Gold Coast Cocoa Farmer*; Ilegbune. "Concessions scramble;" Phillips, *The Enigma*, p. 63.

Chiefs embraced the opportunity so warmly that, by 1912, when Nana Ofori Atta I ascended the throne, alarmingly large tracts of Akyem land had been alienated outright to strangers. The Krobo acquired a vast extent of land from the Begoro stool.[40] Akwapim farmers bought huge tracts of land from the Apapam, Asamankese, and Akanten stools. The Nifahene (one of the divisional chiefs) sold off large tracts of Asiakwa lands.[41] Even Okyenhene Amoako Atta III sold off huge tracts of Akyem Abuakwa lands.[42] The Tafohene was similarly involved in land sales to cocoa farmers.[43] Land sales were so rampant that by 1921, citizens in certain parts of Akyem Abuakwa were beginning to suffer from a shortage of cultivable land.[44]

Soon, incidents of overlapping claims began to occur in both the Ga and Akyem Abuakwa areas. Leaders began to resell land that had already been sold by their predecessors. Others sold the same piece of land repeatedly to more than one person. Yet others sold land that belonged to other leaders and which they knew they had no right to sell. Firmin-Sellers notes that land buyers in Ga "typically found that the plot of land they had acquired had been sold to several other claimants, or that the land had been sold without the consent of the customary owners."[45] She further notes that "unconcerned with legal niceties, the speculators often sold the same tract of land to multiple claimants."[46]

In areas with mineral and timber potential, including Akyem Abuakwa, Ilegbune notes that "some chiefs, in their ambition to make more money, sometimes knowingly conceded" lands that they knew belonged to other chiefs.[47] Some chiefs in Akyem Abuakwa took these activities to an extreme height by selling off lands that were already under cultivation by their citizens.[48] These multiple and overlapping grants render plausible

---

[40] For the sake of clarity, I again quote Rathbone's definition of a stool as referring "firstly to a real stool or throne, upon which a chief sits. It also serves as a synonym for a chief's office and the state or section of state over which he and more occasionally she ruled," *Nkrumah and the Chiefs*, p. 13.

[41] Addo-Fening, *Akyem Abuakwa*, pp. 329, 433.

[42] Robert Addo-Fening, "Chieftaincy and issues of good governance, accountability, and development: a case study of Akyem Abuakwa under Okyenhene Ofori Atta I 1912–1943." Paper presented at International Conference on chieftaincy in Africa, International Conference Center, Accra, January 6–10, 2003, p. 3.

[43] Addo-Fening, *Akyem Abuakwa*, p. 355.

[44] Addo-Fening, *Akyem Abuakwa*, p. 332.

[45] Firmin-Sellers, *The Transformation*, p. 52.

[46] Ibid., p. 31.

[47] Ilegbune, "Concessions scramble," p. 23.

[48] Addo-Fening, *Akyem Abuakwa*, p. 333.

the assessment of the West African Land Committee Draft Report's statement, as quoted by Ilegbune, that in the early 1900s "the chiefs of the
Gold Coast alienated an area which actually exceeded the total area of
the territory itself."[49]

These activities raise interesting questions. Why would sellers want to
sell uncertain rights – the land equivalent of Akerlof's "lemons?"[50] Why
would buyers keep buying these rights of uncertain quality? How profitable have these activities been over the long run? There is a temptation
to attribute these actions to genuine mistakes by chiefs unsure of the
extent of their territories and the location of grants they had already
made.[51] But the widespread, consistent, and long-lasting nature of these
activities suggest that they are better understood as a deliberate style of
dealing in land that deserves further clarification.

Below I present an explanation that exposes both the economic and
political reasons underlying these activities. When land is first commercialized, these activities result from efforts by some chiefs to multiply gains
through short-term exploitation of buyers' trust. Afterward it becomes
an effort by later generations of land-hungry chiefs to benefit from lands
that have already been sold.

As land first became commercialized in the early nineteenth century
buyers paid for what they knew to be rights of certain quality sold by
chiefs. Soon, very cunning chiefs were able to exploit the trust of buyers in
the certainty of the rights being sold in order to multiply the compensation
they received for each plot by selling the same parcel multiple times. As
long as these activities were on a small scale and most chiefs stayed honest,
for a short while the few cheating chiefs were able to make more money
than if they had sold just one strong right to each parcel. This is because
buyers, still believing that chiefs only offered a secure right in each sale,
were willing to offer the prime price.

These activities may have been prolonged a little longer in the Ga
Traditional Area and in Akyem Abuakwa due to the fact that many buyers were new migrant-farmers, concessionaires sometimes coming from
other African countries and Europe, and new arrivals from cities. We can
assume that migrants faced greater information problems than long-term
inhabitants. The causal story here is similar to the occasional sale of over-
priced and worthless stock by companies. As long as most companies play

---

[49] Ilegbune, "Concessions scramble," p. 17. Also see Phillips, *The Enigma*, p. 70.
[50] Akerlof, "The Market for 'lemons'," pp. 488–500.
[51] Ilegbune, "Concessions scramble," p. 23.

within the rules and stock buyers have confidence in the workings of the market, the occasional huckster will be able to swindle some investors.

But we can assume that word soon got out about the existence of these predatory practices of some sellers. Evidence of court cases concerning these issues supports this assumption.[52] Buyers then had two options. They could leave the area and buy land elsewhere or stay and offer lower amounts to compensate for the uncertain character of the good they were purchasing. The presence of minerals, and particularly rich soils in rural Akyem Abuakwa, and the allure of jobs, electricity, water, and other amenities that draw people towards urban areas such as Accra in developing countries ensured that people stayed, and even more kept arriving in these two areas.

After buyers had decided to stay and to buy property, they would have tried to look for more reputable sellers from whom to buy. We see the workings of this dynamic in the Ga Traditional Area now, in which some people who can afford the considerably higher prices try to buy land from the state or from burgeoning real estate development agencies. In the case of the latter, it is assumed that, by the time these developers finish building houses, they will have dealt with most of the conflicting claims on the land.

Because over 60 percent of land in both Ga and Akyem Abuakwa was held by chiefs, people had to approach them for land. But the uncertain nature of the rights they were purchasing would have led buyers to lower the prices to such an extent that land sellers who engaged in multiple sales of the same land might not have been able to make more than they would have from selling one strong right. Again in support of this view, writing of concessionaires in southern Ghana in the nineteenth and early twentieth centuries, Phillips notes that they paid "derisory prices" for land from chiefs.[53]

In some ways the purchase of land in such a situation becomes like a lottery in which buyers purchase not land rights but a certain probability that they will actually acquire those land rights. Lowering bids reduces the amount of money buyers lose, if they end up not getting the land. But, unlike the lottery, the initial purchase is only the beginning of the game. Buyers may have to fight off other claimants and compensate later chiefs who might seek to renegotiate the grant. So paying only a fraction of the price is also a strategy that leaves them with some money that they can

52 Ibid., p. 23.
53 Phillips, *The Enigma*, pp. 64–65.

then use to fend off others and compensate later leaders who might try to resell the land. Phillips notes that concessionaires in colonial Gold Coast often "found themselves paying several times over for the same piece of land."[54]

The struggle to gain and keep land parcels can sometimes be an expensive exercise that involves going to court, developing the land as fast as one can (one consequence of this is the lack of planning in many areas), and employing private enforcers to protect land. In some ways, such a land market redistributes wealth from the weak to the strong in that the weak who pay for, but do not end up receiving land, are subsidizing the powerful who pay a fraction of the price but acquire the land. The powerful can buy land at very low prices and use their muscle to fend off weaker claimants. This might explain why many concessionaires opposed and contributed to the defeat of the Public Lands Bill of 1897, which promised them secure titles in exchange for higher land prices.[55]

If chiefs could not make as much from the repeated allocations of uncertain rights to the same parcel of land as they could by selling one strong claim, then why did they keep reselling already allocated lands and selling the lands of other chiefs? The answer lies in the natural workings of the outright sale of a constant amount of land by generations of chiefs who are almost totally dependent on land for revenues.

Incumbent leaders and their allies tried to sell as much land as quickly as they could to maximize benefits. As noted earlier, the "concessions fever" of the early 1900s alone saw chiefs in the Gold Coast colony, an area including Ga and Akyem Abuakwa, concede "25,000 square miles – greater than its actual area."[56] Since each sale reduced the land available for later grants, unallocated lands were soon exhausted. It is important to note that this stage does not even require the exhaustion of all lands under the control of a chief; only the exhaustion of those lands that people desire at any particular time.

Land users can be extremely myopic in their view of the lands they see as desirable. An example from the United States demonstrates this

---

[54] Ibid., pp. 64–65.

[55] Ibid.

[56] Phillips, *The Enigma*, p. 70. For more on the magnitude pace of land grants, see also Jarle Simensen, "Rural mass action in the context of anticolonial protest: the *Asafo* movement of Akyem Abuakwa," *Canadian Journal of African Studies* 8 (January 1974), p. 29; and Addo-Fening, "Chieftaincy and issues," p. 4; and Firmin-Sellers, *The Transformation*, p. 74.

point. In the late 1830s, while the price of land in the heart of Chicago grew tenfold, land a mere 8–10 miles away received little attention with its price stagnant at the $1.25 an acre first assigned to it by government. Hoyt notes that "apparently even the most vivid speculative imagination of that time could not conceive of a city that grew so far from the river and the lake that these acres would be needed for urban use."[57] And then, as now, there were without doubt many imaginative speculative minds in Chicago, as the accounts of both Hoyt and Cronon indicate.[58]

When desirable land shrank enough, new chiefs faced two choices. They could uphold rights already sold and not receive any resources from that land, or they could resell the land already allocated at the reduced price that buyers were willing to offer for such encumbered lands. Reselling actually involved forcing the occupant to pay another fee for the land or having someone else buy the allocated but not-yet-fully-developed land. *The prime price attached to the reputable sale of one strong right was no longer an option.*

Revenue-maximizing chiefs dependent on land sales preferred reallocating land for the fractional price to not earning any money by upholding earlier grants. Over time, chiefs in a regime where land was sold had more and more of an incentive to abrogate former grants and reallocate rights. Further, chiefs facing land scarcity had an incentive not only to reallocate earlier grants in their realm but also to sell the lands of other chiefs. Because buyers were suspicious and lowered bids anyway, chiefs had little to gain from cultivating a good reputation by not selling the lands of other chiefs.

The political motivations of these sellers, who were, after all, political leaders, render their activities even more understandable. Sometimes the urge to resell came from the need to raise funds on short notice to litigate over, and fund militias to pursue, pervasive and recurring chieftaincy disputes.[59] At other times, claimants of a stool sought to undermine incumbents by laying claim to, selling off, or granting to political allies lands of stool occupants. These political motivations render more plausible the explanation of the activities of traditional leaders, since these calculations might even lead them to forego the higher prices attached

[57] Homer Hoyt, *One Hundred Years of Land Values in Chicago* (Chicago: University of Chicago Press, 1933), p. 36.

[58] Hoyt, *One Hundred Years*; and Cronon, *Nature's Metropolis*.

[59] Rathbone, *Nkrumah and the Chiefs*, pp. 2; and Meek, *Land, Law, and Custom*, p. 172.

to single reputable sales for the political benefits attached to fraudulent sales.[60]

One might object here that this situation should be extremely unlikely. Chiefs should not be able to resell lands. Buyers ought to incorporate the difficulty of securing protection into the price so that only people with the capacity to protect their rights would be likely to buy land, thus making it difficult for chiefs to resell. But this is based on the faulty assumption that land buyers don't frequently misperceive or miscalculate. Like states,[61] which have even more impressive intelligence-gathering capabilities, individuals can miscalculate or misperceive the capacity of chiefs. More importantly, they almost always are ignorant of the capacities of the *unknown* third parties who may buy the same land with catastrophic consequences. In the Ga Traditional Area we see a lot of people who buy land thinking they can protect it only to find out later that they cannot. I have met many people who have fallen victim to these kinds of activities, and unsurprisingly, not one of them has bought land knowing full well that they could not protect it.

In Akyem Abuakwa the direct exploitation of land through sales boosted the power of lesser chiefs relative to the Okyenhene.[62] Proceeds from land sales were one-off, up-front payments that were very easy to hide.[63] This enabled lower chiefs to avoid paying the traditional *abusa*[64] tribute that they owed the Okyenhene and bolstered their economic and political autonomy.[65] The effort by the chief of Asamankese to formally secede from Akyem Abuakwa in 1921 was only one example

---

[60] Bates provides a reminder of leaders' willingness to make such trade-offs between economic efficiency gains and political expediency. Bates, *Markets and States*.

[61] Stephen Van Evera, "The cult of the offensive and the origins of the First World War," in Steven E. Miller, ed. *Military Strategy and the Origins of the First World War* (Princeton, NJ: Princeton University Press, 1985); Jack Snyder, *The Ideology of the Offensive: Military Decision Making and the Disasters of 1914* (Ithaca, NY: Cornell University Press, 1984); Stephen Van Evera, *Causes of War: Power and the Roots of Conflict* (Ithaca, NY: Cornell UniversityPress, 1999); Geoffrey Blainey, *The Causes of War* (New York, N.Y.: The Free Press, 1973).

[62] Addo-Fening, *Akyem Abuakwa*, pp. 330–332, 433; Phillips, *The Enigma*, p. 119; and Firmin-Sellers, *The Transformation*, p. 63.

[63] Addo-Fening, *Akyem Abuakwa*, pp. 320–330, 433.

[64] The *abusa* system required those involved in mining and gathering within the realm of a chief to give a third of what they found to the chief. Hill, *Gold Coast Cocoa Farmer*, p. 10.

[65] Addo-Fening, *Akyem Abuakwa*, pp. 330–332, 433; and Firmin-Sellers, *The Transformation*, p. 63.

of this increasing empowerment relative to the Okyenhene of lower chiefs involved in land sales.[66]

Creating an Enabling Institutional Environment

Like state leaders in Ghana, Kenya, and Botswana, chiefs in the Ga Traditional Area and Akyem Abuakwa set about creating a favorable institutional environment to facilitate how they exploited land. However, as postulated by the theory here, their institutional needs were more similar to those of state leaders in Ghana and Late Kenya because they were all involved in drawing gains that were not mediated by the productive exploitation of land.

Traditional leaders in Ga and Akyem Abuakwa from the mid 1880s to the 1920s thrived on the perpetuation of weak institutions that govern land rights. Strengthening these institutions would have hindered their activities. But an environment of insecure rights in which transaction costs were high for buyers was very convenient. High information, measurement, adjudication, and enforcement costs facilitated activities such as the reselling of land and the sale of land belonging to other leaders.

The absence of credible land information systems such as registries made it more difficult for buyers to check claims of land sellers before they entered into transactions. This made it easier for chiefs to sell fake rights. The absence of these information and documentation systems also deprived landholders of documents that they could use to defend their rights in courts of law. It is in this light that we should view the lack of efforts by many chiefs to document the extent of their lands or the parcels that they had given out.[67] It is also in this light that we should view the deliberate obfuscation of boundaries and rules of land allocation by chiefs and lineage heads in both areas.

The social costs of these predatory sales and the environment of weak rights that facilitated them were extremely high. They led to widespread litigation over land.[68] This motivated the comment of Ormsby Gore, then Undersecretary for the Colonies in 1926, that "land litigation is the curse

---

[66] Robert Addo-Fenning, "The Asamankese dispute 1919–1934," in Robert Addo-Fenning, et al., eds. *Akyem Abuakwa and the Politics of the Interwar Period in Ghana* (Basel: Basler Afrika Bibliographien, 1975), p. 65.

[67] Ilebgune, "Concessions scramble," p. 23.

[68] Meek, *Land, Law, and Custom*, 172; Ilegbune, "Concessions scramble," 23.

of the country."[69] Where chiefs were involved, they externalized the costs of litigation by taxing citizens to pay for court costs. In some communities the taxation was so severe that it led to the flight of labor as some young men ran away from their communities in an attempt to escape taxation or seek employment in mines to pay taxes back home.[70]

People interested in making productive investments in land were deprived of a favorable environment for such investment. They were forced to divert resources into wasteful litigation and the employment of private protection agents. But for chiefs in both areas, the nonfruition and lesser profitability of these agricultural, real estate, and commercial activities did not constitute a tragedy. They drew little from these activities, with their gains from land coming in the form of up-front payments for land allocations. Further, as becomes evident in the discussion of the Ga Traditional Area in the 1990s and 2000s below, the slow development of land caused by conflicts over land rights was beneficial to such leaders because it made it easier to convince new groups of buyers that undeveloped (but allocated) lands were unallocated.

PATHS DIVERGE IN THE 1930S

The Birth and Effects of an Agricultural Chieftaincy in Akyem Abuakwa

Developments in Ga and Akyem Abuakwa diverged with the ascent of Nana Ofori Atta I (1912–1943) to the throne of Akyem Abuakwa. Ofori Atta launched an effort at recentralizing power that caused many traditional leaders to adopt farming and sharecropping arrangements as they sought to maintain their autonomy. In this sense Akyem chiefs became more like state leaders in Botswana and Early Kenya in that they began to draw gains from land through indirect means mediated by the cultivation of land.

The formidable office of the Okyenhene[71] had been badly eroded when Ofori Atta ascended the throne as lower chiefs sold off land and refused to pay tribute to the Okyenhene.[72] He aggressively moved to increase his share of land revenues, reduce the share of lower chiefs, and exert more

---

[69] Cited in Meek, *Land, Law, and Custom*, p. 172.
[70] Ilebgune, "Concessions scramble," p. 24.
[71] The Okyenhene is the king or paramount chief of Akyem Abuakwa.
[72] Addo-Fening, *Akyem Abuakwa*, p. 330.

control over how lower chiefs used their revenues. He tried to enforce chiefs' payment of *abusa* tribute to his office and made the legality of land alienations subject to his signature to keep track of transactions on which he was owed tribute. Further, he later outlawed the outright sale of land.[73]

Forcing chiefs to become farmers and sharecroppers would presumably make it easier for the Okyenhene to monitor chiefs' transactions and capture his share of land revenues. It was easy for lower chiefs to mask the true value of proceeds from land sales or make them disappear altogether.[74] However, the seasonal or yearly proceeds from rentals and sharecropping arrangements created long-term, continual payments that were easier to recognize, monitor, and investigate. When chiefs attempted to hide payments, there was a greater probability of the Okyenhene punishing them by appropriating later harvests. Evidence of this process is seen in the campaign launched by Ofori Atta and his successors to investigate stools farms, distinguish between stool and private farms of chiefs, extract *abusa* tributes from such farms, and punish through seizure of farms those who did not pay the Okyenhene's levy.[75] As in Scott's[76] account of how state leaders seek to render their realms legible, the Okyenhene was trying to make decipherable to his tax collectors assets that his underlings had sought to make indecipherable.[77]

The Okyenhene also sought to control the ways in which lower chiefs spent their share of land revenues in order to limit their capacity to launch political challenges using such funds. In 1928, he created a state treasury to which all chiefs had to contribute 20 percent of their revenues from "farm-rents, gold, diamonds, sale of stool lands," and so on.[78] He led

---

[73] Ibid., pp. 330–336.

[74] Ibid., pp. 328–330, 433.

[75] Baffour Yaw Akese, Odikro of Adubiase wrote to the Okyenhene pleading for the return of a confiscated farm. claiming it was his personal property, not stool property, October 11, 1947, Akyem Abuakwa State Archive, AASA/3/106; and a letter from Kofi Bado of Anyinassing to Nana Ofori Atta II on November 19, 1947, indicated that Ofori Atta I had converted farms belonging Bado's relative, Bafour Dowuona, Odikro of Anyinassing into stool property, November 19, 1947, Akyem Abuakwa State Archive, AASA/3/106. Other letters bearing evidence of the ruthless campaign of Ofori Atta and his successors are present in this file.

[76] Scott, *Seeing Like a State*, pp. 2–3.

[77] This is not to deny the fact noted by scholars that the ban was partly motivated by the threat of landlessness that was facing ordinary Akyem people due to rampart land alienations. See Addo-Fening, *Akyem Abuakwa*, pp. 333–334; Ilegbune, "Concessions scramble," pp. 23–24; Simensen, "Rural mass action," p. 29.

[78] Firmin-Sellers, *The Transformation*, pp. 75–80; Addo-Fening, *Akyem Abuakwa*, p. 436.

the committee that oversaw the treasury and determined how the funds would be spent, giving him some control over how lower chiefs spent their revenues. This control was in addition to his persistent work to collect a third of all their land revenues as *abusa*. To ensure compliancy, he helped create the Native Administration Ordinance (1927) in colonial Ghana, which was subsequently revised. Among other things, the law made it illegal for lower chiefs in Ghana to secede or withdraw allegiance from a higher chief, and it gave paramount chiefs the power to punish rebellious chiefs and to seize stool property from chiefs who tried to convert it into their personal property.[79]

The chiefs of Asamankese and Akwatia opted for overt resistance to these centralizing efforts by boldly declaring their secession from Akyem Abuakwa in 1921.[80] Lacking brute force that equaled that of the Okyenhene's backers, the British colonial administration, many other Akyem chiefs simply resorted to underground resistance using means akin to the "weapons of the weak" discussed by Scott.[81] Their goals were to evade taxation by the Okyenhene and to exercise autonomy over how they spent their land revenues. They turned overwhelmingly towards farming and renting land to sharecroppers.[82] The reorientation towards farming masked their new strategy to evade taxation by the Okyenhene and flout his rules banning the alienation of land. The Okyenhene promoted farming to gain ascendancy in recurrent distributive conflicts, and on the surface it seemed as if he had succeeded as lower chiefs embraced farming. But as I show below, as lower chiefs and citizens embraced farming they fabricated new social arrangements that strengthened their position in these conflicts.[83]

To understand this resistance we should distinguish between two types of farms in Akyem Abuakwa. As Akyem citizens, chiefs could use their personal labor and capital to cultivate *personal farms* on which they owed no tribute to the Okyenhene.[84] These personal farms were different from *stool farms*. Stool farms were established using stool capital and

---

[79] Firmin-Sellers, *The Transformation*, pp. 69–70.
[80] Addo-Fening, "The Asamankese dispute," pp. 64–69.
[81] James Scott, *Weapons of the Weak: Everyday Forms of Resistance* (New Haven: Yale University Press, 1985).
[82] Hill, *Gold Coast Cocoa Farmer*, p. 13; and Addo-Fening, "Chieftaincy and issues," pp. 11–12.
[83] Hill, *Gold Coast Cocoa Farmer*, p. 16; and Amanor and Diderutuah, *Share Contracts*, p. 2.
[84] Hill, *Gold Coast Cocoa Farmer*, p. 14.

belonged not to the sitting chief, but to that stool as an institution.[85] The Okyenhene was owed tribute on stool farms. To avoid paying these tributes, many chiefs established farms using stool capital and declared them personal farms, instead of stool farms.[86]

Some chiefs even adapted these new arrangements to alienate land outright against the laws of the Okyenhene. Earlier sharecropping arrangements demanded that the produce, not the land, be shared once crops had borne fruit. At each harvest, the landlord and sharecropper would simply be assigned their area to harvest, with the farm remaining intact. Under the new system chiefs sometimes shared the farm upon maturation of the cocoa crop, creating two farms, one belonging to the tenant and the other to the landlord. This constituted alienating the land without actually selling it for cash.[87] Ofori Atta and his successor Ofori Atta II quickly recognized and sought to clamp down on these new methods of resistance through widespread farm seizures.[88]

Many chiefs exploited their control of stool lands to establish personal and stool farms.[89] Sharecropping arrangements proliferated. Chiefs became divided between taking advantage of this new economic opportunity and performing their increasing administrative duties. The new involvement of chiefs in cocoa farming was so intense that people began to complain of chiefs neglecting their duties to concentrate on farming.

---

[85] Addo-Fening, *Akyem Abuakwa*, pp. 404–436; interview with a traditional chief in Akyem Abuakwa (Gh 57), December 14, 2004; and Firmin-Sellers, *The Transformation*, p. 75.

[86] Bafour Yaw Akese, Odikro of Adubiase, in a letter to Ofori Atta II pleading for the return of a farm transformed into a stool farm by Ofori Atta I, claimed he had established this farm in his private capacity using private resources, October 11, 1947, Akyem Abuakwa Stool Archive, AASA/3/106. Bafour Kwadjo Akai II, Odikro of Kyea, in a letter to Ofori Atta II took a different approach and argued for the return of one of his converted farms on humanitarian grounds, November 28, 1947, AASA/3/106.

[87] Hill, *Gold Coast Cocoa Farmer*, p. 13; and Amanor and Diderutuah, *Share Contracts*, pp. 1–2.

[88] Baffour Yaw Akese, Odikro of Adubiase wrote to the Okyenhene pleading for the return of a confiscated farm claiming it was his personal property, not stool property, October 11, 1947, Akyem Abuakwa State Archive, AASA/3/106; and a letter from Kofi Bado of Anyinassing to Nana Ofori Atta II on 11–19–1947 indicated that Ofori Atta I had converted farms belonging to Bado's relative, Bafour Dowuona, Odikro of Anyinassing, into stool property, November 19, 1947, Akyem Abuakwa State Archive, AASA/3/106. Other letters bearing evidence of the ruthless campaign of Ofori Atta and his successors are present in this file.

[89] Addo-Fening, *Akyem Abuakwa*, pp. 388–390; interviews with an official of the Office of the Administrator of Stool Lands in a town in Akyem Abuakwa (Gh 56), December 14, 2004; and an official of the Cocoa Swollen Shoot Virus Disease (CSSVD) Control Unit in a town in Akyem Abuakwa (Gh 58), December 14, 2004.

In a way these complaints were similar to other complaints about the deep involvement of state officials in land-intensive productive businesses in Botswana and Early Kenya discussed in Chapters 3 and 5. Finding it difficult to reconcile the two, at least one chief is known to have resigned from the stool to pursue cocoa farming full time in 1919.[90] Nifahene Nana Kwaku Agyeman cited the fact that cocoa farming was more profitable in his decision to resign his divisional stool to become a full-time cocoa farmer.[91]

As chiefs and elders turned toward agricultural production, they developed preferences for, and sought to create, strong institutions that clarified and better enforced property rights in land, just as state leaders in Early Kenya and Botswana had. The most important shift by Akyem leaders was their attention to delineating and following clear rules for allocating and transferring land that created predictability.[92] This shift was logical because the preexisting environment of insecurity would have undermined agricultural activity and the seasonal produce from which chiefs now drew revenues.

The anthropologist Polly Hill, who did significant field research in these cocoa-growing areas, provides us with a direct causal link between the new interest of chiefs in the seasonal agricultural produce and their investment in property rights security. Writing of the new tranquility in these areas in 1956, she noted that "the chiefs have willingly agreed that the stranger-farmer shall be immune from disturbance and shall enjoy the same perpetuity of tenure as the indigenous cultivator, provided the agreed-upon proportion is regularly paid to the native authorities."[93]

To borrow from Bates's reflections on property elsewhere, chiefs had "attach[ed] their political future to [the] economic performance" of these farms, giving them – like leaders in Botswana and Early Kenya – an incentive to protect property rights.[94] New generations of chiefs inherited stool farms and personal farms from relatives and established new farms. These gave them an investment in the seasonal crop and an interest in ensuring an environment of security that facilitated agricultural production.

---

[90] Addo-Fening, *Akyem Abuakwa*, pp. 388–390.
[91] Addo-Fening, "Chieftaincy and issues," p. 12.
[92] Hill, *Gold Coast Cocoa Farmer*, p. 11; and Addo-Fening, *Akyem Abuakwa*, p. 431.
[93] Hill, Gold Coast Cocoa Farmer, p. 12.
[94] Robert Bates, "On *The Politics of Property Rights* by Haber, Razo, and Mauer," *Journal of Economic Literature* XLII (June 2004), p. 497.

THE INSTITUTIONAL CONSEQUENCES OF CONTINUING
LAND SALES IN GA

The shift to the exploitation of land through farming in Akyem Abuakwa was in stark contrast to Ga leaders' continued direct exploitation of land through sales.[95] Had The Office of the Administrator of Stool Lands (OASL)[96] worked well in the Ga Traditional Area, it would have had an effect similar to that of stool farms. It would have made Ga chiefs' gains from land dependent on its productive use.

In line with state laws prohibiting the outright sale of customary land, the OASL required chiefs to grant leaseholds to people. The OASL, which started operation in 1996, would then collect, manage, and distribute annual rents and royalties from lands allocated by chiefs. Land users would, in effect, have been paying annual rents drawn from the industrial, commercial or residential uses to which they put land. But the OASL has not had much success. Incumbent chiefs prefer to sell or grant capitalized leases and pocket the total amount for leaseholds up-front rather than risk losing most of the money through death or dethronement. The fact that the OASL is supposed to disburse to chiefs only 22.5 percent of those rents has further made chiefs unwilling to give up land sales in exchange for annual rents.[97]

Because many land users pay chiefs up-front for the land at the time of allocation, users refuse to pay annual rents to the OASL. An official of the OASL informed me in 2004 that the institution was collecting rents from only a fourth of registered landholders in the Greater Accra area, and that the vast majority of landholders in the Ga Traditional Area had not registered leases anyway. He noted that many registered leaseholders cited the fact that they had bought capitalized leases from chiefs as justification for their refusal to pay annual rents.[98]

The prices involved in these purchases keep rising and can assume sizable proportions,[99] even though they are still referred to as *nsa* or

---

[95] Gough and Yankson, "Land markets," p. 2492.

[96] The OASL was most recently provided for under section 267 (2–8) of the 1992 Constitution of the Republic of Ghana.

[97] Interview with an official at the Lands Commission, Accra (Gh 2) September 24, 2004. Many chiefs in Akyem Abuakwa similarly resist the OASL for this reason.

[98] Interview with an official of the Office for the Administration of Stool Lands, Accra (Gh 3), September 24, 2004.

[99] Roth, Cochrane, and Kasanga, *Land Markets*, p. 17; and Gough and Yankson, "Land markets," p. 2494.

drinks money. Nsa in Twi means drink(s) and is a reference to the symbolic drinks that were offered to consummate grants of free parcels of
land before land became commercialized. But, to borrow Furnivall's 1909
expression, land in the Ga Traditional Area is no longer a "free gift of
nature."[100] The bottles of schnapps now have to be accompanied by hefty
sums of money that constitute the capitalized leasehold fee. Some traditional authorities even insist on payment in U.S. dollars for some parcels.
The OASL has failed to make chiefs' gains from land dependent on its
productive use.

Below, I present estimated land prices from various peri-urban areas
of Accra as supplied by a Principal Valuation Technician at the Land Valuation Board in Accra in 2002. This table has obvious shortcomings. The
attempt to state fixed prices for land anywhere in Ghana is problematic.
Land really has no definite price, and how much one gets it for depends
on a host of factors that range from relations between the grantor and
grantee to how much the grantee can afford. Further, the estimates were
supplied by a state official and are not prices reported by land buyers
or sellers. Also, they are prices for only one point in time and do not
demonstrate what most needs to be shown here: increasing land values
over time.

However, this table is still useful because we can take, as an anterior
point, a time a few decades ago when land in peri-urban areas such as
Gbawe, Amasaman, and New Bortsianor was agricultural land "in the
bush," far from the capital. At that time, locals received parcels for free
from chiefs, and many buyers would not have been willing to buy them
given their distance from the city.

The difficulty of getting quotes for land prices over time in the Greater
Accra area is itself part of the politics of land. Land buyers and sellers have
an incentive to mislead, and they often do so. Chiefs understate the price
to mask how much they make from such sales. They do likewise to reduce
potential liability when they sell land to more than one person. Buyers
try to reduce their valuation taxes by reporting extremely low prices
described as "ridiculous amounts" by the principal valuation technician
who gave me the prices indicated in Table 4.1.

As occurred during the concessions scramble in the nineteenth century,
sitting Ga chiefs and elders have tried to sell off as much land as possible
as soon as buyers have begun to show interest in any parts of their realm.

---

[100] J. S. Furnivall, "Land as a free gift of nature," *The Economic Journal* 19 (December
    1909).

TABLE 4.1. *Prices for Undeveloped Plots Around Peri-Urban Accra in 2002*

Area	Price Range
Ashaley Botwe	USD 2600–4000
Mempeasem	USD 4000 and up
Gbawe	USD 3300
Baatsonaa/Spintex Road	USD 2000–5300
Okpoi Gonno, Ajiriganor, East Legon Extension	USD 4600–8000
La Bawaleshie	USD 8000 and up

Source: Principal valuation technician, Land Valuation Board, Accra, 2002.

These hasty sales often take disturbing proportions. In 2005, many people who could not get land closer to Accra turned their attention to the old Ga settlement of Ningo. The chief of New Ningo seized the opportunity and quickly sold off all available lands in the community. But people were still interested in buying land in New Ningo, so the sitting chief began to sell already-allocated lands. He even cavalierly sold off the not-yet-used portions of the community's "Christian cemetery" and "pagan cemetery." As it turned out, he died immediately after these sales, leaving his successors with no source of land revenues as well as the quandary of where to inter him. He was eventually buried in his room.[101]

Many chiefs invariably try to avoid this problem of "finished lands" by treating already-allocated lands as if they are unallocated. They challenge the rights of grantees and resell such lands or pounce on the lands of neighboring chiefs. One strategy involves claiming that the original grantor had no right to alienate the land in the first place. The *Ghanaian Chronicle has* noted in this regard that "sometimes, when a chief dies, his successor, out of greed, tries to nullify the allocation of his predecessor. All sorts of unfair charges of wrongful allocation are trumped up and lessees with proper leases are asked to submit them for inspection."[102]

Another ploy involves claiming that the grantee had abrogated a development covenant, giving chiefs the right to repossess the land. At other times, they covertly sell it to someone else or threaten to give it to another buyer if the holder does not pay more. Even the same chief who originally allocated the land can later try to reclaim part of the land from

---

[101] "Chief sells cemetery to developers...and dies," www.ghanaweb.com: General News; November 11, 2005. http://www.ghanaweb.com/GhanaHomePage/NewsArchive/printnews.php?ID=94049. (Accessed, December 19, 2007.)

[102] "Chiefs, plots and the Lands Department," *Ghanaian Chronicle* (Accra), December 10, 2001.

the buyer. Reporting on these issues, the *Ghanaian Chronicle* noted that "some chiefs try to take away a portion of the plot they have allocated on the grounds that the plot is too big, as if they had their eyes closed when the layout was being planned."[103]

In 2004, a *Daily Graphic* editorial noted that "there is a tendency among some Ghanaians to sell lands they do not own or even when they are the owners, to sell the same piece of land to as many willing buyers as possible."[104] The *Ghanaian Chronicle* similarly noted the "unscrupulousness and greed of certain chiefs and family heads [that has] led to land disputes" as they "sell a plot to more than one person."[105]

In the case of New Ningo discussed above, community members came together under the banner of the Great Ningo Development Forum. Upon the death of the chief they branded land users to whom he had sold lands as "intruders" and swore to take back their property on the grounds that the dead chief had no right to sell them in the first place.[106]

Another case in which chiefs tried to reclaim allocated land took a more tragic turn. In October 2007, Agric-Cattle Lakeside Estate Limited was developing a 1.5-billion-cedi residential estate in Ashaley-Botwe, a peri-urban area of Accra, on land they had acquired in 1995 from the then-acting-chief Nii Afotey Odai IV. That month *landguards* attacked and burnt down the estate. The company pointed fingers at the sitting chief, Nii Otu Akwetey IX of Katamanso and other claimants who had been allocated the same land. They revealed that the destruction of their estate was the culmination of continuous pressure put on them by Nii Otu Akwetey IX, among others.[107]

Interestingly, a *landguard* with whom I conducted multiple interviews and toured various peri-urban areas informed me that the invocation of the development covenant was the most common trick that chiefs and *landguards* use to justify the repossession of lands. He said that once land in a highly desirable area has been exhausted, they would routinely invoke the breach of a development covenant to justify allocating this same land

---

[103] Ibid.
[104] "Landguards menace," *Daily Graphic* (Accra), December 22, 2004.
[105] "Chiefs, plots, and the Lands Department," *Ghanaian Chronicle* (Accra), December 10, 2001.
[106] "Chief sells cemetery to developers . . . and dies," www.ghanaweb.com: General News; November 11, 2005. http://www.ghanaweb.com/GhanaHomePage/NewsArchive/printnews.php?ID=94049. (Accessed, December 19, 2007.)
[107] "1.5bn property destroyed at lakeside estate," *Daily Guide* (Accra), October 25, 2007. http://www.dailyguideghana.com/portal/modules/news/article.php?storyid=4275. (Accessed December 20, 2007.)

to new buyers, even when the two years designated for development had not elapsed.[108]

Some have pointed to the Ghanaian state's compulsory acquisition of about a third of the lands in the Ga Traditional Area as the cause of these activities by chiefs.[109] These acquisitions and the lack of adequate compensation from the state are undoubtedly unjust. But this explanation overlooks the fundamental problem of the continued dependence of generations of traditional leaders on the outright sale of a good of fixed quantity, which encourages these fraudulent activities.

If the state returned all compulsorily acquired lands in the Ga Traditional Area now, these lands would be completely alienated in a few weeks or months by sitting traditional leaders, and the process of reallocations would simply begin again. In fact, traditional leaders have already sold off large parts of lands compulsorily acquired by the state. When the NPP government of President Kuffour took power in 2000, the Minister of Lands Kasim Kasanga expressed his desire to return to chiefs some of the lands that had been compulsorily acquired by the state. In accordance with this, the Lands Commission did a survey of the 120-acre Accra Training College land to see how much could be given back to chiefs. It was discovered that 70 acres had already been developed by people who had claimed that they had bought the land from chiefs in the area.[110]

To facilitate these activities, Ga chiefs and elders continue to perpetuate insecure land rights, investing little in surveys, records systems, and adjudication mechanisms that would provide security to land buyers.[111] Instead, they have created an environment that has allowed them to continue to squeeze money out of even lands that they have already allocated. They exert a corrupting influence on police and judicial officials by routinely offering bribes in money and land parcels to undermine cases brought against them and their agents.[112]

The main enforcement agents of these chiefs are armed *landguard* units that perpetuate much of the insecurity in the Ga Traditional Area.

[108] Interview with a *landguard* in the Ga Traditional Area (Gh 7), October 4, 2007.
[109] Roth, Cochrane and Kasanga, *Land Markets*, p. 10.
[110] Interview with an official of the Lands Commission in Accra (Gh 1), September 24, 2004.
[111] Interviews with an official of the Lands Commission in Accra (Gh vi), July 4, 2002; and an employee of a real estate development agency in Accra (Gh iii), July 3, 2002; and "Chiefs, plots and lands department," *Ghanaian Chronicle*.
[112] Interviews with a *landguard* in the Ga Traditional Area (Gh 7), October 4, 2004 (Gh 7); and another *landguard* (Gh 11), October 6, 2004.

Landguards in the pay of chiefs serve many functions. They protect land users who have the approval of chiefs. They also facilitate the reallocation of already-sold lands by slowing down development. Making it harder for people to develop their land brings grantees closer to breaching development covenants that give chiefs the right to repossess such lands if they are not developed within a specified period. It is also easier for sellers to convince new buyers that lands are unallocated if they are undeveloped. Further, when chiefs ask landholders to pay more money for their continued enjoyment of rights, *landguards* exert the necessary pressure on people to comply.

Landguards employ disruptive and violent strategies. Sometimes they simply threaten people to scare them off the land. At other times they physically assault developers and land claimants or destroy their property. The case of Agric-Cattle Lakeside Estate Limited cited above is an example. Occasionally, they engage in armed confrontations with other *landguard* units or the police.[113] Many of the officials and land users that I interviewed shared a common distrust of chiefs' and *landguards'* land-market activities.[114]

Landguards have also taken center stage in the conflicts between competing land users in the Ga Traditional Area.[115] Because the judiciary is suffocated by land cases and corruption is rampant in the police and among judicial officials, many Ghanaians rely on *landguards* to contest and protect land rights.[116] Writing of land disputes, the *Accra Mail* noted that they involve the

hiring of *landguards* and "machomen" (muscularly built men) by feuding parties to brutalize their opponents and claim disputed land for them.... The illegal operations of *landguards* has [sic] become an issue of national concern because of the havoc they are wreaking on society. Their operations have become so fearsome and perpetrated [sic] that many Ghanaians are beginning to fear that they would eventually metamorphose into a rebel group in the nearest [sic] future.[117]

---

[113] "Menace of land guards evokes fear in capital," *Africanews*; "Trouble looms in Oblogo over chieftaincy, land sales," *Ghanaian Chronicle* (Accra), February 15, 2001; "Ablekuma saga continues, *landguards* still terrorizing Bortianor locals," Ghanaian Chronicle (Accra), May 18, 2001.

[114] Interviews with an official of the Lands Commission (Gh 2), September 24, 2004; an official of the Office of the Administrator of Stool Lands (Gh 3) September 24, 2004; an employee of a real estate development agency (Gh 10), June 10, 2004; and a residential land user (Gh 12), October 6, 2004.

[115] Center for Democracy and Development (Ghana), *Corruption and Other Constraints*, p. 19.

[116] Ibid.

[117] "Menace of land guards evokes fear in capital," *Africanews* 40–42, July 20, 1999, http://lists.peacelink.it/afrinews/msg00022.html. (Accessed April 18, 2007.)

These *landguards* are not only hired by chiefs and poor, ordinary Ghanaians. When the reputable Home Finance Company was locked in a dispute over a 60-acre parcel of land in Kwedonu with other claimants, it hired *landguards* to protect its interests.[118] Similarly, the MP for Asikuma/Odoben/Brakwa who was embroiled in a land disputes with his neighbors in Dome in 2001, is alleged to have hired *landguards* from Amasaman to intimidate his opponents.[119]

A draftsman in one real estate agency told me about how a chief sold them land that had already been sold to others in the 1990s. One of the other parties deployed *landguards*, who beat up their construction workers with shovels and warned them to never return to the land again.[120] The case was still in court in 2004. A residential land user interviewed in Accra similarly told me that she abandoned a plot she had bought after *landguards* hired by a rival claimant severely beat up her construction workers, who had to be hospitalized for months.[121]

Some *landguards* whom I interviewed boasted about their immunity from punishment. They claimed that, as servants of chiefs, they enjoyed their protection, and the police and the state could do little to them.[122] One *landguard* detailed how he had been arrested repeatedly by the Odorkor police for assault and racketeering in New Weija. He explained that the chief he served gave police officers plots, and they always released him after a few hours. His return to the area after such short stints in prison always reinforced his reputation and made land users even more scared of him.[123]

The activities of the *landguards* are most evident in developing, peri-urban areas such as Nmai Dzorn, Oyibi, Ablekuma, Oblogo, Aplaku, Bortsianor, and Amasaman, where land sellers are involved in a rush to defraud as many people as possible before lands become fully developed.[124] In August 2004, the Minister of the Interior directed the police

---

[118] "Guards arrested...as tension mounts over 60-acre land," *Ghanaian Chronicle* (Accra), July 12, 2001. http://allafrica.com/stories/200107120238.html. (Accessed December 20, 2007.)

[119] "MP at loggerheads with Dome residents," *Ghanaian Chronicle* (Accra), February 1, 2001.

[120] Interview with a senior employee of a real estate development agency in Ghana (Gh 8), October 6, 2004.

[121] Interview with a residential land user (Gh 12), October 6, 2004.

[122] Interviews with a *Landguard* in Accra (Gh 7), October 4, 2004; and another *landguard* (Gh 11), October 6, 2004.

[123] Interview with a *landguard* in Accra (Gh 7), October 4, 2004.

[124] "Menace of land guards evokes fear in capital," *Africanews;* "Trouble looms in Oblogo over chieftaincy, land sales," *Ghanaian Chronicle* (Accra), February 15, 2001;

to "launch an all-out war against the *landguards*," citing their violent and disruptive activities as justification.[125] This announcement had little effect on *landguards'* activities. When the police sent a Highway Patrol Unit to confront *landguards* in Amasaman in December 2004, the *landguards* killed one of the policemen.[126]

Why are chiefs willing to tolerate the highly disruptive effects of such unstable property relations on commercial, real estate, and industrial activities in the Ga Traditional Area? The answer is that they draw few gains from these activities. On the contrary, the development of land represents the cessation of gains from those lands for chiefs. In the Ga Traditional Area, developed land, or what the *landguards* I interviewed kept referring to as "finished land," constitutes a big loss for chiefs. Development makes it difficult for them to sell these lands.

Perpetuating the disruptions that hinder real estate development in many peri-urban areas is beneficial in that it allows for repeated allocations. In Akyem Abuakwa the transition to sharecropping arrangements and farming meant that chiefs got nothing from the allocation of land. Their gains were drawn from the productive uses to which land was put. Perpetuating an environment of insecurity disruptive to farming would have been catastrophic for Akyem chiefs, just as it would have been for ordinary land users. It would have hurt the seasonal harvest in which they were heavily invested.

Evidence from the 1930s

The argument of this book is that, as with state leaders in Botswana, Ghana, and Kenya, the ways in which traditional leaders have drawn gains from land has influenced their preference for different types of institutions governing land rights. This argument will be buttressed by evidence that traditional leaders' ways of using land also affected their other public policy decisions. We can find such evidence if we look back at

---

"Ablekuma saga continues, *landguards* still terrorizing Bortianor locals," *Ghanaian Chronicle* (Accra), May 18, 2001; and "Nmai Dzorn land developers advised," *New-timesonline.com*, February 3, 2006. http://newtimesonline.com/index.php?option=com _content&task=view&id=1337&Itemid=245. (Accesses April 4, 2007.)

[125] "Landguards banned with immediate effect," Ghanaweb.com, August 4, 2004. http:// ghanaweb.com/GhanaHomePage/NewsArchive/printnews.php?ID=63233. (Accessed December 20, 2007.)

[126] "Tragedy near Amasaman: cop shot dead," *Daily Graphic* (Accra) December 18, 2004.

the 1920s and 1930s, when Ghanaian cocoa farmers tried, with great success, to withhold their cocoa from exporters. The involvement of Akyem chiefs in farming and sharecropping arrangements influenced the roles that they played in the cocoa hold-ups in the 1920s and 1930s.

In 1937, the cocoa-exporting Royal Niger Company and the African and Eastern Trading Corporation negotiated a buying agreement that apportioned quotas to buyers and set a ceiling on cocoa prices in the Gold Coast and Nigeria. African farmers detested this arrangement. They executed a cocoa hold-up, barring farmers from selling cocoa to the companies, that disrupted the export of cocoa and trade in European goods throughout the Gold Coast colony.[127]

The commission established by the British government to investigate the hold-ups discovered that chiefs played an important role in facilitating collective action and in voicing the grievances of farmers because of their deep interests in the cocoa sector.[128] The Okyenhene Nana Ofori Atta and the Asantehene led the charge in publicly condemning "the selfish and inimical policy enunciated by the trading firms."[129] Chiefs had become the official spokesmen of the cocoa farmers. Led by Ofori Atta, chiefs wrote protest letters to, and held a series of meetings with, colonial authorities to argue on behalf of farmers. Chiefs played the invaluable role of facilitating collective action among farmers by administering traditional oaths to prevent farmers from defecting. They also denounced, threatened, tried, and even punished farmers who sold cocoa in violation of the hold-ups. They prevented the community from honoring social obligations, such as the payment of adultery fees,[130] to such defectors.[131] Farther north, the powerful Asantehene proclaimed – threateningly – that farmers who defected were "trying to betray the country."[132]

The Committee on the Marketing of West African Cocoa was to conclude, like the European buyers, that the leading role of chiefs was not surprising given their "considerable stake" in the cocoa sector as farm owners, landlords to sharecroppers, buyers, middlemen, and moneylenders.[133]

---

[127] Great Britain, *Report of the Commission*, pp. 66–69; and Austin, "Capitalists and chiefs," pp. 79–86.
[128] Great Britain, *Report of the Commission*, pp. 66–69.
[129] Ibid., 54.
[130] Adultery fees are levies that a court forces a man who has had an affair with a married woman to pay to her husband. See Penelope Roberts, "The court records of Sefwi Wiawso, Western Region, Ghana," *History in Africa* 12 (1985), pp. 381–382.
[131] Great Britain, *Report of the Commission*, pp. 54–69.
[132] Austin, "Capitalists and chiefs," p. 86.
[133] Great Britain, *Report of the Commission*, pp. 66–69.

This championing of the interests of cocoa farmers by chiefs was akin to the wide-ranging efforts by cattle-owning BDP state leaders in Botswana to promote big cattle interests in their country. It provides further evidence of how the productive interests of these leaders influence their other public policy choices, thus supporting the argument that these interests also influence their approach to institutions that govern land rights.

SOME ALTERNATIVE EXPLANATIONS

A Question of Distributive Conflicts?

The argument in this book, which focuses on different ways of drawing value from land to explain how leaders handle property rights institutions, goes against a revisionist literature that explains property rights security in terms of distributive conflicts.[134] The distributive conflicts literature claims that, even though all parties want secure property rights in the face of rising land values, insecurity can persist because parties cannot settle on how rights in land should be defined or distributed. It is only when these conflicts are settled either through outright victory by one party or mutual agreement that secure rights are created.

For instance, in her study of Akyem Abuakwa and the Ga Traditional Area, Firmin-Sellers[135] portrayed secure property rights in Akyem Abuakwa during the reign of Ofori Atta as the effect of his ability to win distributive conflicts over land with the help of the British colonial authorities. None of the contending Ga factions is said to have been able to achieve a similar victory, hence the persistent insecurity in the Ga Traditional Area. After winning the distributive conflict, the Okyenhene is said to have credibly committed to respecting the rights of lesser chiefs and citizens to encourage them to invest in agriculture.[136]

On an empirical level, the claim that distributive conflicts were definitively settled in favor of Okyenhene Ofori Atta, even if only temporarily, is problematic. Various efforts by the Okyenhene to stop land sales and force lesser chiefs to pay him tributes did not stop people from selling land or from refusing to pay tributes. This only forced them to evolve new instruments of subversion to evade taxation and alienate land against the Okyenhene's orders.[137] As the widespread seizures of the farms of

[134] Firmin-Sellers, *The Transformation*; and Knight, *Institutions and Social Conflict.*
[135] Firmin-Sellers, *The Transformation*, p. 17.
[136] Ibid. pp. 71–83.
[137] Hill, *Gold Coast Cocoa Farmer*, p. 14; and Amanor and Diderutuah, *Share Contracts*, p. 2.

recalcitrant chiefs by the Okyenhene[138] show, his reign was marked by heightened distributive conflicts, rather than their absence. These seizures also cast serious doubt on the claim that increased farming in Akyem Abuakwa was due to the victorious Okyenhene credibly committing to the land rights of his subjects.

As argued above, lower chiefs' investment in agriculture was a means of resisting the Okyenhene's control, not the result of trust in his commitments. Further, relatively secure property rights in Akyem Abuakwa have persisted despite the serious blows by the government of Kwame Nkrumah, which thoroughly weakened the position of the Okyenhene and strengthened pro-Nkrumah lower chiefs in the late 1950s and early 1960s.[139]

Theoretically, these distributive conflicts over the ownership and control of land are not critical to understanding people's willingness to build strong institutions that govern property rights in land. The view that we can gauge whether or not people prefer strong public institutions that secure property rights by simply looking at the distribution of, and struggles over, the ownership and control of that resource is problematic. This view is founded on the assumption that the urge to protect property is the main motivation behind the creation of property rights institutions. But, as de Soto has noted, "formal property's contribution to mankind is not the protection of ownership; squatters, housing organizations, mafias, and even primitive tribes managed to protect their assets quite efficiently."[140]

Unfortunately, the focus on distributive conflicts to explain preferences for formal property rights institutions has widespread currency and is one of the issues on which liberal and Marxist analyses coincide.[141] The preference for strong or weak formal property institution is more directly

---

[138] Baffour Yaw Akese, Odikro of Adubiase wrote to the Okyenhene pleading for the return of a confiscated farm claiming it was his personal property, not stool property, October 11, 1947, Akyem Abuakwa State Archive, AASA/3/106; and a letter from Kofi Bado of Anyinassing to Nana Ofori Atta II on November 19, 1947, indicated that Ofori Atta I had converted farms belonging to Bado's relative, Bafour Dowuona, Odikro of Anyinassing into stool property, November 19, 1947, Akyem Abuakwa State Archive, AASA/3/106. Other letters bearing evidence of the ruthless campaign of Ofori Atta and his successors are present in this file.

[139] Rathbone, *Nkrumah and the Chiefs*, Chs. 8 and 9.

[140] de Soto, *The Mystery of Capital*, p. 59.

[141] Firmin-Sellers, *The Transformation*, pp. 12–13; Sonin, "Why the rich," p. 716; Karl Marx, "The Communist Manifesto," in David Mclellan, ed. *Karl Marx: The Selected Writings* (Oxford: Oxford University Press, 1977), pp. 229–230.

tied to how people extract value from land than their ownership or control of land. This is especially true for such fluid institutional environments where the ownership of a resource does not guarantee benefits from it, and one can benefit from a resource without owning or controlling it.

Distributive conflicts over land proliferated in Akyem Abuakwa among various levels of chiefs, citizens, tenant farmers, and state agencies such as the Lands Commission and the OASL during and after the reign of Ofori Atta. However, since the reign of Ofori Atta, disputants have continually sought to pursue these conflicts through means that do not promote insecurity.[142] This is because they are enmeshed in a complex, conflict-ridden web of relations that draws sustenance from seasonal produce. This web ensures the persistence of distributive conflicts but compels all to strive to pursue them in peaceful ways.

A chief in Akyem Abuakwa might give a tenant farmer a parcel of land to cultivate cocoa. During the 4–7 years before the cocoa trees bear fruit, the tenant would have the right to intercrop the cocoa with food crops to which the landlord has no rights. The landlord might also be obligated to give the tenant monies for sustenance. He or she will only receive a token amount from the tenant farmer to consummate the transaction. The landlord only begins to benefit when the cocoa trees begin to bear fruit. For the tenant, he or she invests up to seven years of labor and some capital in the farm as well as the token *drinks money*[143] given to the landlord to seal the transaction. Given the need for long-term investments of this sort, it would be irrational for either of these parties to create insecurity that would prevent the maturation of crops and the seasonal harvest of produce.

But this relationship also dooms both parties to perennial distributive conflicts as each tries to get more out of the relationship over time. For instance, having acquired land for cocoa production, some tenants use various excuses to delay planting cocoa for a year and instead cultivate

---

[142] Hill quotes the draft report of the West African Land Committee, which noted that "chiefs have willingly agreed that the stranger-farmer shall be immune from disturbance and shall enjoy the same perpetuity of tenure as the indigenous cultivator, provided the agreed-upon proportion is regularly paid to the native authorities." *Gold Coast Cocoa Farmer*, p. 12.

[143] *Drinks money* in Ghanaian parlance is the amount a tenant gives to a landlord to consummate a land transaction. Initially, this took the form of alcoholic beverages, *nsa*, and was a symbolic indication of the transfer of land and the gratitude of the tenant. Once land was commercialized, drinks took the form of money and it was not long before the term "drinks money" was coined. Drinks money sometimes runs into thousands of U.S. dollars these days.

food crops such as cassava and plantains knowing that they will be solely entitled to all of the produce. They may also plant cocoa, but they may plant less than the land can hold to increase the amount of food crops they can intercrop. The landlord may push the tenant to plant enough cocoa on the land as fast as possible to maximize gains from the land.

When the cocoa begins to bear fruit, the landlord might rig the sharing of the seasonal crop by manipulating the division of the farm. For instance, he or she might, through trickery, use a longer rope to measure one part of the farm and a shorter rope to measure the other part, knowing that a landlord is entitled to choose first which part to harvest. The tenant might retaliate by pilfering the landlord's portion once the farm is divided for harvesting.[144]

Despite these pervasive and persistent conflicts, tenant farmers, chiefs, and other citizens have sought with great success to ensure an environment of security that allows the cultivation of the crop that they fight over. The environment of secure property rights that makes Akyem Abuakwa very attractive to Ghanaian farmers is not the result of the absence of distributive conflicts. It is the result of the willingness of parties involved in such conflicts to channel them through institutions such as adjudication mechanisms that reduce their unpredictable, disruptive, and violent character.

In sharp contrast, in the Ga Traditional Area, similar distributive conflicts over land rights often form a façade behind which chiefs engage in various disruptive activities that fundamentally undermine land rights security. At other times they deliberately manufacture and deploy claims to the lands of others to facilitate their fraudulent activities. It would be a mistake to regard these conflicts as the causal variables that explain whether or not chiefs create property rights security. The prevalent disputes are, in many cases, the effects of how chiefs exploit land.

For example, land in New Weija that was attached to the Weija stool was claimed by the divisional chief of Sempe in the early 1990s. While the case was in court, Sempe and Weija leaders simultaneously sold off the same lands under dispute. Violence flared in the area as rival *landguards*

---

[144] This account is a composite of information obtained from interviews with an official of the OASL in a town in Akyem Abuakwa (Gh 56), December 14, 2004; another official of OASL in Akyem Abuakwa (Gh 63), December 16, 2004; an official of the CSSVD Control Unit in Akyem Abuakwa (Gh 58), December 14, 2004; an official of CSSVD Control Unit in Akyem Abuakwa (Gh 64), December 17, 2004; and an official of the Okyenhene's land secretariat, Kyebi (GH 55), December 17, 2004.

clashed.[145] Despite all appearances, this was not a case of distributive conflicts over the ownership and control of land leading to losses for all. One of the *landguards* who spearheaded the Sempe effort informed me that his bosses knew they had no justifiable claims to New Weija lands and that their goal was not to win rights to the land in court. They had fabricated the conflict and subsequent insecurity as a cover under which they could sell off those lands, and they were happy to abide by the court ruling against them after they had finished selling the land.[146]

Interestingly, such invention and exploitation of distributive conflicts was also present in pre-Ofori Atta Akyem Abuakwa, where chiefs were involved in land sales. As cited by Ilegbune, in the *Atta* case of 1905, J. Purcell decried the willingness of chiefs eager to profit from land sales to lay claim to land to which they had "no possible earthly right."[147] In the *Kufour* case of 1909, Ilegbune quotes the same presiding justice's condemnation of the defendant chief for "concoct[ing] very foolish untruths" to justify his claims to the land of another chief.[148]

Since the 1930s Akyem chiefs have ceased to exploit distributive conflicts to perpetrate fraud. Further, they have sought to manage the multiplicity of existing and new disputes through arbitration systems in which the Okyenhene plays a central role.[149] Giving the same land parcel to two sharecroppers simply hinders both from farming it, and such action denies the landlord of a share of the harvest.

A Rural–Urban Divide?

It is tempting to regard the difference in how traditional leaders handle property rights in these two areas as the effect of a rural–urban divide. One might argue that there is advanced commercialization of urban land in the Ga Traditional Area, which leads chiefs to sell land against the dictates of customary law. Further, the need to invest large amounts in urban buildings and businesses may well have forced urban chiefs to sell land outright because buyers would be unwilling to invest significant resources in land if it would revert to chiefs and their communities as dictated by customary law. It might also be argued that rural land in

---

[145] Interviews with a *landguard* in the Ga Traditional Area (Gh 7), October 4, 2004; and a *landguard* in the Ga Traditional Area (Gh 11), October 6, 2004.

[146] Interview with a *landguard* in the Ga Traditional Area (Gh 11), October 6, 2004.

[147] Ilegbune, "Concessions scramble," p. 23.

[148] Ilegbune, "Concessions scramble," endnote 27, p. 29.

[149] Interview with an official of the customary land secretariat of Okyeman, in Kyebi (Gh 55), December 13, 2004.

Akyem Abuakwa is subject to less commercialization, allowing chiefs to adhere to the "traditional" norms of only granting user rights, farming, and entering into sharecropping arrangements. Therefore, it is possible that the rural–urban divide has an impact on the key independent variable here: how traditional leaders use land.

In fact, a usufruct system in which rights are secure is quite compatible with both urban and rural development, and a freehold system in which rights are insecure is a danger to both urban and rural development. Given that cocoa is a long-term crop, if we follow the logic of the initial objection, we could just as well argue that rural farmers would be unwilling to invest in its production without permanent rights.

The dynamic comparison design used here enables us to effectively eliminate this potential explanation. If a rural environment has the effects ascribed to it in this objection, then the commercialization of land and proliferation of land alienation should never have occurred in Akyem Abuakwa, which has been predominantly rural throughout the period under consideration in this book.

As indicated above, the sale of land to farmers, mineral concessionaires, and timber extractors proliferated in Akyem Abuakwa in the late 1800s and early 1900s before the reign of Ofori Atta. Chiefs there did not only sell land, but they often sold it repeatedly, and they occasionally degenerated into the sale of even their own subjects' cultivated fields.[150]

Reminiscent of land booms taking place around the same period in far away Chicago in the United States,[151] there was a mad rush of Ghanaian and foreign land speculators to Akyem Abuakwa in the late 1800s and early 1900s. The speculators were mostly interested not in the minerals that lay under the ground or the timber that stood above it, but in making money through betting on land prices.[152] Speculation in rural Akyem lands often took place in sophisticated ways in distant areas like Britain.

When the British India Rubber Exploration Company, Ltd. placed ads in Britain in 1887 indicating that it owned "500 square miles at Appaboomah, rich in 450,000 trees, with land titles duly registered at the colonial office," the British administration in the Gold Coast took notice. This was because the company did not operate in the colony, the district name was fictitious, lands were not that endowed with timber, and the registration of titles was not yet possible in the colony.[153]

[150] Addo-Fening, *Akyem Abuakwa*, p. 333.
[151] Hoyt, *One Hundred Years*.
[152] Ibid., p. 352.
[153] Phillips, *The Enigma*, p. 63.

Such speculation in rural Gold Coast land was so prevalent that the British repeatedly contemplated prohibiting it with legislation, fearing that "the colony would become identified with purely speculative, even fraudulent capital, and that serious investors would be frightened away."[154]

Given the co-existence of a rural environment, and the commercialization of land and subversion of property rights in pre-Ofori Atta Akyem Abuakwa, we cannot attribute the variation in either how chiefs used land or their attitudes towards rights institutions to the rural nature of Akyem Abuakwa. A rural environment was compatible with both the sale of land and farming by chiefs. Similarly, an urban environment is compatible with the sale of land and real estate development and management by chiefs. Instead of selling land or issuing capitalized leases, Ga leaders could have issued leases on which they would collect monthly or annual rentals from the proceeds of real estate development, which would make them the urban equivalent of sharecroppers. Also, they could have used the land for real estate development and rentals, thus making them similar to farmer chiefs in the Akyem Abuakwa traditional area.

Varying Capabilities?

The imposition of a Ghanaian state along with highly divisive national politics has uniformly undermined the capacity of traditional leaders in both areas, reducing the potential explanatory power of variations in capacity. Interestingly, how leaders use land has directed the ways in which they have deployed the limited capacity that they have. Ga leaders have had more impact than Akyem chiefs because it takes far less capacity to disrupt and undermine property institutions than to create and strengthen them. Thus, even though Ga leaders lack significant capacity, their disruptive influence on the land market in the Ga Traditional Area gives the initial impression that they are, in fact, very capable.

Traditional leaders of precolonial entities such as Akyem Abuakwa and Ga have operated as sovereign overlords of independent entities with rights to police, imprison, tax, and wage wars. Colonialism drastically reduced their power to do these things.[155] The British left them with only the authority to control local populations on behalf of the

---

[154] Ilegbune, "Concessions scramble," pp. 26–27; and Phillips, *The Enigma*, p. 63.
[155] Kwame Arhin, *Traditional Rule in Ghana: Past and Present* (Accra: Sedco, 1985), Ch. 5.

colonial administration.[156] The governance of customary land is one of the few areas in which the state left chiefs with significant policymaking authority.[157] But the ability of chiefs to actually administer land in these two areas was diminished by an inability to centralize authority over lesser chiefs, incessant disputes over chieftaincy, and constant interference in chieftaincy issues by national politicians.[158] The traditional legitimacy of the institution of chieftaincy similarly suffered from these incessant disputes.[159] This general decline in chiefly capability has limited the ability of Ga and Akyem chiefs to administer land.

Chiefs in Akyem Abuakwa and Ga – some of the chiefs with better resources – were also similarly matched in their revenue streams and coercive force. Since the mid-1880s, Ga chiefs have benefitted significantly from the sale of some of the most valuable lands in Ghana. In the same period, Akyem chiefs have also drawn significant resources from land sales and more recently from sharecropping arrangements and mining and timber royalties.[160]

In both areas, *asafo* companies, who formed the main fighting bands in these communities, had, by the late 1900s, asserted themselves as autonomous activist organizations available for hire by those seeking coercive force to influence policy.[161] Ga chiefs and lineage heads have used their limited revenues to cultivate and provide cover for remnants of these *asafo*, who became known as *landguards*, to selectively settle and evict land users.[162] Akyem leaders have not used their limited resources to cultivate and protect disruptive enforcement agents such as the *landguards* in the Ga Traditional Area. Instead, they have sought to clarify rules, create rudimentary documentation systems, and support adjudication systems. Because of their limited capacity, the success that Akyem

---

[156] Frederick Lugard, *The Dual Mandate in British Tropical Africa* (Edinburgh: W. Blackwood and Sons, 1926); Mamdani, *Citizen and Subject*; and Asante, *Property Law*, pp. 40–47.

[157] Roth, Cochrane, and Kasanga, *Land Markets*, pp. 5–6.

[158] Rathbone, *Nkrumah and the Chiefs*, Ch. 10; Arhin, *Traditional Rule in Ghana*, p. 119; and Firmin-Sellers, *The Transformation*, 36–48.

[159] "House of Chiefs to minimize chieftaincy disputes," *Ghanaian Chronicle* (Accra), November 22, 1999.

[160] Office of the Administrator of Stool Lands, "Requirements and procedures for collection and disbursement of stool land revenue" (information leaflet, Accra, n.d.); and interview with a chief in Akyem Abuakwa (Gh 57), December 14, 2004.

[161] Rathbone, *Nkrumah and the Chiefs*, Ch. 10; Simensen, "Rural mass action," p. 29; and Addo-Fening, *Akyem Abuakwa*, pp. 445–449.

[162] Interview with a long-term employee of a real estate development agency in Accra (Gh iv), July 13, 2002.

chiefs have achieved is due more to the willingness and efforts of many chiefs and citizens to cultivate an environment of security than the capability of any one chief to impose an environment of security on the land market in the area.

The weak capacity of Akyem chiefs has compromised the extent to which they have been able to reinforce institutions that secure rights. The evolution of the Okyenhene's land office, first created by Nana Ofori Atta, provides us with a good example. This office was meant to serve as a central land administration office for issuing "native leases" and keeping information on land interests in Akyem Abuakwa. Unfortunately, the full potential of this office was never realized due to the limited financial and enforcement capacity of the Okyenhene. Many lower chiefs, unwilling to reveal to the Okyenhene their revenues from land grants issued their own indentures and sent grantees who were willing and able to formalize land transactions straight to the Lands Commission.

The ability of these chiefs to evade the Okyenhene's lands office has been aided over time by the willingness of state agencies such as the Lands Commission to endorse documents not approved by the Okyenhene. One effect of this decentralized structure is that it undermines the effort to put together a master information system similar to what state leaders in Botswana are seeking to create with the TLIMS and the SLIMS.

CONCLUSION

Employing subnational units of analysis is particularly important in the study of the political economy of Africa because it builds on a literature that laments the problems of states in Africa. Given that some states do not guarantee property rights, I pose the next logical question: How have people approached property rights institutions within the context of a state that allows local leaders great latitude? Analyses that simply point out the failure of states without examining subnational outcomes can end up with overly pessimistic accounts of the situation in these societies. Sometimes the political economic situations in these societies are not as dire as state-centric analyses portray them because local actors try to provide goods such as property institutions.

By focusing on subnational elites, this chapter reflects on a divisive debate in the study of postcolonial African politics: what should be the role of traditional chiefs in governance? Some scholars and policymakers see chiefs as legitimate and accountable representatives who deserve more governing responsibilities.[163] Others see them as despotic and corrupt leaders who should be excluded from power.[164]

By considering the activities of chiefs in two adjacent areas of Ghana, this book demonstrates that, like their state counterparts, these traditional leaders are not essentially good or essentially bad. Instead, their governing practices are influenced by how they are integrated into both local and global political economies. Thus, calls for centralization or decentralization of authority should be tempered by empirical analysis of the specific situation of subnational and national elites in each society.

[163] Leslie Bank and Roger Southall, "Traditional leaders in South Africa's new democracy," *Journal of Legal Pluralism and Unofficial Law*, pp. 37–38 (1996), pp. 407–430.

[164] Lungisile Ntsebeza, *Democracy Compromised: Chiefs and the Politics of the Land in South Africa*. Vol. 5, *Afrika-Studiecentrum Series* (Leiden: Brill, 2005), pp. 16–31.

5

Building and Then Demolishing Institutions in Kenya

INTRODUCTION

In August 1961, Kenya was on the verge of independence, and colonial authorities with a multitude of issues on their hands were being harassed by the stubborn complaints of a certain European settler. Then safely ensconced in the European settler redoubt of Salisbury (now Harare), Southern Rhodesia (now Zimbabwe), Mr. E. F. P. Hill was pestering the office of the governor of Kenya with compensation demands for his farm, cattle, and farm tools.[1]

Hill was seeking compensation because of what he saw as the abrogation of his titles to Stratton Estate in Kenya, contrary to earlier state assurances that they would not be abrogated "except for good reason and subject to the payment of full compensation."[2] Interestingly, unlike many estates, Hill's farms had not been targeted for acquisition by the state or threatened by squatters. Hill had faced no apparent threat to his person or property. The deracialization of the former White Highlands was what he saw as an abrogation. As he pointed out to the governor, "farms [in the vicinity] whose Title Deeds state they are to be sold to those of pure European descent only, have now been sold to Africans – surely that constitutes abrogation."[3]

Thus, to wisely escape Kenya's "second retrograde step" of independence, after the first "retrograde step" of "internal self-government," Hill ran off to Southern Rhodesia and requested compensation in full.[4]

---

[1] E. F. P. Hill to His Excellency the Governor of Kenya, July 2, 1963. Kenya National Archives (KNA) BN/81/150.

[2] Ibid.

[3] Letter from E. F. P. Hill to His Excellency the Governor of Kenya, August 14, 1963. Kenya National Archives (KNA) BN/81/150.

[4] Ibid.

The 1960s and 1970s witnessed a massive quantity of disputes, claims, and counterclaims on land parcels, many of which were at least slightly more reasonable than that of Mr. Hill. As many white settlers fled what they saw as the scourge of black rule for the more hospitable climes of Southern Rhodesia, apartheid South Africa, and the United Kingdom, there was a frantic rush by black Kenyans to acquire lands that had earlier been seized by colonial administrations for exclusive European use. People with state-issued titles clashed with those making historical claims to land. Former laborers on European farms who had long resided on those farms resisted eviction by the new owners who had bought the farms from fleeing white settlers. Peasants squabbled for parcels in the multiple settlement schemes created by the state. Members of private land-buying companies struggled over the division of lands acquired with their pooled resources. Senior politicians and bureaucrats grabbed large swathes of land around the country.

What is remarkable about this period in Kenyan history is that the state was able to create and reinforce various institutions that facilitated transactions in land, offering many Kenyans reasonable levels of property rights security. Senior state officials of KANU who ruled the country from independence in 1963 to the multiparty elections of 2002 reinforced property rights institutions in the period that I term Early Kenya (1963 to late 1990).

Interestingly, KANU officials later switched and significantly subverted the very institutions that they had created in what we call in this book the Late Kenya period (early 1991 to 2000). The case of path switching here is interesting. Why did national ruling elites in Kenya gradually switch to subverting property rights institutions that they had earlier invested in creating and reinforcing?

This book argues that, given leaders' similar levels of capacity in the two periods, we can find an answer to this question by examining the ways in which they have extracted gains from land. Leading politicians and senior bureaucrats in the early independence period became heirs to the agricultural, real estate, and tourism concerns of many white settlers who left the country as it moved towards independence in 1963.[5]

As it did for Batswana leaders and chiefs in post–Ofori Atta Akyem Abuakwa, drawing gains from land in such an indirect manner gave leaders in Early Kenya a strong preference for an environment of secure property rights akin to those of earlier European settlers. They used their

---

[5] Holmquist, Weaver, and Ford, "The structural development," p. 79.

high levels of capacity to reinforce property rights institutions. But by the 1990s, like Ghanaian leaders, many KANU government officials facing increasing pressure during the era of re-democratization began to draw political gains from land that was unmediated by its productive use. To facilitate these new ways of exploiting land, senior government officials and state bureaucrats began to undermine property rights institutions. Their success at this subversion was facilitated by their relatively high capacity.

BACKGROUND AND CHANGING RESPONSES

Kenya's 581,751-sq-km land mass is about the same size as that of Botswana, but its population in 1999 stood at 20 million, about seventeen times that of Botswana.[6] Kenya's natural beauty, its potential for agricultural development, and its location between the Indian Ocean and Britain's prized asset – Uganda – led to Britain's eventual colonization of the country in 1885. That year, the Protectorate of East Africa was created, and it is that entity that later became Kenya.[7]

Colonization in Kenya was an attempt to reap the fruits of the land through productive means. The deliberate encouragement of European settlement in Kenya by the colonial administration over time attracted a sizable European settler community that numbered around 61,000 in 1960.[8] The British East Africa Company and the colonial administration encouraged commercial agriculture by European settlers, going as far as to threaten "forfeiture by the crown if they [the lands granted] remained undeveloped without reasonable excuse."[9] Settler agriculture was supposed to increase traffic along the Uganda–Indian Ocean railway that had been constructed at enormous financial and human cost. It was also intended to provide the colonial government with agricultural tax revenues that would aid administration and military campaigns against local groups bent on resisting colonial expropriation of their lands.[10]

---

[6] Kenya, *Report of the Commission of Inquiry into the Land Law System of Kenya*, p. 15.

[7] Guy Arnold, *Kenyatta and the Politics of Kenya* (London: Dent, 1974), p. 11.

[8] Arthur Hazlewood, *The Economy of Kenya: The Kenyatta Era*, Economies of the World (Oxford: Oxford University Press, 1979), p. 4; and Arnold, *Kenyatta and the Politics of Kenya*, p. 54.

[9] Meek, *Land, Law, and Custom*, p. 80.

[10] Bruce Berman and John Lonsdale, *Unhappy Valley: Conflict in Kenya and Africa*, Eastern African Studies (London: J. Currey, 1992), pp. 35, 89; Hazlewood, *The Economy of Kenya*, p. 1.

The colonial government soon began to institutionalize European rights to lands expropriated from Africans to facilitate the agricultural activities of European settlers. Settlers argued that they needed secure titles to benefit from investment in agriculture and to enable them to secure loans for investment in farming using their lands as collateral.[11] Agitators for secure titles included the Settlement Committee, the Convention of Associations, and the Nairobi Chamber of Commerce. Interestingly, even the "Representatives of the church of England, Mohammedan, and Hindu communities" advocated secure freehold titles to ensure the permanent dedication of land parcels to the service of God, as they put it![12]

The colonial administration responded by creating survey departments and title and deeds registries. Efforts at registering titles of Europeans to lands seized from Africans on a large scale were in progress by 1919.[13] Discontent over such expropriations sparked numerous rebellions by groups including the Nandi, Babukusu, and Pokot, among others.[14] These rebellions culminated in the bloody Mau Mau war against British colonialism in the 1950s.[15]

While Britain brutally suppressed these rebellions,[16] the administration realized that the dream of creating a "Whiteman's country"[17] characterized by white privilege and the rule of a white minority in Kenya could only be maintained at an intolerable military, economic, and political cost.[18] In 1963, Britain granted independence to Kenya under a KANU government headed by Jomo Kenyatta.[19] Over the following years, KANU leaders first reinforced and then later subverted institutions that secure rights in land. Below, I contrast how leaders handled these institutions in two periods of the country's history.

---

[11] Kenya, Land Tenure Committee, *Report 1941* (Nairobi: Government Printer, 1941), pp. 10–11.

[12] Ibid., p. 14.

[13] Meek, *Land, Law and Custom*, pp. 93–94.

[14] Bethwell Ogot, "Britain's Gulag." *The Journal of African History* 46 (November 2005).

[15] Ibid.

[16] Caroline Elkins, *Britain's Gulag: The Brutal End of Empire in Kenya* (London: Jonathan Cape, 2005).

[17] The reference to Kenya as a "Whiteman's country" was popularized by Elspeth Huxley in her book *White Man's Country: Lord Delamere and the Making of Kenya* (London: Macmillan and Co. Limited, 1935).

[18] Holmquist, Weaver, and Ford, "The structural development," p. 73.

[19] Holmquist, Weaver, and Ford, "The structural development," p. 73; Bethwell Ogot, "Britain's Gulag," pp. 495–497; and Arnold, *Kenyatta and the Politics of Kenya*, p. 12.

Rules Governing Land Transactions

At independence the state made efforts to impose standardized rules on how people could acquire and dispose of land rights. Land control boards created throughout the country[20] played a significant role in examining the documents of sellers and approving transfers, making sure that people actually transferred the rights they purported to transfer. The Ministry of Land's Department of Land Adjudication and Settlement (DLAS) also operated in many areas around the country, facilitating the acquisition of land by Kenyans.[21] DLAS had settled 48,000 families on 1.7 million acres by 1969.[22]

KANU leaders fundamentally undermined these rules and systems for acquiring land in the 1990s. They also allowed district commissioners and divisional officers to allocate land, making procedures unclear and subverting the authority of the DLAS and the land control boards.[23] Many land control boards were not provided with supplies such as paper for their work or even paid their allowances, thus leading some board members to refrain from work or resort to graft.[24]

Land Information Systems

KANU leaders invested heavily in creating and updating land information systems after independence. The DLAS moved into the countryside, spearheading this drive even as they created settlement schemes in many parts of the country. They undertook the meticulous work of mapping

---

[20] Karuga, "Land transactions," p. 6; and Nyaga Mwaniki, "Social and economic impacts of land reform in Mbeere," Vol. No. 391, *Working Paper* (Nairobi Kenya: Institute for Development Studies University of Nairobi, 1982), p. 15.

[21] Kenya, *Report of the Mission on Land Consolidation and Registration in Kenya, 1965–1966* (Nairobi: Printed by Print. Percent Packaging Corp, 1966); and "Recent land reforms in Kenya." Paper to be given by the Kenya delegate at the seminar on Land Law Reforms in East Africa, June 4, 1968, Kenya National Archives, BN/81/87.

[22] Henry Bienen, *Kenya: The Politics of Participation and Control* (Princeton, NJ: Princeton University Press, 1974), p. 167.

[23] Kenya, *Report of the Commission of Inquiry into the Illegal/Irregular*, p. 132; interviews with an official of a divisional office in the Uasin Gishu District (Ken 33), April 20, 2005; and an official of one of the land administration agencies in the Uasin Gishu District (Ken 34), April 20, 2004.

[24] Discussions during a meeting with three land control board members in the Nyeri District (Ken 26), March 9, 2005; and an interview with an official of a divisional office in the Nyeri District (Ken 2), March 7, 2005.

land, demarcating plots, and documenting interests.[25] The state increased staff levels in the DLAS by 65 percent from 1967 to 1968, and the Survey of Kenya was well funded by the state.[26] Land title registries were also created in most district capitals in the country, allowing people to document interests and providing the state with valuable land information.

In Late Kenya, state leaders forced many of these institutions off course by getting them to deviate from their normal operating procedures. The phenomenon of land registries issuing multiple titles to different people for the same plot became common.[27] Similarly, government agencies began to produce multiple maps for the same area, creating conflicts over land interests.[28] As district commissioners and divisional officers began to compete with DLAS to allocate land in settlement schemes, many schemes were established without the initial, meticulous work of documenting interests that the DLAS was best known for.[29]

Beyond this, efforts were made to undermine existing record systems. Many transfers were not recorded, and entries in registers were changed or removed all together. This reduced the extent to which registers reflected actual realities on the ground, diminishing their usefulness to land buyers and those who were tasked with adjudicating land disputes.[30] A commission of inquiry set up to investigate land transactions in 2003 condemned the doctoring of land records and decried the extent to which it hampered efforts by the commission to uncover many illegal land deals.[31]

---

[25] Interviews with an official of the Ministry of Lands and Settlement, Nairobi (Ken 5), February 18, 2005; and another official of the Ministry of Lands and Settlement, Nairobi (Ken 29), March 15, 2005.

[26] Kenya, *Report of the Mission on Land Consolidation;*" and Ministry of Lands and Settlement, "Ministry of Lands and Settlement: an overview" (publicity pamphlet, Nairobi, n.d.); and "Recent land reforms in Kenya."

[27] Kenya, *Report of the Commission of Inquiry into the Illegal/Irregular*, pp. 37, 40, 75; and interview with an official of the Ministry of Lands and Settlement, Nairobi (Ken 1), February 14, 2005.

[28] Interview with a divisional officer in the Uasin Gishu District (Ken 35), April 21, 2005.

[29] Interviews with a divisional officer in the Uasin Gishu District (Ken 33), April 20, 2005; and an official of one of the land administration agencies in the Uasin Gishu District (Ken 34), April 20, 2005.

[30] Interviews with an official in the Ministry of Lands and Settlement, Nairobi (Ken 1), February 14, 2005; an official of one of the land administration agencies in the Nyeri District (Ken 8), March 1, 2005; an official of an NGO involved land issues Kenya, Nairobi (Ken 3), February 17, 2005; and another official of an NGO involved in land issues (Ken 6), February 21, 2005; and "DO sought in land title racket," *Daily Nation* (Nairobi), October 4, 2004.

[31] Kenya, *Report of the Commission of Inquiry into the Illegal/Irregular*, p. 38.

Adjudication

Given the prevalence of disputes during Kenya's energetic land market of the 1960s and 1970s, adjudication mechanisms were in high demand. The DLAS took the lead in such adjudication. After creating settlement schemes, it adjudicated disputes there until landowners took possession of titles after paying off their loans from the state. Titleholders could then go to the land registrar and the courts. Outside of settlement schemes, the DLAS deployed various layers of adjudication in trust land areas subject to land adjudication and consolidation across the country. These different adjudication mechanisms meant that by the time titles were produced, most of the disputes had been settled, reducing the pressure on the normal judicial system.[32] Titleholders could appeal either to the land registrar or the normal courts for dispute adjudication.[33]

In Late Kenya, the creation of land dispute tribunals under the Land Disputes Tribunal Act of 1990 gave the impression of further investment in land adjudication by state leaders. These tribunals were supposed to be located in rural areas with appeals going to a provincial land dispute tribunal.[34] Unfortunately, the state did not pay the allowances of tribunal members and failed to provide them with adequate logistical supplies. This meant that tribunals in most areas existed only on paper.[35] Further, the involvement of the provincial administration in the creation of new settlements and in the allocation of plots in the 1990s subsequently undermined the ability of the DLAS to resolve disputes in those areas.[36]

Enforcement

In Early Kenya, district officers led the administration police in enforcing property rights. They evicted those seen by the state as squatters,

[32] Interviews with an official of Ministry of Lands and Settlement in Nairobi (Ken 5), February 18, 2005; and an official of one of the land administration agencies in the Uasin Gishu District (Ken 34), April 20, 2005.

[33] Interviews with an official of one of the land administration agencies in the Nyeri District (Ken 7), March 1, 2005; and an official of one of the land administration agencies in Nyeri District (Ken 8), March 1, 2005.

[34] Interview with an official of a divisional office in the Nyeri District (Ken 19), April 3, 2005.

[35] Interviews with an official of a divisional office in the Nyeri District (Ken 24), March 8, 2005; a member of a land dispute tribunal in the Nyeri District (Ken 28a). March 10, 2005; and an official of a divisional office in Kiambu District (Ken 31), April 6, 2005.

[36] Interviews with an official of a divisional office in the Uasin Gishu District (Ken 33), April 20, 2005; and an official of one of the land administration agencies in the Uasin Gishu District (Ken 34), April 20, 2005.

protected those recognized by the state as legitimate holders, and separated disputing parties.[37] They also provided land administration officials such as those of the DLAS with protection as they performed their duties.[38] Apart from the police, the DLAS deployed officers in settlement schemes to monitor and enforce the installation of corner posts and the occupation of appropriate plots by settlers.[39]

In Late Kenya, leaders transformed enforcement institutions into instruments for the selective enforcement of decisions. State leaders often deliberately withheld protection from many land users. In the 1990s, the security forces refrained from protecting hundreds of thousands of people who were seen as supporters of opposition parties when they were evicted during land clashes across the country.[40]

The glaring variation in how leaders in Early and Late Kenya handled institutions that govern land rights is due to differences in how these leaders extracted gains from land in the two periods.

INHERITING PRODUCTIVE INTERESTS

Like BDP leaders in Botswana and unlike Ghanaian state leaders, KANU politicians and senior bureaucrats in this early period drew significant gains from the productive exploitation of land. They inherited much of the agricultural, real estate, and tourism concerns of white settlers who fled when Kenya achieved independence. In the massive transfer of assets from white settlers to black politicians and senior bureaucrats that followed independence, President Kenyatta, like previous colonial governments, insisted on productive use as a condition for the state's recognition of land rights.[41] These interests gave many black politicians the preference previously held by white settlers for secure property rights that would facilitate these productive concerns.

---

[37] J. K. ole Tipis, the MP for Narok East wrote a letter to the Rift Valley Provincial Commissioner protesting the eviction of "illegal occupants" on land in Narok by the Administration Police during which, the gunfire from the Administration Police caused a pregnant woman to abort, April 20, 1966, Kenya National Archive, BN/83/10.

[38] Interview with an official of the Ministry of Lands and Settlement in Nairobi (Ken 5), February 18, 2005.

[39] Interview with an official of one of the land administration agencies in the Nyeri District (Ken 7), March 1, 2005.

[40] Kenya, *Report of the Parliamentary Select Committee to Investigate Ethnic Clashes in Western and Other Parts of Kenya 1992* (Nairobi: Government Printer, 1992), pp. 71–73.

[41] Arnold, *Kenyatta and the Politics of Kenya*, p. 195.

Various factors allowed members of the new elite to acquire some of the biggest farming, real estate, and tourism enterprises in the country. The policy of Africanizing the civil service and business played a key role in this. The agriculture, real estate and tourism sectors were key targets of this Africanization policy. Kenyatta also insisted on a willing buyer–willing seller policy in the transfer of property from whites to blacks, privileging politicians and bureaucrats who were able to raise capital.[42]

Politicians and bureaucrats took advantage of this *laissez-faire* environment. As educated people well situated in the state machinery, they understood and were able to exploit the system to their advantage.[43] Also, they knew what land was available before everyone else did.

The manipulation of the Settlement Fund Trustees (SFT)[44] provides a good example. The SFT bought lands from Europeans for the creation of settlement schemes in many areas of the country in which mostly poor Kenyans were supposed to be settled. But, SFT parcels sometimes ended up in the hands of politicians and bureaucrats free of charge.[45] For instance, the 26,000-acre Sukari Limited farm in Ruiru was purchased to settle landless people from Gatundu in 1975. Before the land was parceled out to the poor, the Minister of Lands and Settlement Jackson Angaine wrote a letter to the Director of Settlement instructing him to set aside 6000 acres of the farm for President Kenyatta.[46] The Z-Scheme gave politicians another opportunity to acquire highly subsidized land that should have gone to less-privileged members of society. Parcels in these settlement schemes were 100 acres large and included a farmhouse. The recipients of these parcels were supposed to act as model farmers to the community around them, but instead many politicians grabbed these parcels.[47]

Other politicians and bureaucrats used the market to acquire land. As senior state officials with political clout, they could obtain loans without collateral.[48] Private banks and the state's Agricultural Finance

---

[42] Ibid., p. 66.
[43] "Moi suspends land allocations, raises hopes about land reform," *Weekly Review* (Nairobi), September 22, 1978.
[44] The SFT was a government trust created to acquire lands to create government settlement schemes. Plots in these schemes will then be given out to people who will repay overtime.
[45] "No cheer," *Weekly Review* (Nairobi), August 7, 1981.
[46] Letters from J. H. Angaine, Minister for Lands and Settlement, to the Director of Settlement, January 7, 1975, Kenya National Archives, BN/81/135.
[47] Bienen, *Kenya*, p. 169.
[48] Interview with a consultant on and informed observer of the Kenyan elite (Ken 75), June 18, 2005.

Corporation[49] gave generous loans to politicians and senior bureaucrats. Because of the lack of collateral, when some of these politicians failed to repay loans, banks were left with little recourse. For instance, when the influential politician Paul Ngei defaulted on loans from various banks it prompted lengthy and complicated legal disputes in the 1970s and 1980s. One of his creditors, Standard Bank Ltd admitted that it held no collateral on some of its loans to the influential politician.[50]

Through these diverse means, leading politicians and bureaucrats acquired staggering numbers of farms, apartment buildings, hotels, office blocks, and vacant lands in various parts of the country. The holdings of the families of the presidents of Kenya during this period provide us with an idea of the extent of these possessions. When Jomo Kenyatta passed away in 1978, he left a vast estate to his family that is said to equal Kenya's Nyanza Province in size.[51] The most important in these holdings is Gicheha Farms in Bahati (Nakuru District) and Gatundu (Kiambu District).[52] They also owned Ziwani Estate in the Taveta subdistrict, which covers 24,000 acres.[53] At various points these lands have been used for farming maize and tobacco, horticulture, nursing seedlings, and raising cattle and sheep.[54] The Ziwani estate also has an ecotourism facility.[55] The family further owns the sprawling Sukari Estate on Thika Road in Nairobi, opposite Kenyatta University. It is now prime residential and commercial real estate.[56]

President Daniel arap Moi, who succeeded Jomo Kenyatta, is similarly well propertied and is known to be one of the politicians who take their farming activities more seriously.[57] He owns a ranch in Ol Pejeta in the Samburu district. He grows maize, wheat, and flowers on his Ziwa farm

---

[49] The Agricultural Finance Corporation was a parastatal created to provide loans to private people willing to invest in the purchase of farms.

[50] "Watch out," *Weekly Review* (Nairobi), April 4, 1980.

[51] Jackson Mwalulu, "The Ndung'u report political dynamite," *Darubini*, Issue 4 (September–December 2004), p. 1.

[52] "Land: Who owns Kenya?" *East African Standard* (Nairobi), October 1, 2004.

[53] "Land: Who owns Kenya?" *East African Standard* (Nairobi), October 1, 2004; and interview with an official of one of the land administration agencies in the Taita-Taveta District (Ken 63), May 13, 2005.

[54] Interviews with an official of one of the land administration agencies in the Taita-Taveta District (Ken 58), May 11, 2005; and another official of one of the land administration agencies in the Taita-Taveta District (Ken 63), May 13, 2005.

[55] Interview with an official of one of the land administration agencies in the Taita Taveta District (Ken 63), May 13, 2005.

[56] "Land: Who owns Kenya?" *East African Standard* (Nairobi), October 1, 2004.

[57] Ibid.

in the Uasin-Gishu District.[58] He raises dairy cattle and cultivates maize and wheat in his 1,600-acre Kabarak Farm in Rongai constituency in the Nakuru District. Moi also owns a large tea farm in Olenguruoni, which houses the Kiptakich Tea Factory. His 3000-acre farm in Bahati on the Nakuru-Nyahururu road is used to grow coffee.[59]

Other politicians and bureaucrats during that period similarly acquired vast productive interests in land.[60] One example is Kenneth Matiba, who had spearheaded the country's Africanization drive as permanent secretary in the Ministry of Commerce and Industry beginning in 1965.[61] He partnered with S. G. Smith to form Alliance Investments Ltd., which came to own interests in a string of hotels including African Sea Lodge, Jadini Beach Hotel, Outrigger Hotel, and Naro Moro River Lodge. Matiba also owned the prestigious Alliance Schools.[62] Another example is Duncan Ndegwa who was head of the civil service and first African governor of the Bank of Kenya. He jointly owned the Insurance Company of East Africa and its impressive ICEA Building, the prestigious Riverside Apartments on Waiyaki Way, the Information House, and the Hughes Building, all in Nairobi. The Kiriani Tea Estate in Kiambu also belonged to him.[63] Eliud Mahihu, the very influential Provincial Commissioner of Coast Province during the Kenyatta era, had extensive interests in African Safari Club, Giriama Apartments, and Bahari Beach Hotel in Mombasa.[64] Njenga Karume, nominated MP from Kiambu, owned the Jacaranda Hotel as well as several farms in Kiambu.[65]

---

[58] Interview with a divisional officer in the Uasin Gishu District (Ken 35), April 21, 2005; and "A choice of seven grand homes: which will Moi opt for? *Daily Nation* (Nairobi), January 28, 2002.

[59] 'Land: Who owns Kenya?' *East African Standard* (Nairobi), October 1, 2004.

[60] "Who is who in the exclusive big land owners register" *East African Standard* (Nairobi), October 4, 2004.

[61] David Himbara, *Kenyan Capitalists, the State, and Development* (Boulder, CO: L. Rienner Publishers, 1994), p. 96; and Kenneth Matiba, *Aiming High: The Story of My Life* (Nairobi: People Ltd, 2000). Matiba also served as permanent secretary in the ministries of Home Affairs and Education. He also acted at various times as Secretary to the Cabinet and Permanent Secretary in the Office of the President.

[62] "Who owns what in Kenya," *Weekly Review* (Nairobi), March 8, 1991.

[63] "Who owns what in Kenya," *Weekly Review* (Nairobi), March 8, 1991; and interview with a consultant on and keen observer of the Kenyan national elite (Ken 75), June 18, 2005.

[64] "Shake-up in the parastatals," *Weekly Review* (Nairobi), May 16, 1980; and 'Who owns what in Kenya,' *Weekly Review* (Nairobi), March 8, 1991.

[65] "Who owns what in Kenya," *Weekly Review* (Nairobi), March 8, 1991; and interview with officer of Kiambu Municipality Divisional Office, Kiambu (Ken 31), April 6, 2005.

The massive involvement of state bureaucrats and politicians in these agricultural, real estate, and tourism concerns prompted criticism from many. As in Botswana and Akyem Abuakwa, the extensive involvement of politicians in business activities created concerns over conflicts of interests and officials' commitment to their public duties.[66] These concerns motivated the formation of the Ndegwa Commission in 1965 to examine the involvement of politicians and bureaucrats in business. The commission was headed by Duncan Ndegwa, first secretary to the cabinet and later, governor of the Central Bank of Kenya. Kenneth Matiba served as the secretary to the commission.

In many ways, this was like assigning wolves to guard the sheep. Ndegwa and Matiba were two of the leading businessmen–politicians in Kenya.[67] It was thus not surprising when the Ndegwa Commission wholeheartedly gave approval to leading politicians' and bureaucrats' participation in business in 1972. It recommended that public servants be allowed to participate in private business activities.[68] Reflecting on the work of the Ndegwa Commission later, Matiba argued that the decision made sense in the context of Africanization. He argued this because civil servants "were the educated people, the people with means. They were the people who could be credit worthy. And if we were going to Africanize business as I had originally intended, civil servants were the people."[69]

Kenyan leaders were similar to Batswana elites and chiefs in post–Ofori Atta Akyem Abuakwa who were also heavily involved in productive means of exploiting land. Processes in Kenya during this period and in Botswana were very similar and even related. When the Leno Affair scandal, discussed in Chapter 3, concerning the involvement of state officials in a big real estate deal broke out in Botswana, the Minister for Local Government and Lands, Mr. Balopi, tried to justify the involvement of state leaders in business. He pointed to Personal Directive No. 7 of 1984,[70] which legitimized the involvement of Batswana politicians and senior bureaucrats in business just as the Ndegwa Commission did for elites in Kenya. He further stated that this directive was issued after fact-finding missions by Batswana officials to Malawi and Kenya.[71] Batswana

---

[66] Nyong'o, "State and Society in Kenya," p. 241.

[67] Himbara, *Kenyan Capitalists*, p. 96; and Matiba, *Aiming High*.

[68] Nyong'o, "State and society in Kenya," p. 246.

[69] "Oral history documentation from former Kenya civil servant Kenneth Matiba," 1985 (p. 69), Kenya National Archive.

[70] "Leno Real Estates is clean-Mmusi," *Daily News* (Gaborone), February 25, 1986.

[71] "Enclave plot allocation cleared." *Daily News* (Gaborone), April 23, 1986.

leaders were, in this respect, copying their Kenyan counterparts not only in their aggressive participation in the productive exploitation of land, but also in their use of various state instruments to justify and support their activities.

The Reinforcement of Facilitating Institutions

As in Botswana and Akyem Abuakwa, as KANU officials acquired these productive interests in land, they moved to embrace and further reinforce facilitating property rights institutions.[72] As in Botswana, the promoters of these efforts at institutional reinforcement went beyond national bureaucrats and politicians to include district-level officials such as district commissioners, regional government agents, district agricultural officers, and civil secretaries.[73] They had also acquired productive land interests and were eager to create institutions that will facilitate their exploitation.

Their correspondence was full of rationalizations that included the need to promote land titling to secure farmers' rights and enable them to use their land as collateral for loans.[74] Officials always dwelled on the ways in which titling would benefit ordinary farmers and business people. But they also had the promotion of their own productive activities very much at heart. When the inhabitants of Rabai refused to allow the registration of lands in their area in 1964, the Regional Government Agent in the Kilifi District set out to try to convince them to change their minds. In a revealing letter from that district official to the Civil Secretary of Coast Region, he suggested that

Perhaps the President [Kenyatta] himself might be interested in helping to win back the agreement that had been achieved from the local people. This will

---

[72] Bienen, *Kenya*, pp. 164–170; and M. Tarmakin, "The roots of political stability in Kenya," *African Affairs* 77, No. 308 (1978), p. 307.

[73] For instance, see letter from the District Agricultural Officer, South Nyanza, to all Assistant Agricultural Officers instructing them to identify "possible areas where land adjudication could be opened in 1968/1969" on October 22, 1968. Kenya National Archives (KNA) BV/156/2.

[74] Masai MPs and country councillors wrote a letter to President Kenyatta urging him to bring land adjudication and consolidation to the Narok District so people could get titles that would allow them to secure loans to develop land, Kenya National Archives, Murumbi Africana Collection Part III, MAC/KEN/100/2; and a letter from the District Agricultural Officer, South Nyanza, to all assistant agricultural officers directing them to identify and give priority to areas with high agricultural potential and progressive farmers who would buy titles to secure loans for investment in land adjudication and consolidation processes, October 22, 1968, Kenya National Archives, BV/156/2.

especially concern him [President Kenyatta] personally as he himself is going to find it necessary to get his neighbors in Mariakani to accept registration so that it will be possible to obtain title for his cattle ranch there. I believe the R. A. [Regional Assembly] Board has made a stipulation regarding his application for a loan to develop the ranch.[75]

As in Botswana, state officials reinforced property institutions because secure rights facilitated the farming, real estate, and tourism concerns that they had acquired around the country.

Many people in Kenya embraced the state's effort at reinforcing rights and sent government agents letters inviting them to undertake registration, consolidation, and adjudication in their areas. For instance, on June 22, 1966, a group calling itself the Presidents of the Kanyango/K'Okal Land Committee wrote to the Land Consolidation Officer of Homa Bay requesting "a surveyor and recorder for our clan. We are ready with clean paths and . . . bridges and are eagerly waiting [sic] your team."[76]

But such warm embrace of the state's efforts was not universal. The cases in which people resisted state titling efforts are important. They demonstrate in glaring ways the deep commitment of KANU officials to the reinforcement of property institutions in this period. Where such resistance occurred, people often had deep-seated suspicions regarding state designs on their land and objected to the remaking of social realities that state efforts entailed. In the face of such resistance, officials launched stubborn offensives that involved trumpeting the virtues of titles in ways uncannily similar to the more recent efforts of de Soto and other recent proponents of titling systems.[77] They also harshly condemned those who opposed such reforms and tried to deprive them of local platforms on which to express their attacks on state titling efforts. In Lower Mbeere, exasperated government officials blamed local resistance to land titling and consolidation efforts on the "laziness and backwardness of the people who do not understand the value of an individual freehold title."[78]

The people of Rabai Location in the Kilifi District, Coast Province, proved to be particularly tough nuts to crack. In May 1964, the touring adjudication officer of the Taita District noted with satisfaction that

---

[75] Letter from the Regional Government Agent, Kilifi to the Civil Secretary, Coast Province, June 24, 1964, Kenya National Archives, CA/10/12.

[76] KNA, BV 156/2.

[77] de Soto, *The mystery of capital.*

[78] Mwaniki, "Social and economic impacts," p. 12.

during his meeting with the people of Rabai, they "showed that they are interested in land registration."[79]

But it later turned out that these people were merely being polite to a visiting powerful and enthusiastic state official. As it afterward became evident, the adjudication officer had mistaken their polite and patient attention to his proselytism as acceptance of his message. Wa-Rabai (the people of Rabai) later fiercely resisted title registration, prompting J. G. Mackley, the Civil Secretary of the Coast Region, to label them "reactiona[ries]." He suggested that Jibana Location be targeted instead for registration because they had "an enlightened and energetic chief."[80]

Government officials were, however, determined to register titles in Rabai as in most parts of the country. In June 1964, they once again organized a "three-hour *baraza*" (meeting) to convince wa-Rabai of the benefits of registration. To the chagrin of the assistant regional government agent present at the meeting, wa-Rabai again "objected point blank.... Long explanations were given but one could as well explain the facts to a stone wall." He suggested bringing in the influential Coast Province politician Ronald Ngala "to remove these illusions that people have about land registration."[81] One of these "illusions" was that the installation of cement beacons by land agencies during land surveying and demarcation would mean "adding Rabai to Mombasa."[82] Given the recent history of European expropriation of lands and the extent to which the expansion of state land administration efforts went along with the appropriation of land by leading bureaucrats and politicians, these "illusions" by peasants were by no means totally unfounded.

In a show of dogged determination, the assistant regional government agent made another attempt to convince wa-Rabai of the sweet fruits of title registration in August of that same year. At the slightly longer, 4.5-hour meeting on August 18, many state and local dignitaries were brought in to address the "very well attended" *baraza* on the benefits of registration and assure them that the government had no untoward designs on their lands. But while people listened patiently and applauded

---

[79] Letter from the Adjudication Officer, Taita District, to the Regional Government Agent, Kwale District, May 22, 1964. KNA, CA/10/12.
[80] Letter from J. G. Makley, Civil Secretary, Coast Province to Acting Principal Consolidation Officer, Ministry of Lands and Settlement. KNA CA/10/120.
[81] Letter from Assistant Regional Government Agent, Kaloneli to Regional Government Agent, Kilifi, June 11, 1964. KNA CA/10/120.
[82] Ibid.

intermittently, their minds were still unchanged, as the frustrated government official was to note.

From the applauses, cheers, and the general mood of the crowd, it looked as if all was well and the land registration programme was an accepted thing in Rabai. However, when the final showdown came, it was obvious that our four and half hours had been fruitless. The Kaya elders as usual adamantly rejected the idea.

The "very lame excuse" they gave this time was that they had to consult their brothers from the neighboring Ruruma Location. Even more worryingly, they even refused to select representatives to go on the government-organized and sponsored tour of other registration areas in the country. This caused the disappointed official to decry the "chronic ignorance and conservatism" of Rabai leaders.[83] But Rabai leaders were not alone in this resistance. After the government sponsored 25 skeptical community leaders from Kilifi and Kwale districts to tour faraway Central Nyanza to see firsthand the benefits of registration, they still refused to accept titling in their areas. In his anger, the regional government agent in Kwale ordered officials involved in organizing community meetings to prevent such unconvinced elders from speaking at local meetings held to discuss land registration.[84]

The stubborn determination of state officials in the face of such resistance demonstrates their steadfast commitment to reforming property rights institutions in the country.

THE MOVE TOWARDS UNMEDIATED GAINS

This determination was to vanish later. When Kenya reintroduced multiparty democracy under local and international pressure in 1991, leading KANU politicians began to exploit political gains from land that were not mediated by productive activities. Like generations of Ghanaian state leaders, they used land to reward supporters, punish opponents by putting their land rights in jeopardy and maintain support by threatening the rights of would-be opponents. They even went beyond the actions of Ghanaian leaders by moving voters around to change the voting character of constituencies. Weak institutions governing property rights, which gave politicians arbitrary power over the land rights of

---

[83] Letter from Assistant Regional Government Agent, Kaloneli to Regional Government Agent, Kilifi, August 18, 1964. KNA CA/10/120.

[84] Letter from Regional Government Agent, Kwale, to Adjudication Officer, Ministry of Lands and Settlment, November 2, 1964. KNA CA/10/120.

the populace, were vital for these activities. Consequently, like Ghanaian state leaders and chiefs in the Ga Traditional Area who also drew gains from land that were unmediated by productive activities, KANU leaders launched stunning attacks to undermine the institutions that they had earlier invested in creating.

The announcement of the return to multiparty democracy and scheduling of the 1992 parliamentary and presidential elections saw the defection of many politicians from the ruling KANU to form opposition parties. In this new political environment, many members of the smaller ethnic groups in the country, such as the Masai, Turkana, and Kalenjin, continued to strongly support KANU.[85]

New opposition parties such as the Democratic Party and Forum for the Restoration of Democracy tended to draw significant support from the larger ethnic groups such as the Luo, Gikuyu, and Luhya.[86] Because many members of these larger groups had settled in areas seen as the traditional homelands of the smaller groups, politics in many parts of the country pitted indigenous groups seen as supportive of KANU against people seen as settlers from other parts of the country that often supported opposition groups.[87]

Sometimes members of the groups perceived as settlers outnumbered those thought of as indigenous to those areas, and the "settlers" tried to assert themselves politically by voting for opposition parties and parliamentary candidates from their own group.[88] For example, Gikuyu seen as settlers in the Narok District were thought to outnumber the indigenous Masai in urban areas and even in some rural areas such as Enoosupukia, Enabelilel, Illaiser, and Kojonga.[89]

Beleaguered KANU politicians turned to the exploitation of land to keep the opposition at bay. A key strategy involved the use of land to buy political support. Regarding this strategy, the Ndung'u Commission of Inquiry was to note that, in the 1990s, the allocation of land became a "political reward."[90] The lands thus allocated for political support included "prominent public sites, including schools, bus stations, roads,

---

[85] Jacqueline Klopp, "Can Moral Ethnicity Trump Political Tribalism? The Struggle for Land and Nation in Kenya," *African Studies* 61 (2–2002).

[86] "Gikuyu settlers in other districts," *Weekly Review* (Nairobi), March 1, 1991.

[87] Rok Ajulu, "Politicised ethnicity, competitive politics and conflict in Kenya: a historical perspective," *African Studies* 61 (February 2002), p. 264.

[88] "Narok: background to ethnic conflict," *Weekly Review* (Nairobi), March 1, 1991.

[89] "Narok: background to ethnic conflict," *Weekly Review* (Nairobi), March 1, 1991.

[90] Kenya, *Report of the Commission of Inquiry into the Illegal/Irregular*, p. 8.

parking lots, markets, police stations, forests, mortuaries, cemeteries, and public toilets."[91]

In rural settlement schemes designed to provide land for the landless and those with particular farming skills, parcels often went to "district officials, their relatives, members of parliament, councillors, and prominent politicians from the area, Ministry of Lands and Settlement Officials, other civil servants and the so-called 'politically correct.'"[92]

To facilitate these practices, the Office of the President along with its Provincial Administration began to establish its own settlement schemes in total disregard of the Department of Land Adjudication and Settlement, which was tasked with that job.[93] Klopp attributes the intensification of the use of land to buy political support partly to the shortage of resources from other revenue streams such as foreign aid during this period.[94] To increase the amount of political support that could be purchased with each parcel, leaders began dishing out the same parcel to more than one person. Furthermore, multiple state officials, including district commissioners, provincial commissioners as well as officials of the Ministry of Lands and parliamentarians would each give the same land to different parties.[95]

Politicians also sold land to garner funds for electioneering. State officials would sell land and then convert the money into a political resource by using it to buy votes, organize campaigns, etc. To increase the amount accrued from each parcel, the office of the Commissioner of Lands and the Provincial Administration began to sell multiple land allocation notes for the same piece of land to different buyers.[96] To facilitate these activities, the Ministry of Lands included a disclaimer in letters of allotment in 1993 absolving itself of the responsibility to give people alternative plots of land where allotted parcels were already occupied by others.[97]

More sophisticated rackets involved transforming the state into a "captive buyer."[98] The Ministry of Lands or another state agency would sell property to a politically connected person at a pittance. The buyer would then immediately sell the parcel to another state agency at a highly

---

[91] Klopp, "Pilfering the public," p. 8.
[92] Kenya, *Report of the Commission of Inquiry into the Illegal/Irregular*, pp. 126–127.
[93] Ibid. p. 132.
[94] Ibid.
[95] Kenya, *Report of the Commission of Inquiry into the Illegal/Irregular*, p. 14.
[96] Kenya, *Report of the Commission of Inquiry into the Illegal/Irregular*, pp. 9–14 and 80. Interestingly, the state simultaneously bought lands at highly inflated prices from allies of leading politicians who had acquired these parcels from the state at very low prices.
[97] Interview with an official of the Department of Lands (Kenya 1), February, 14, 2005.
[98] Kenya, *Report of the Commission of Inquiry into the Illegal/Irregular*, p. 14.

inflated price. Since the head of the second state agency and other officials responsible for guaranteeing these transactions were all in on the deal, the buyer could charge unrealistically high prices. For instance, Continental House, L.R. No 209/9677 was sold by the Attorney General's office for 225 million shillings in June 1996 to a certain Archways Holdings Ltd., which then sold it to the National Assembly for 580 million shillings 3 months later with no improvements. Interestingly, the National Assembly had made a bid when it was first put up for sale by the attorney general's office.[99] At other times, houses belonging to the state were given to favored people as gifts. These people then sold the houses at very high prices to various state agencies.[100]

To influence voting outcomes, politicians unable to redraw constituency boundaries nonetheless gerrymandered them by manipulating property rights. The strategy was to purge constituencies of voters seen as hostile by abrogating their land rights. Supporters could then be settled on land in the area. Sometimes the lands on which supportive groups were settled already belonged to others, creating violent disputes.[101] Many Gikuyu residents in Likia, for instance, claimed that the state sought to influence the outcome of voting there by settling 318 Kalenjin families in the area before the 1997 elections.[102]

The expulsion of "politically incorrect" populations from certain constituencies in pursuit of such gerrymandering goals often took violent dimensions, leaving at least 1,500 dead and 300,000 internally displaced by 1993.[103] Violence instigated by political leaders led to the eviction of many Kenyans holding state-issued land title deeds from their homes around the 1992 and 1997 elections.[104]

In Narok, Gikuyu farmers were evicted from Enoosupukia. In Turkana, Nandi, Kericho, Uasin Gishu, Taita, etc., violent ethnic clashes led to destruction of property, deaths, and mass expulsions of Gikuyu and Luo communities.[105] After the elections, politicians made the return of the displaced contingent on their "correct" political behavior.[106] In 1997, the

---

[99] Ibid., p. 116.
[100] Ibid., p. 115.
[101] Kenya, *Report of the Commission of Inquiry into the Illegal/Irregular*, pp. 37, 40, 75; IDMC, "I am a refugee in my own country," pp. 13–20.
[102] IDMC, "I am a refugee," p. 20.
[103] Ibid., p.13.
[104] Klopp, "Can moral ethnicity," pp. 269–275; and Ajulu, "Politicised ethnicity," p. 264.
[105] Kenya, *Report of the Judicial Commission Appointed to Inquire into Tribal Clashes.*
[106] "The indigenous and the natives," *Weekly Review* (Nairobi), July 9, 1993; and "The end of tribal talks," *Weekly Review* (Nairobi), September 15, 1995.

late Nandi parliamentarian Kipkalya Kones vowed not to allow displaced title-bearing Gikuyu to return to Nandi district until political questions between the communities were settled.[107]

The 1992 multiparty elections were held in December 1992, but by April 29 of that year all pro-opposition, non-Kalenjin residents of Olengu-ruone in Nakuru District had fled the area, leaving only their pro-KANU Kalenjin neighbors behind to vote.[108] They were fleeing organized attacks from well-armed and uniformed "Kalenjin warriors" intent on purging them from the area. As attackers raided farms, torched homes, stole cattle, and maimed and killed Gikuyu and other non-Kalenjin people in the area, the district commissioner instructed the security forces not to shoot at the attackers. By the end of April, the area had been cleansed. Victims were so scared that they did not return to cast votes there in either the 1992 or 1997 elections. Many had not returned to their farms by 1999.[109]

The urge to influence election outcomes in certain constituencies was even more apparent in earlier attacks in the Molo Division, also in the Nakuru District. Molo was very cosmopolitan like many areas in the Rift Valley Province, with Kalenjin, Gikuyu, Luo, Kisii, and other groups living alongside each other peacefully.[110] After the introduction of multiparty democracy, Kalenjin residents began to protest the recruitment of non-Kalenjin members by opposition parties such as the Forum for the Restoration of Democracy.[111] They saw these activities as hostile to the incumbent KANU president, Daniel arap Moi, who was also a Kalenjin. That same month anonymous leaflets were distributed advising all non-Kalenjin to leave the area or face attacks. Police refused to respond to the leaflets.[112]

On March 14, an attack on Kenya Nguirubi Farm, owned by Gikuyu, marked the onslaught of "well-organized and coordinated" attacks by uniformed and armed Kalenjin attackers.[113] They killed, maimed, stole, and destroyed houses. Attackers pointed to earlier anti-KANU remarks made by Gikuyu leaders in a March meeting to justify their activities.[114]

---

[107] "End of tribal talks," *Weekly Review* (Nairobi), September 15, 1995.
[108] Kenya, *Report of the Parliamentary Select Committee*, p. 17.
[109] Kenya, *Report of the Judicial Commission Appointed to Inquire into Tribal Clashes*, pp. 123–126.
[110] Kenya, *Report of The Parliamentary Select Committee*, p. 11.
[111] Ibid., p. 15.
[112] Ibid., p. 15.
[113] Kenya, *Report of the Judicial Commission Appointed to Inquire into Tribal Clashes*, pp. 119–120.
[114] Ibid., p. 16.

They also stated their intention to punish and expel Gikuyu and Kisii residents opposed to the re-election of KANU's incumbent President Moi.

In the midst of the attacks in April, KANU-nominated MP Wilson Leitich is said to have warned that "there would be no fire" if voters supported KANU, but that there would be fire if they supported opposition parties.[115] These attacks quickly spread to other areas of Molo such as Kapsumbeiwa, Chemaner, Kipsonoi, Nyota, and Teemoyetta. Gikuyu who tried to undertake retaliatory attacks were overwhelmed by well-organized Kalenjin militia as the security forces looked on without intervening. Many non-Kalenjin fled the area.[116]

Similar attacks aimed at influencing, punishing, and purging opposition supporters from certain constituencies reoccurred during the 1997 elections. In Nakuru clashes during the 1997 elections shifted to the areas of Njoro, Lare, and Mauche.[117]

FASHIONING A FACILITATING INSTITUTIONAL ENVIRONMENT

Most of these activities by politicians depended on the existence of a very specific, permissive institutional environment. KANU leaders realized, as generations of colonial and postcolonial state leaders in Ghana had long known, that the blatant manipulation of property rights to muster support depended on an environment in which politicians had arbitrary powers over land rights, and autonomous institutions such as title registries and adjudication systems did not work well. Functional registries, tribunals, and land control boards were advantageous to elites when they were confined to exploiting land through productive activities such as farming, real estate development, and the operation of tourism concerns. But these institutions would have hindered the new ways in which KANU leaders used land. The stringent enforcement of rights would have made the eviction or issuance of threats against the properties of political opponents difficult. Functional registries would have made the sale of fake rights to fill campaign chests tricky because buyers would have been able to check before paying for encumbered rights. The individuals who bought land cheaply in "captive buyer" schemes would have been able to walk out of such arrangements with the properties once they received them, with little to fear from the politicians who facilitated such schemes. Generally,

---

[115] Kenya, *Report of the Parliamentary Select Committee*, p. 19.
[116] Ibid., p. 121.
[117] Kenya, *Report of the judicial commission appointed to inquire into tribal clashes*, p. 119.

grantees in the political exchange of land for support would have been able to disobey politicians once they had received land, with little to fear of retaliation.

An environment devoid of institutions guaranteeing property rights, which left arbitrary power over rights in the hands of politicians, better facilitated these new ways of exploiting land. Compromised title registers made it difficult for land buyers to verify ownership rights before paying for land, enabling politicians to swindle them more easily. Flawed registers also increased the flexibility that politicians had in deciding which rights to enforce. Since registers provided no conclusive evidence as to who owned rights, politicians could pick and chose which rights to enforce based on criteria such as the political persuasion of property holders. Like colonial and postcolonial state leaders in Ghana, Kenyan leaders realized that, in the absence of strong institutions that guaranteed property rights, maintaining the goodwill of state leaders was of paramount importance to those interested in keeping or acquiring property rights.

With these considerations in mind, leading KANU politicians launched full frontal attacks on property rights institutions. William ole Ntimama, the KANU Narok North MP and Minister for Local Government, was one of the leaders of the assault on institutions. He aimed his attacks at the heart of the bundle of institutions that governed property rights in Kenya: title registries. To the consternation of many Kenyans, he proclaimed in 1993 that land titles were "mere pieces of paper."[118]

The panic this statement evoked at the time was reflected in the response of the opposition Masai politician John Keen that devaluing land title deeds was "like opening a Pandora's box and ultimately means that no one has a right to own anything in Kenya."[119] But Keen had misunderstood. Ntimama was not out to deny that Kenyans owned property. He was just making it known that, from then on, the important question of who owned or enjoyed what property would be determined not by autonomous title registers, but by politicians using the political behavior of landholders as their main consideration.

This verbal assault on property rights institutions was accompanied by various efforts at rendering title registers and other land information systems obsolete. Many land deals went unrecorded. Some entries in registers were expunged or changed, and others were fabricated.[120] These

---

[118] "The indigenous and the natives," *Weekly Review* (Nairobi), July 9, 1993; and "The end of tribal talks," *Weekly Review* (Nairobi), July 9, 1993.

[119] 'The indigenous and the natives,' *Weekly Review* (Nairobi), July 9, 1993.

[120] Kenya, *Report of the Commission of Inquiry into the Illegal/Irregular*, p. 75.

actions made these registers less reflective of social realities, thus reducing the extent to which they could instruct land buyers, the judiciary, banks, etc. Hampered by this shortage of records in its investigations, the Commission of Inquiry into Illegal/Irregular Allocation of Public Lands was to conclude in 2004 that the lack of information "was no accident and no reflection on the general competence and accuracy of the Records Department. It seemed to be deliberate."[121]

When senior government officials engaged in these modes of dealing with property institutions, they were bringing to the heart of the state practices first adopted by less central actors who had invented various ways of squeezing political gains out of land in the 1970s. Their contributions to changes in land documentation are the subject of Chapter 6.

CAPACITY: TRANSFORMING PREFERENCES INTO OUTCOMES

Kenyan leaders were able to transform their preferences into outcomes in both Early and Late Kenya because they possessed relatively high levels of capacity. Starting at independence Kenyatta and his allies were able to firmly control the relatively capable state apparatus they had inherited from the British.[122] This enabled them to adamantly reinforce property rights institutions. The capacity of elites declined in Late Kenya,[123] but elites were still able to subvert institutions because the decline was slight and it is much easier to undermine than to build these institutions.

Strong Elites in Early Kenya

In Early Kenya, KANU elites had access to significant financial resources that enabled them to undertake the expensive task of reinforcing institutions. As the capitalist bastion in a volatile region, Kenya has received significant aid from Western countries and institutions.[124] Donor funding has been particularly important because most of it has gone directly into state coffers and consequently into the hands of state leaders.

---

[121] Ibid., p. 38.

[122] Bienen, *Kenya*, pp. 27–59.

[123] David Throup, "The construction and destruction of the Kenyatta state," in Michael Schatzberg ed. *The Political Economy of Kenya* (New York: Praeger, 1987), p. 72.

[124] Stephen Brown, "Authoritarian leaders and multiparty elections in Africa: how foreign donors help to keep Kenya's Daniel arap Moi in power," *Third World Quarterly: Journal of Emerging Areas* 22 (May 2001), p. 726.

Significantly, some of this aid has been directly targeted at the land sector. The British government and the World Bank, among others, have provided loans to buy and redistribute European settler farms.[125] A good proportion of this money has gone directly into building land administration institutions such as title registries and survey departments that would undertake this task of redistributing land.[126]

This financial capacity has been buttressed by the coercive capacity of state leaders, which have kept them in office and given them the ability to forcibly implement policy where it has been needed. Because of the need to suppress uprisings resulting from land expropriations, British colonial authorities had built up the King's African Rifles and the police.[127] Importantly, the capacity of these forces included the ability to gather, process, and deploy information in ways necessary to monitor and regulate the movement of people who had been expelled from their homes or forced into special villages created by the colonial authorities to contain rebellions against land expropriations. These skills proved invaluable in the arduous task of reinforcing land administration agencies.

Kenyatta brought these forces under his control by placing many of his ethnic Gikuyu kinsfolk in positions of command. As BDP leaders had done in Botswana, Kenyatta integrated leading men in these forces into the politico-business elite and maintained British officers after independence to monitor newly empowered officers.

In the 1960s, he created the elite paramilitary General Service Unit (GSU),[128] loyal first not to the state but to the president and KANU.[129] While Ghana had experienced three successful coups by 1975, there were no successful coups in Early Kenya. The coercive and administrative capacities of the military, police, and GSU were heavily buttressed by the Provincial Administration and its coercive arm, the Administration Police. Created by the British to penetrate deep into society the Provincial Administration provided a strong monitoring, enforcement, and implementation tool to Kenyan leaders.[130]

---

[125] Atieno-Odhiambo, "Hegemonic Enterprises," p. 240; Leys, *Underdevelopment in Kenya*, p. 74; and Kenya, *Report of the Commission of Inquiry into the Illegal/irregular*, p. 123.

[126] Nicholas Nyangira, "Ethnicity, class, and politics in Kenya," in M. Schatzberg, ed., *The Political Economy of Kenya* (New York: Praeger, 1987), p. 26; Kenya, *Report of the Mission on Land Consolidation*.

[127] Bienen, *Kenya*, p. 31; and Tarmakin, "The roots of political stability," p. 300.

[128] Tarmakin, "The roots of political stability," pp. 300–301.

[129] Throup, "The construction," p. 41.

[130] Tarmakin, "The roots of political stability," p. 306.

KANU elites were able to direct these financial and coercive instruments towards their preferred ends because of their stranglehold on the legislative and policymaking processes in the country. After victory in pre-independence elections in 1963, KANU incorporated the leaders of the opposition Kenya African Democratic Union and the Kenya African Union, thus effectively transforming the country into a one-party state.[131] Of 34 MPs that broke away from KANU in 1966 to form the Kenya People's Union, only 9 were returned to parliament in the Little Elections of 1966.[132] The Kenya People's Union was later banned and its leaders imprisoned in 1969. This restored the *de facto* one-party system until 1982, when Moi changed the country into a *de jure* one-party state.[133] KANU firmly controlled policymaking power and was thus able to make policies concerning land administration with no serious challenges.

Even though KANU's avowed respect for the rights of title-bearing landholders was resented by many poorer Kenyans, Kenyatta appropriated the legitimacy of the Mau Mau war against British rule to crack down on opponents. There is little evidence that Kenyatta was connected to the violent Mau Mau war,[134] but he wrapped himself in its glorious mantle once the war ended. Ironically, he used this mantle effectively to disempower and suppress real Mau Mau fighters who advocated the expropriation of European settler lands and free distribution of land to Kenyans.[135]

KANU's firm control over the legislature allowed them to both maintain a battery of colonial laws that were initially meant to protect settler land interests and to add new laws to the collection. Legislators who opposed these laws such as Oginga Odinga, Bildad Kaggia, and J. M. Kariuki were singled out for severe punishment and even death in the case of J. M. Kariuki.[136] The large influx of donor funds targeted at land reform enabled KANU to strengthen and propagate institutions such as land control boards, land registries, and land adjudication and settlement units. The strong coercive capacity of elites enabled them to

---

[131] Ajulu, "Politicised ethnicity," p. 258; and Holmquist, Weaver, and Ford, "The structural development," p. 77.

[132] Ibid.

[133] Makau wa Mutua, "Justice under Siege: The Rule of Law and Judicial Subservience in Kenya," *Human Rights Quarterly* 23 (January 2001), p. 97.

[134] Throup, "The construction," p. 38.

[135] Tarmakin, "The roots of political stability," p. 316; and Holmquist, Weaver, and Ford, "The structural development," p. 75; Atieno-Odhiambo, "Hegemonic enterprises," p. 239.

[136] wa Mutua, "Justice under siege," p. 97; Nyong'o, "State and society in Kenya," p. 248; and Ajulu, "Politicised ethnicity," p. 260.

enforce rights in the face of omnipresent squatter invasions and pervasive landlessness. The GSU, Kenya Police, and administration police were heavily involved in evictions during this period as people struggled over land rights across the country. The Provincial Administration was particularly useful because of its presence on the ground throughout the country. District and divisional officers played key roles in various land administration bodies such as the Land Control Boards and the DLAS. They coordinated and facilitated the activities of these bodies on the ground and provided valuable feedback on the working of various policies.[137]

Moderate Decline in Late Kenya

State leaders in Late Kenya had to operate with slightly less capacity than those in Early Kenya. The country did not totally escape the decline in state capacity that affected many postcolonial African states beginning in the 1970s. But its decline was moderate compared to that of the Ghanaian state, which tottered on the verge of collapse in the late 1970s and early 1980s.

There was a decline in the revenues available to ruling KANU elites in Late Kenya. International loans to pursue land reforms dried out in the 1980s. This blow to the coffers of Kenyan elites was exacerbated by the earlier decline in the performance of the Kenyan economy in the 1970s and 1980s because of oil crises and falling commodity prices.[138] However, Kenya's economy was cushioned from the worst effects of these global processes because of its larger tourism sector and stronger manufacturing base compared to those of other African countries.[139] Nevertheless, these economic problems fuelled popular discontent[140] and reduced leaders' ability to co-opt and pacify people through the provision of jobs and decent wages. Fortunately for KANU elites, Kenya continued to receive financial support from Western countries and international financial institutions due to its position as a stable capitalist country in a region in which Somalia, Ethiopia, Sudan, and Uganda were all embroiled in persistent conflict.[141]

---

[137] Bienen, *Kenya*, p. 37.
[138] Nyong'o, "State and society in Kenya," pp. 245–246; and Holmquist, Weaver, and Ford, "The structural development," p. 90.
[139] Holmquist, Weaver, and Ford, "The structural development," p. 79.
[140] Ibid., p. 91.
[141] Brown, "Authoritarian leaders," p. 726; Michael Chege, "Introducing race as a variable into the political economy of Kenya debate: An incendiary idea," *African affairs* 97 (387–1998), p. 227.

Moi was able to maintain control over the coercive forces in the country. When he succeeded Kenyatta in 1978 he brought large numbers of his Kalenjin kinsmen into the armed forces, police, and GSU and promoted Kalenjin officers while retiring senior Gikuyu and Kamba officers.[142] This purge was partly facilitated by the failed coup plot of 1982, which gave him a pretext to shed disloyal members of the security forces and promote his allies.[143] Moi's efforts paid off. There were no other coup attempts in the country after the 1982 attempt, and by 1985 his rule had been stabilized.

KANU leaders' ability to deploy their financial and coercive resources in their preferred directions was ensured by their continued domination of legislative and policymaking in the country. Moi invigorated KANU and used party district branches as instruments to control politicians.[144] He forced KANU district branches to suspend politicians who proved troublesome in parliament. Once suspended by their district offices, they lost the ability to contest for or sit in parliament. Such suspensions became even more potent when he made Kenya into a *de jure* one-party state in 1982.[145]

Moi also cracked down on social groups such as the "tribal associations" headed by middle-class and upper-class Kenyans that could have asserted influence on policymaking.[146] Moi paid particular attention to the powerful Gikuyu, Embu, and Meru Association (GEMA), which was formed in 1970. It was launched as a "tribal association" aimed at furthering the cultural and welfare interests of the Gikuyu, Embu, and Meru peoples of central Kenya. GEMA membership was thought to be up to 3 million by 1977.[147] It established a commercial arm – GEMA Holdings Ltd. – which by 1979 had total assets worth around 50 million Kenyan shillings, including ranches, buildings, and a pottery factory.[148]

Leading GEMA executives and members were senior bureaucrats, influential politicians, or other notable people who were Kenyatta loyalists. They included Julius Kiano (Minister for Commerce and Industry),

---

[142] Ajulu, "Politicised Ethnicity," p. 262.
[143] Ajulu, "Politicised Ethnicity," p. 262; and wa Mutua, "Justice under Siege," p. 98.
[144] Holmquist, Weaver and Ford, "The structural development," p. 94.
[145] Atieno-Odhiambo, "Hegemonic enterprises," p. 228.
[146] Throup, "The construction," p. 60; and wa Mutua, "Justice under Siege."
[147] 'Is tribalism in Kenya increasing, decreasing?' *Weekly Review* (Nairobi), November 21, 1977.
[148] "GEMA speaks out on politics," *Weekly Review* (Nairobi), May 19, 1975; "What went wrong at GEMA Holdings?" *Weekly Review* (Nairobi), February 2, 1979; and "Gema Holdings Assets," *Weekly Review* (Nairobi), February 2, 1979.

Duncan Ndegwa (Governor of the Bank of Kenya and former Permanent Secretary in the Ministry of Education and Ministry of Commerce and Industry), Wilson Macharia (wealthy businessman), Kihika Kimani, Njenga Karume (nominated MP from Kiambu), Njoroge Mungai (Minister of Defense), Mwai Kibaki (Minister of Finance), and Jackson Angaine (Minister of Lands and Settlement).[149]

With such a heavy concentration of politicians, it was not surprising when GEMA began to enforce support for Kenyatta among its members. In 1975, Njenga Karume, GEMA chairman, made statements downplaying the murder of the Nyandarua North MP, J. M. Kariuki, and denouncing rumors that implicated senior Kenyatta officials in his death.[150] They threatened action against members who opposed Kenyatta and even formed a committee to select parliamentary candidates in forthcoming elections.[151] They also threatened to intervene against those whose actions could destabilize the country. Further, they organized oath-taking ceremonies in Kenyatta's Gatundu home to encourage people to commit to making sure power stayed in the House of Mumbi, an allusion to Kenyatta's Gikuyu group.[152]

Moi organized a leaders' conference in 1980 that called for the dissolution of all ethnic associations.[153] He subjected the affairs of these groups to judicial scrutiny and brought many of their executives to court for not properly filing company returns.[154] Subsequent pressure led to the disbandment of all of these groups. The grasp of KANU on the Kenyan state apparatus was only threatened with the introduction of multiparty democracy in 1992, but Moi was able to keep the opposition at bay and win elections in 1992 and 1997.

KANU efforts at containing opposition parties after redemocratization in 1991 exploited the historical concerns held by members of smaller

---

149 "What went wrong at GEMA Holdings?" *Weekly Review* (Nairobi), May 19, 1975; "Is tribalism in Kenya increasing, waning?" *Weekly Review* (Nairobi), November 21, 1977; and "GEMA can do it, why can't KANU," *Weekly Review* (Nairobi), January 12, 1976.

150 "Gema speaks out on politics," *Weekly Review* (Nairobi), May 19, 1975.

151 "Is tribalism in Kenya increasing, waning?" *Weekly Review* (Nairobi), November 21, 1975.

152 "Gema has big credibility gap," *Weekly Review* (Nairobi), October 3, 1980. Mumbi is the mythical ancestor of all Gikuyu people and references to keeping power in the house of Mumbi is a code for ensuring the dominance of Gikuyu over the Kenyan state.

153 "Pressure on tribal unions to wind up," *Weekly Review* (Nairobi), August 8, 1980.

154 "A lesson to others: prosecution has no room for technicalities, *Weekly Review* (Nairobi), February 2, 1979.

ethnic groups in Kenya regarding Gikuyu domination of land.[155] KANU leaders perversely exploited the fears and grievances of smaller ethnic groups such as the Masai, Kalenjin, Turkana, and Samburu, who had been marginalized in the redistribution of land under Kenyatta that was thought to have disproportionately favored the Gikuyu.[156] Politicians such as Nicholas Biwott, Kipkalya Kones, and Ntimama used the theme of resistance to Gikuyu domination to discourage support for opposition parties and to instigate violence against those seen as supportive of the opposition.

The relative ease of subverting property rights institutions as opposed to creating and reinforcing them allowed state leaders to achieve much more with their slightly compromised capacity. They made policy changes that further muddied the rules on how to transact in land. This control also allowed them to undermine the operating procedures of land allocation offices such as that of the land commissioner.[157] It allowed them to undercut the efficacy of DLAS by deploying the Provincial Administration in a rival role. They also used their control over the security forces to selectively enforce property rights and withhold the protection of the state from thousands of assumed opposition supporters who were violently evicted from their homes.

THE RED HERRING OF CAPACITY

One could object here that the decline of property rights institutions was simply the result of declining state capacity and the subsequent inability of the state to maintain these costly institutions. Such an objection would tie in neatly with a substantial literature on the political economy of Africa that decries the weak capacity of African states.[158] The slight decline in the capacity of the Kenyan state could be used as evidence for this argument. A focus on how elites use land would then be mistaken or at best redundant in explaining changing outcomes. However, I argue that the slight decline in the capacity of the Kenyan state means that we can essentially hold state capacity constant. Further, I present theoretical and

---

[155] Ajulu, "Politicised ethnicity; Klopp, "Can moral ethnicity."
[156] Klopp, "Can moral ethnicity," pp. 273–274; Atieno-Odhiambo, "Hegemonic enterprises," p. 241.
[157] Kenya, *Report of the Commission of Inquiry into the Illegal/Irregular.*
[158] Herbst, *States and Power*, p. 18; Grindle, *Challenging the State*, p. 1; and Robert Jackson, *Quasi-states: Sovereignty, International Relations, and the Third World* (New York: Cambridge University Press, 1990).

empirical reasons showing that elites have wanted weaker institutions and have deliberately striven to achieve this.

This book provides a theoretical argument for why leaders in Late Kenya along with state leaders in Ghana and traditional chiefs in the Ga Traditional Area have preferred weak institutions that govern land rights. The detailed empirical evidence provided also includes actions and pronouncements by Kenyan state leaders that are clear testaments to a deliberate effort to undermine property rights institutions. These actions and statements cast doubt on an argument that would attribute their behavior to weak capacity.

There was a verbally articulated logic to the subversion of property rights institutions. When the Minister of Lands and Local Government, William ole Ntimama, said land titles were "mere pieces of paper," he was not commenting on the inability of the state to enforce rights. He was trying to shake opposition-supporting Gikuyu in his constituency out of the dangerous delusion that *mere* possession of state-issued land titles would save them from violent eviction if they continued with their anti-KANU activities. Ntimama was driving home the point that the state was willing to guarantee the rights only of those involved in "correct" political behavior, and that the efficacy of rights would now depend on such "correct" political behavior instead of autonomous institutions such as title registries and courts.

In a similar vein, in 1991 Ntimama also warned the Gikuyu in his constituency to "lie low like an envelope or face grave consequences."[159] Again, he was not warning of a lack of state capacity to protect them from eviction from their lands. He was indicating to them the willingness of the KANU state to use its capacity to abuse the rights of those involved in opposition activities.

Contrary to the objection raised here, the subversion of property rights was in many ways *a clear exercise in coercive and administrative capacity* in the face of organized and sometimes armed resistance by many communities singled out for eviction. Klopp is right in noting that, in the struggle between state agents seeking to expel people and the victims of such evictions, the former have had a significant advantage: a "monopoly on violence."[160] They have used their control over the security forces to selectively enforce property rights, withhold protection from hundreds of thousands, and forcefully transport these evictees to areas more

---

[159] "Masai hawk," *Weekly Review* (Nairobi), March 1, 1993.
[160] Klopp, "Can moral ethnicity," p. 287.

acceptable to state leaders.[161] They also have used their control of the executive to make policy changes that have further obfuscated the rules on how to transact in land and issue multiple titles for the same land parcel.[162]

CONCLUSION

Increased political competition has encouraged many KANU elites to adopt direct ways of exploiting political gains from land. But this transition was only partial as many of these leaders still have extensive productive land interests. Leading politicians such as Biwott, Ntimama, and Moi still own significant agricultural, real estate, and tourism concerns.[163] The challenge these elites have since faced has been the difficulty of destabilizing property rights in certain areas of the country without undermining the whole structure of property rights institutions from which they still benefit tremendously.

Thus, when Mwai Kibaki, another member of the propertied elite, defeated KANU and became president in 2002, he vowed to reinforce property institutions and established a commission of inquiry into abuses of land administration structures in the country. But the report produced by this commission was doctored before it was released. The version eventually released was left largely unimplemented, and Kibaki could not resist exploiting land in eerily similar ways when he was locked in a tightly contested referendum over a proposed constitution in 2005.[164]

The ways in which elites in Late Kenya have used their high levels of legitimacy, economic, coercive and policymaking capacity to aggressively undermine property rights institutions requires us to reflect on the flourishing literature on states in Africa. Recent political works have reflected much on the capacity and functioning of African state. Scholars have mostly decried the weak capacity of the African state. They have

---

[161] IDMC, "I am a refugee," p. 14.

[162] Kenya, *Report of The Commission of Inquiry into the Illegal/Irregular*, p. 75.

[163] "Who is who in the exclusive big land owners register," *East African Standard* (Nairobi), October 4, 2004; "A choice of seven grand homes: which will Moi opt for," *Weekly Review* (Nairobi), January 28, 2002; and "A story of wealth and power," *Weekly Review* (Nairobi), November 22, 1991.

[164] Mwalulu, "The Ndung'u report political dynamite," p. 1; "Orange team stunned by Kibaki land move," *East African Standard* (Nairobi), October 4, 2005; "President in move to allay fears over land," *East African Standard* (Nairobi), October 15, 2005; and "Kibaki gives out land for 'Yes' review vote," *East African Standard* (Nairobi), October 3, 2005.

assumed that capable states will necessarily do good things and be good for society; they have assumed that more capable states are necessarily better.[165] In these analyses the ills in society are then seen as the effects of weak or collapsed states.

These works gloss over the critical question raised by Kohli[166] of whether state officials are in fact agents of development. Thus, much of this literature sheds only partial light on the possibility of positive political economic transformation in these societies. Late Kenya reminds us of the downsides of a capable state with malevolent intentions. Indeed, the behavior of the Hutu power regime in Rwanda in the early 1990s, the activities of the Sudanese state in Darfur, and the actions of Nazi Germany provide ample evidence for the point I am making here. High state capacity is not necessarily good. Many in these societies would have been better off if the malevolent states under which they lived had been less capable of inflicting murderous violence on them.

[165] Grindle, *Challenging the State*, p. 7; World Bank, *The State*, p. 3; and Herbst, *States and Power*.

[166] Atul Kohli, "Centralization and powerlessness: India's democracy in a comparative perspective" in Joel Migdal, Atul Kohli, and Vivienne Shue, eds., *State Power and Social Forces* (New York: Cambridge University Press, 1994), p. 90.

6

Endogenous Contributions to Institutional Change

This chapter moves on from the theme of institutional choice that has preoccupied the previous empirical chapters to explore the issue of institutional change. More specifically, the subject of endogenous contributions to institutional change is explored. As stated in Chapter 2, considering endogenous change is particularly interesting to this study because institutions that govern land rights display clear positive feedback effects. The specific case of land documentation in Kenya is used to illustrate what in Chapter 2 was called the contradictory potential of institutions. By this is meant the ability of the same institution to simultaneously generate forces dedicated to its reinforcement while also spawning and supporting actors that thrive on its subversion.

As noted in Chapter 2, the goal here is not to deny other sources of change in self-reinforcing institutions. As was discussed in Chapter 2, exogenous shocks that either changed the leadership of societies or drastically altered the environment to which leaders responded were at the root of burgeoning institutional change in Ghana in 2000 and drastic institutional transformation in Akyem Abuakwa just before the middle of the 1900s. As shown in Chapter 5, Kenya had the exogenous shock of re-democratization to blame for drastic changes in how leading state leaders exploited land and their consequent attitudes toward the institutions that govern land rights.

This chapter fills the gaps in the story of institutional change in Kenya by examining what more marginal characters who were not in the upper echelons of state power and policymaking did with these property rights institutions. This is a necessary exercise if we are to avoid the "big man trap" – the view that social realities are always simply the sum of what the people at the apex of the state apparatus want them to be. As the work of Scott demonstrates, even when social realities appear on the surface to be so, they are most often not merely what the most powerful actors in society wish them to be.[1] Similarly, in his reflections on entanglements between states and peasants in Africa, Hyden shows that "what government proudly initiates can easily be undone by the peasant,"[2] and that "the winners of these games are by no means always the rulers."[3]

Although the focus here is not on peasants, the attention to the scheming of less central actors throws new light on the theoretical conceptions of institutional change as well as on the history of Kenyan political economy. In Chapter 5, we noted that Kenyan state leaders were supportive of and built strong institutions that secure land rights up to the 1990s when democracy was reintroduced in the country. The exogenous shock of re-democratization led leaders to exploit land rights in very disruptive ways and encouraged them to weaken institutions such as title registries to facilitate this.

By focusing on the activities of a diverse group of lesser actors, I argue here that the land documentation institutions constructed by state leaders, beginning with colonial administrators, created groups invested in their persistence over time. But they also simultaneously produced actors dedicated to the subversive exploitation of these institutions by creating a widespread and exploitable belief in the ability of various pieces of paper to grant rights to land. The subversive activities of these actors over time eroded confidence in land documents, but also engineered very subversive ways of exploiting land documents that state leaders were to adopt in the 1990s.

Ordinary con men seeking to make some money from the active land market of the1960s first seized on the widespread belief in the efficacy of land documents to hawk useless pieces of paper that they passed off as land titles. These petty con operations inspired politicians in the 1970s to extend the exploitation of land documents to the political sphere. When state leaders adopted their methods in the 1990s, land documents were already under serious suspicion in Kenya. The system of land documentation that had generated more and more support over time had

---

[1] Scott, *Domination and the Arts of Resistance*, pp. 188–195; and Scott, *Weapons of the Weak*, p. xvii.

[2] Hyden, *Beyond Ujamaa in Tanzania*, p. 210.

[3] Ibid., p. 213.

also fostered subversive con men whose activities had, gradually, eroded confidence in land documentation.

THE RISE AND POSITIVE FEEDBACK EFFECTS OF LAND DOCUMENTATION

As used here, land documentation is a system whereby information about the location of, dimensions of, and interests in land parcels are recorded, thus capturing rights to various land parcels on paper. In Kenya, land documents included land titles, letters of allotment, and letters of offer issued by the Ministry of Lands[4] as well as share certificates issued by private land-buying companies.[5] This broad definition has been adopted instead of a narrow one focused only on land title deeds partly because people employ many forms of documents as indicators of rights to land.[6]

Laws such as the East African (Lands) Order in Council (1901), the Crown Lands Ordinance (1902 and 1915), and the Land Titles Ordinance (1908) paved the way for the documentation of the land rights of Europeans in colonial Kenya.[7] Land documentation was extended to the Native Reserves, where Africans were allowed to possess land by the Swynnerton Plan in 1954. This was during the Mau Mau liberation war.[8] It was a counterinsurgency device aimed at creating a class of prop-ertied black Kenyans, each of whom, as a colonial official wrote, would "become the anchor of the tribe, the solid yeoman farmer, the land owner who knows that he has too much to lose if he flirts, however lightly, with the passions of his nationalistic friends."[9] The postcolonial government under President Kenyatta embraced land documentation at independence with laws such as the Land Adjudication Act (Cap 284), the Land Consol-idation Act (Cap 283) and the Registered Land Act (Cap 300), allowing for the issuance of 3.1 million titles by 1999.[10]

---

[4] Kenya, *Report of the Commission of Inquiry into the Illegal/Irregular*, 13.

[5] "Vanity shares," *Weekly Review* (Nairobi), June 20, 1980.

[6] Evidence of transactions in allotment letters; the length for which some hold share certificates; many different forms of documentation in Botswana.

[7] Kenya, *Report of the Commission of Inquiry into the Land Law System of Kenya*, pp. 21–23; Meek, *Land, Law, and Custom*, pp. 93–94.

[8] Atieno-Odhiambo, "Hegemonic enterprises," p. 238.

[9] Daniel Branch, "Loyalists, Mau Mau, and elections," p. 28. Also see Ngugi, "Re-examining the role," p. 500; Atieno-Odhiambo, "Hegemonic enterprises," 238; and Bienen, *Kenya*, 1974.

[10] Kenya, *Report of the Mission on Land Consolidation*; interview with an official of the Ministry of Lands and Settlement, Nairobi (Ken 5), February 18, 2005; and "Recent land reforms in Kenya" (paper to be given by the Kenya delegate at the seminar on Land

Some of the literature on the workings of property rights institutions creates the expectation that land documentation will have very strong positive feedback effects. Land documentation distributes land in certain ways and makes certain methods of using land easier and more profitable.[11] Thus, it gives more economic resources to certain actors who can then transform some of these resources into political instruments to further perpetuate the structure and integrity of land documentation. The incentive structure that land documentation creates also attracts new constituencies to use land in the ways facilitated by institutions,[12] thus transforming them into supporters of the continued strength of documentation.

There is evidence that land documentation in Kenya had these positive feedback effects. Talk of the sanctity of land titles quickly spread from its initial base within the European settler community to swathes of the black Kenyan community.[13] Leading politicians and bureaucrats who exploited their familiarity with and influence on the processes of land documentation to secure vast estates, as described in Chapter 5, became ardent supporters of the system of documentation.[14] Small landholders who had received new land titles under the Swynnerton Plan and ongoing settlement and adjudication schemes similarly began to support the sanctity of land titles.[15] Many banks also became supporters of land documentation as they increasingly gave out loans to farmers, real estate developers, and tourism operators with land titles as collateral.[16] Apart from securing their loans, efficacious titles facilitated the productive activities from which debtors were supposed to make payments to these banks.

The British had succeeded in creating a class of black Kenyans who would "assume the mantle of the European settler"[17] by defending the

Law Reforms in East Africa, June 4, 1968), p. 10, Kenya National Archives (KNA), BN/81/87; "How to get out of the quagmire," *East African Standard* (Nairobi), March 11, 2002.

[11] Ngugi, "Re-examining the role," p. 477; de Soto, *The Mystery of Capital*, pp. 6–7; and World Bank, *Building Institutions for Markets*, pp. 4–8.

[12] de Soto, *The Mystery of Capital*, pp. 6–7.

[13] Ngugi, "Re-examining the role," p. 502; and Kenya, *Report of the Commission of Inquiry into the Illegal/Irregular*, p. 16.

[14] Ngugi, "Re-examining the role," p. 502; and "Moi suspends land allocations, raises hopes about land reform," *Weekly Review* (Nairobi), September 22, 1978.

[15] Branch, "Loyalists, Mau Mau, and elections," p. 43.

[16] "How should the Ndungu Report recommendations be implemented? What Kenyans say," *Land Update*, Nakuru (Kenya): Kenya Land Alliance. October–December 2004 (p. 13). Also see Kenya, (2004), p. 66.

[17] Branch, "Loyalists, Mau Mau, and elections," p. 28.

"sanctity" of titles.[18] In 1964, the Mbari ya Kagwima group wrote to Minister for Lands and Settlement, Jackson Angaine, seeking the restitution of land in Limuru based on historical grounds. In his response, Angaine informed them that others had "been given titles to this land. I regret that my Ministry could not countenance any move to reject the security given by a title to land, and therefore I am not prepared to take any action in this matter."[19] Many people with historical claims to the lands on which they were living were forcibly evicted by others who had registered titles in those lands. As a state commission of inquiry was later to note, some had made efforts to stamp "an imprimatur of legal invincibility" on land title deeds over the years.[20]

Interestingly, the rise of this dominant constituency in support of efficacious land documentation developed alongside a marginal constituency that thrived on the subversive exploitation of land documentation to damaging effects to those institutions.

THE SUBVERSION OF LAND DOCUMENTATION IN KENYA

Land documentation, which displayed positive feedback effects, had contradictory potential. The aggressive expansion of land documentation by colonial and postcolonial governments created an exploitable belief system that aided the activities of subversive agents who thrived on actions that undermined the efficacy of land documentation.[21] People gradually came to accept pieces of paper as encapsulating rights to certain pieces of land.

The increasing belief in the power of land documents presented fraudsters with a favorable political opportunity. In a society lacking very capable police and judicial structures, the increasing belief in the efficacy of land documents made it much easier for con men to defraud land buyers. Ingenious con men created authentic-looking papers and passed them

---

[18] Arnold, *Kenyatta and the Politics of Kenya*, p. 65.

[19] Letter from J. H. Angaine to The Mabari ya Kagwima, February 28, 1964. KNA VQ/10/12.

[20] Kenya, *Report of the Commission of Inquiry into the Illegal/Irregular*, p. 16.

[21] Ngugi also argues that land registration in Kenya faced significant opposition. But his argument concerns how various social actors sought to blunt some of the implications of land registration that posed significant challenges to existing social arrangements. He points out that, "These social sectors refused to accept all the implications of registration, such as near-absolute powers of the individually registered owner. They organized, invented and mobilized customary norms to frustrate complete operation of the new formal regime of tenure arrangements." "Re-examining the role," p. 472.

off as valid land documents in exchange for money and political support. They did not have to bear the extra costs of settling people on land or even visiting plots with buyers to pretend they were actually going to pass on real rights. This was what made it possible for a single individual to defraud thousands across the country within a few months, as is shown below.

This alternative institutional logic came closer to the center of state power in the 1970s when powerful land-buying-company executives refined these techniques for subversively exploiting land documents and extended them to the political sphere. The issuance of fake documents became an excellent way of raising cash to sponsor electoral campaigns, buying the support of various individuals and groups, and dissuading would-be opponents. Issuing documents to people without actually giving them land turned out to be an effective way of getting them to attend political rallies, and it allowed politicians to change the voting complexion of electoral constituencies.

Land documentation was thus already under serious stress when re-democratization occurred in the early 1990s. The embrace of these strategies by KANU state leaders bent on political survival during the era of re-democratization, described in Chapter 5, only brought this logic more firmly into the mainstream of Kenyan political economy.

THE SMALL-TIME ORIGINATORS

As is often the case in such instances of innovation in the face of dominant institutions,[22] the initial process of introducing new ways of manipulating the structure of land documentation was started on the fringes of society by small-time operators with a bad reputation. By 1968, fraudsters were already exploiting the opportunities for profit presented by the increasing faith in and use of land documents in Kenya. These were petty con men with no political clout or ambitions who were simply out to benefit economically from the hyperactive Kenyan land market of the 1960s. Their schemes revolved around creating and selling fake land documents that purportedly granted land-hungry buyers rights to land.[23]

---

[22] See the interesting work of Leblebici et al. on how alternative logics and structures are first innovated at the periphery and gradually seep into the center. *Institutional Change*, p. 345.

[23] Letter from Chief of Chimba North Location to District Commissioner of Kwale discussing the illegal sale of state land by con men in Msulwa. October 18, 1968; p. 277. KNA CC/12/47; letter from J. C. Kariuki to the District Commissioner of Kwale

One Kariuki was defrauded of monies he had paid for 200 acres of land in Lunga Lunga Location in 1970 when he was "sold" Crown Land that the seller had no right to transfer.[24] In Shimba North Location, Kamba people bought land belonging to the Location from three men from Diani Location who then disappeared into thin air.[25] In Kwale, the proliferation of fraudulent sales forced the district commissioner to write chiefs in the district requesting their assistance in stifling the practice.[26]

With time these institutional entrepreneurs began to invent arrangements of more complexity to exploit the credulity created by land documentation. The "company" that called itself the Kenya Express Land and Estate Agent of P. O. Box 12954 was a sophisticated example of this trend. With an eye-catching name and a postal address in Nairobi, it set about its business of harvesting the fruits of citizens' greater trust in land documents. It placed at least two adverts in the influential *Taifa Leo* newspaper on March 23 and April 5, 1968 purporting to sell 50-acre parcels of land in Kwale District. It invited people to bring or send the 1,170-shilling price for the land as well as a 20-shilling registration fee, 2-shilling stamp fee, and 200-shilling agent fee "in one lump sum – no installment," it emphasized.[27] Their letter on April 5, 1968, to one customer prominently noted that buyers would be issued with "title-deed[s]."[28] When a would-be buyer in Garissa inquired about visiting Kwale to see the plots, he was informed that "owing to unforeseen circumstances the land in question is not yet available and therefore it will be a waste of time for you to come to Nairobi. We will inform you in the future if it will be necessary for you to come."[29]

concerning 200 acres of land on May 29, 1970. KNA CC/12/47; and letter from the District Commissioner Kwale to the District Officer of Coast Division, Kwale on April 4, 1968. KNA CC/12/47.

[24] Letter from J. C. Kariuki to the Ministry of Lands and Settlement, May 15, 1970. KNA/CC/12/47.

[25] "Msulwa report," by the Shimba North Location Chief to the District Commissioner, Kwale, October 18, 1968. KNA CC/12/47.

[26] Letter from the District Commissioner Kwale to the District Officer of Coast Division, Kwale on April 4, 1968. KNA CC/12/47.

[27] Letter from J. M. Masesi of Garissa to Minister for Lands and Settlement on June 25, 1968. KNA CC/12/47.

[28] Letter from the Managing Director of the Kenya Express Land and Estate Agent to Mr. James Crispus on April 5, 1968. KNA CC/12/47.

[29] Letter from J. M. Masesi of Garissa to Minister for Lands and Settlement on June 25, 1968. KNA CC/12/47.

At other times they passed themselves off as the agents of a fictitious "Local Government of Kwale."[30] At least a few actual and would-be victims wrote authorities, including the District Commissioner of Kwale and the Minister of Lands and Settlement, inquiring or complaining about this company. The District Commissioner's representative sent the same taciturn but pointed response to each of these inquiries: "There are no 50-acre plots being sold in Kwale at all. Watch out for rogues who go around deceiving people that they have lands to sell."[31]

These subversive institutional innovations by sleazy "land merchants" along the periphery would gradually move closer to the mainstream of institutional practice with their adoption by land-buying company executives in the 1970s.

"VANITY SHARES":[32] THE REFINEMENT AND EXPORTATION OF TECHNIQUES

Because such innovations by marginal actors do not necessarily attain dominance, it is important to distinguish between institutional innovations by peripheral actors and the attainment of a space in the mainstream of politics by these institutional innovations. How did the methods invented by these marginal crooks move from the periphery where they were deliberately hidden from the glare of the law to become a part of the mainstream of Kenya's political economy? An important step in the movement from the periphery to the mainstream was the adoption of these forms by actors with more clout who were looking for institutional methods to solve new problems. These actors could use their power to shield these new ways of exploiting institutions from attack in ways that marginal actors could not. Further, because of their influential positions, their engagement in these institutional practices encouraged imitation. In Kenya in the 1970s, land-buying-company (LBC) executives in the Central and Rift Valley provinces with political ambitions performed this critical task of moving the fraudulent exploitation of land documentation closer to the center of state power.

---

[30] Letter from Kinuthia Njoroge to the District Commissioner of Kwale on May 4, 1968. KNA CC/12/47.
[31] Letter from the District Commissioner of Kwale to J. K. Ithagu on May 4, 1968. KNA CC/12/47.
[32] This was the title of a story in the *Weekly Review* (Nairobi), June 20, 1980.

The leading LBC executives were aspiring politicians seeking to harness the economic and political possibilities of LBCs to achieve their political ends. Because of their political ambitions, they found the economic exploitation of land documents useful, but they needed to maximize its political effectiveness. To this end, they impressed on people the idea that the documents they held were worth little without the support of political actors.

Like state leaders in Ghana and KANU leaders in 1990s Kenya, they sapped the guarantee of rights from various land documents that they had sold people. They evicted errant landholders and settled compliant ones. This gave politicians the benefits of money and support rendered up-front for papers. It also had the added advantage of transforming such document holders into captive populations who had to obey politicians over the long term so as to have the rights promised by various land documents delivered.

The evolution of LBCs presents an interesting case of what Thelen[33] has called "functional conversion." LBCs were registered under the Companies Act (Cap 486). Because many departing white settlers sought to sell their farms in large chunks, poor peasants could not enter the land market individually. LBCs were devised as a means of allowing people to pool resources by buying shares in companies. The revenues from share sales could then be used to buy farms that would be subdivided among shareholders according to the shares they held.[34] Because of this, LBCs became very popular in the 1960s and 1970s.[35] Initially, many people joined and acquired land through LBCs, thus creating widespread trust in these institutional mechanisms that aspiring politicians were later able to exploit. The initial success of LBCs is important for understanding why many people invested in the fraudulent schemes that aspiring politicians later turned LBCs into.

The institutional structure of the LBC was later taken over by fraudsters and politicians and put to political ends through the systematic subversion of land documentation. Many aspiring parliamentarians and local politicians formed LBCs. Ngengi Muigai, MP for Gatundu formed

---

[33] Thelen, "Timing and temporality," p. 105.

[34] Wanjohi, *The Politics of Land*, p. 13; Kenya, *Report of the Commission of Inquiry into the Land Law System of Kenya*, p. 38 of Appendix.

[35] "Bogus companies," *Weekly Review* (Nairobi), May 23, 1980; and "Ultimatum: directors told to end land problems," *Weekly Review* (Nairobi), August 29, 1980.

the Gatundu Development Company.[36] John Michuki, aspiring Kangema MP, formed the Kangema Farlands Company.[37] George Mwicigi, the Assistant Minister for Agriculture and Livestock Development, formed the Kandara Investment Company.[38] Waruru Kanja, Nyeri MP and Assistant Minister for Local Government and Development, formed Burguret Arimi Limited.[39] Kihika Kimani, aspiring MP in Nakuru, formed the notorious Ngwataniro Land Buying Company. Towards the end of the 1970s there were up to 73 LBCs in the Nyeri District alone.[40] Ngwataniro is estimated to have had as many as 30,000 members in 1979.[41]

Land-buying-company executives sold and exploited "vanity shares" to amass money for local political campaigns, influence whether people attended political rallies, and manipulate how and where they voted.[42] "Vanity shares" were share certificates that were supposed to but did not always give people access to land. When shareholders got land, they sometimes found that access to their land depended not on possession of the share certificates, but on performance of other services such as rendering political support to LBC executives. These "vanity shares" led to widespread doubts over the legitimacy of LBC share certificates. In 1980, 30,032 people registered with the District Commissioner of Nyeri alone claiming they had been defrauded by LBC executives.[43]

Many LBC executives issued share certificates for which there were no corresponding land parcels, leaving people with worthless documents. Others put multiple papers with the same plot number into boxes from which shareholders were supposed to randomly pick plots. This led to more than one person drawing "rights" to the same piece of land. Members of the Githunguri Constituency Ranching Company actually received land title deeds from their executives but found no corresponding lands.[44]

[36] "Land issue," *Weekly Review* (Nairobi), May 9, 1980; and "Opting out," *Weekly Review* (Nairobi), March 26, 1980.

[37] "Michuki takes the plunge," *Weekly Review* (Nairobi), Mary 4, 1979.

[38] "Mwicigi resigns," *Weekly Review* (Nairobi), January 25, 1985.

[39] "Bogus Companies," *Weekly Review* (Nairobi), May 23, 1980.

[40] "Act Two: Nyeri land squabbles continue," *Weekly Review* (Nairobi), September 5, 1980.

[41] "Shocking revelations: company allegedly lost millions of shillings," *Weekly Review* (Nairobi), March 30, 1979.

[42] "Campaign against JM rumors," *Weekly Review* (Nairobi), May 5, 1975; and "Bogus Companies," *Weekly Review* (Nairobi), May 23, 1980.

[43] "Vanity shares," *Weekly Review* (Nairobi), June 20, 1980.

[44] "No hanging on Moi tells land buying companies," *Weekly Review* (Nairobi), April 4, 1986.

There were widespread allegations that some of the proceeds from these fraudulent activities by LBC executives had been used "in the last two parliamentary and civic elections."[45]

By delaying the distribution of land to shareholders, LBC executives transformed share certificates and titles into mechanisms for holding shareholders as political captives whom they could manipulate in various ways. They could summon crowds for campaigns and other political meetings by announcing that land parcels, land titles, or share certificates would be issued or discussed. This was the route that John Michuki, who was to become the powerful Interior Minister of Mwai Kibaki in 2007, took. In 1979, he called a meeting of his 6000-member Kangema Farlands Company at his home, ostensibly to issue share certificates. In a well-orchestrated process, attendees were first treated to "light refreshment" after which "speaker after speaker, representing the various locations and sub-locations in the division, made ... speeches calling on Michuki to contest the seat and pledging their support." Michuki's heart eventually softened, and he made a long speech agreeing to run for the seat! Incidentally, no share certificates, titles, or land parcels were distributed at that meeting.[46]

Kihika Kimani, head of the notorious Ngwataniro LBC, contributed to this repertoire by being one of the first politicians to use land documents to change the voting complexion of constituencies. Baiting shareholders with the promise of land, he trucked people around the vast estates of his Ngwataniro LBC during voter registration exercises to influence the voting complexion of constituencies and so control politicians in the Nakuru District.[47]

Armed with these instruments, Kihika Kimani executed a move that replaced three of four Nakuru MPs with Ngwataniro members in the 1974 elections.[48] As the dominant force in Nakuru politics in the 1970s, he initiated a meeting in 1977 of the Change the Constitution Movement aimed at preventing Vice President Moi from automatically succeeding President Kenyatta in the event of his death.[49]

---

[45] "Bogus companies," *Weekly Review* (Nairobi), May 23, 1980.

[46] "Michuki takes the plunge," *Weekly Review* (Nairobi), May 4, 1979.

[47] "Ngwataniro at crossroads as internal problems surface," *Weekly Review* (Nairobi), December 12, 1977.

[48] "Campaign against JM rumors," *Weekly Review* (Nairobi), May 5, 1975; "Mr. 100 per cent," *Weekly Review* (Nairobi), January 12, 1979; and "Shocking revelations: company allegedly lost millions of shillings," *Weekly Review* (Nairobi), March 30, 1979.

[49] "1977 limping to the finish in Kenya," *Weekly Review* (Nairobi), December 26, 1977.

The political significance that LBCs had come to assume was not lost on state leaders. When Moi succeeded Kenyatta, one of his first moves was to crack down on the LBCs that his opponents had used as a base from which to launch the anti-Moi Change the Constitution Movement. Moi realized, correctly, that the power of these MPs depended on their captive LBC shareholders, and that liberating these shareholders would fundamentally undermine his opponents.[50] He meticulously reinforced institutions that govern land rights in the areas where LBC executives held sway to hinder their efforts at exploiting land to garner political support.

Moi publicly denounced LBCs and their fraudulent activities.[51] He also forced them to register all shareholders with the registrar of companies and not only executives as members.[52] Not registering these "sleeping members," who numbered in the thousands, left them at the mercy of executives of these companies since they were not legal shareholders. Once they were registered shareholders, they could use the court system to hold company executives accountable. Further, Moi forced LBCs to subdivide their farms and issue titles to their members.[53] When companies were slow to comply, as in the case of the Gatharakwa Land Buying Company in Kieni West Division, Nyeri District, he deployed state officials to survey and subdivide farms and give members titles.[54] In April 1983, he travelled to Bahati in Nakuru to personally distribute share certificates to members of the Ngwataniro LBC.[55] In addition, he pronounced that these LBCs should be deregistered and disbanded as soon as they had finished allocating lands to members.[56] Moi's effort was, in effect, an attempt to liberate tens of thousands of people from the control of LBC executives.

[50] Wanjohi, *The Politics of Land*, p. 14.
[51] "Beware conmen," *Weekly Review* (Nairobi), October 5, 1979.
[52] "Company rules tightened: sleeping partners to get protection," *Weekly Review* (Nairobi), February 23, 1979.
[53] Wanjohi, *The Politics of Land*, p. 14; "Company rules tightened: sleeping partners to get protection," *Weekly Review* (Nairobi), February 23, 1970; "Beware conmen! President warns Kenyans, *Weekly Review* (Nairobi), October 5, 1979; and "Ultimatum: directors told to end land problems," *Weekly Review* (Nairobi), August 29, 1980; and "Progress," *Weekly Review* (Nairobi), April 22, 1983.
[54] Interview with an official of a land control board in Nyeri District (Ken 26), March 9, 2005; "Action for Gatarakwa," *Weekly Review* (Nairobi), June 13, 1986; and "Progress," *Weekly Review* (Nairobi), April 22, 1983.
[55] "Progress: Ngwataniro members finally get share certificates," *Weekly Review* (Nairobi), April 22, 1983.
[56] "No hanging on, Moi tells land companies," *Weekly Review* (Nairobi), April 4, 1986.

Not surprisingly, once Moi had liberated these captives, many LBC executives saw a drastic decline in their political fortunes. Kihika Kimani's dramatic demise exemplifies this. On April 21, 1979, his long reign as director of Ngwataniro LBC ended when he refrained from contesting new elections for company director under pressure from his opponents.[57] When Moi nullified KANU Nakuru Branch elections in 1979, Kihika Kimani declined to contest his long-held seat, thus allowing Moi's favored Kariuki Chotora to run unopposed.[58] That same year, he lost his Nakuru North parliamentary seat to Koigi wa Wamwere, who received three times as many votes as he did.[59] But Kihika's fall from power was not yet complete. In 1985 he was tried and jailed for mismanaging Ngwataniro funds.[60]

Moi's deliberate effort at reinforcing property rights institutions in areas controlled by LBCs to undermine LBC executives opposed to him is of great significance here. It provides evidence for two points that have been made repeatedly in this book. It shows that increasing political competition and increasing threats to the positions of leaders do not always have a negative impact on property institutions. Further, it shows that the political exploitation of land rights does not always have a detrimental effect on property institutions.

Increasing political competition led Moi to strengthen property rights in the areas of Kenya under the influence of his LBC opponents. As we saw in Chapter 5 of this book, competition in the 1990s led Moi and his KANU allies to fundamentally subvert rights in various parts of the country. This included areas of Nakuru formerly under LBC executives such as Kihika Kimani where he had earlier advocated and acted to secure the rights of LBC members.

The specific effect of competition on institutions depended on the contextual factor of who was in a position to benefit from weak institutions by exploiting rights. When Moi and his allies were in a position to do so, they happily undermined institutions. When their opponents were in a position to do so, as during the era of LBCs, Moi aggressively reinforced institutions to handicap his opponents. It is for this reason that we cannot simply use the security of leaders' hold on power to explain their preferences for secure or insecure rights, as was argued in Chapter 2.

---

[57] "Kihika Kimani to face uphill battle," *Weekly Review* (Nairobi), April 27, 1979.
[58] "Kihika steps down," *Weekly Review* (Nairobi), June 8, 1979.
[59] "Dixon Kihika Kimani bids for come-back," *Weekly Review* (Nairobi), November 19, 1982.
[60] "Kihika appeals," *Weekly Review* (Nairobi), January 31, 1985.

This insight also speaks to the broad question of the policy effects of increased political competition. Some argue that increasing political competition (sometimes through the introduction of multiparty democracy) forces political leaders to make better public policy choices by allowing electorates to hold them accountable.[61] Others point out that competition may actually lead to worse public policy choices by shortening the time horizons of leaders.[62] Here we show that differences in local dynamics within the same country impact how increasing political competition impacts leaders' institutional preferences.

Moi's crackdown on the fraudulent activities of LBCs also showed the flawed nature of the dichotomy often drawn between the good effects of economic motivations and the bad effects of political motivations on public policy. Moi's actions were highly politically motivated. They were not primarily geared towards boosting the economy or even protecting poor Gikuyu peasants who were being exploited by LBC executives. His efforts at reinforcing property rights institutions were meant to break the backs of his LBC opponents. He was politically exploiting property rights to subvert his opponents, and this took the form of strengthening institutions that secure land rights.

Land documents in Kenya were already under tremendous attack by 1991, when the most powerful state officials responsible for policymaking and policy implementation launched an outright assault on the efficacy of land documents. Even though most of this earlier subversive exploitation of land documents was not done by officials at the center of state power, it was already having a serious effect on people's trust in LBC share certificates.

Land titles were not immune from such exploitation or the resultant decline in public confidence either. In 1991, the high court nullified hundreds of title deeds issued after a land adjudication program in Mosiro, Kajiado District. Various officials in the Ministry of Lands had exploited their positions to issue titles to people who had no rights to land in that area in exchange for money. Ministry officials and their relatives also received titles to lands to which they had no conceivable rights.[63] The cancellation of these titles by the high court led a writer in the

[61] World Bank, *Governance and development* (Washington D.C.: The World Bank, 1991); and Claude Ake, *Democracy and development in Africa* (Washington D.C.: The Brookings Institute, 1996).

[62] Robert Bates, "Institutions and development," *Journal of African Economies* 15 (April 2006), pp. 30 & 57.

[63] "Land questions," *Weekly Review* (Nairobi), May 24, 1991.

Weekly Review to question the validity of the popular assumption "that a title deed gives the holder irrevocable ownership of a piece of land" in an article aptly titled, "What Value a Title Deed?"[64]

ARRIVING AT THE HEART OF THE MAINSTREAM

The exogenous shock of re-democratization in Kenya did not suddenly create an opportunity for the subversion of land documentation, as argued by many students of Kenyan political economy and policymakers.[65] That process was already underway. What it did was give central state leaders a huge incentive to embrace modes of manipulation that had been invented by more marginal actors and were already having serious effects by 1991. As discussed in Chapter 5, the activities of central state leaders in the 1990s eerily mirrored those of LBC executives, thus raising the possibility that the innovations of marginal con men in the periphery had finally come to influence mainstream political economic processes.

The deliberate subversion of land titles and allocation notes by politicians during the era of re-democratization went along with continuing efforts by con men to exploit widespread trust in the efficacy of land titles in order to sell nonexistent rights. In collaboration with some officials at the Ministry of Lands and the Government Printer in Nairobi, "brokers," as these con men were known, manufactured and sold titles to nonexistent rights. This practice was so prevalent and the techniques of these "brokers" so sophisticated that the state introduced serial numbers for each district and imported paper on which to print titles. But this did not defeat the efforts of con men. They would search title registers and print titles for properties. Pretending to be the owners of the parcel, they would then tell their victims to inspect the register if they had doubts. They would then sell the title and change the entry in the register with the help of officials at the Ministry of Lands. Victims then clashed over the land and ended up going to the police and courts. The high quality of their titles and the compromised nature of registers often made these cases very difficult to resolve.[66] The Uasin Gishu District Lands Office

---

[64] "What value a title deed," *Weekly Review* (Nairobi), May 31, 1991.

[65] Jacqueline Klopp, "Pilfering the Public," pp. 8–9; IDMC, "I am a refugee," p. 13. There is a popular discourse ascribing the subversion of land documents and other forms of corruption in the land market to re-democratization in the 1990s. Various interviewees held this view. These included a staff member of an NGO involved in advocacy on land issues (Kenya 2), February 15, 2005; and an official of the Department of Lands (Kenya 1), February 14, 2005.

[66] Interview with a long-time employee of the Department of Lands (Kenya 8), March 1, 2007.

decided to restrict the ability of members of the public to inspect the land register to curb such fraud.[67]

Efforts to clamp down on the work of these con men by state officials deeply involved in undermining property rights institutions in the 1990s is understandable. The power to exploit land documentation presents state officials with a potent instrument that they can use to entrench their power. But to maximize its effects, state officials need to monopolize this ability to exploit documentation. If everyone can similarly exploit documentation, the belief in land documentation that facilitates such exploitation will disappear fast. Further, the exploitation of documentation by those who are opponents of state officials eliminates the advantage that state officials gain from such exploitation.

A government commission of inquiry in 2004 recognized what was widely known in the country. There were often multiple titles in the hands of different people for the same piece of land. Like many Kenyans who I interviewed in 2005,[68] this commission noted that, "while the title deed in Kenya has largely been reliable," these activities have "seriously thrown into question the degree to which members of the public can rely on it as a valid legal document." "This uncertainty," it noted "has the potential of disrupting the land market and jeopardizing the general development of the country."[69]

CONCLUSION

This chapter builds on an understanding of the contradictory potential of institutions to demonstrate the way in which the aggressive introduction and promotion of land documentation in Kenya contributed to its own gradual subversion. I argue that the institution of land documentation in Kenya produced and sustained dominant agricultural, real estate, and tourism interests that were dedicated to the "sanctity of land titles." But the success of land documentation created a trust in the efficacy of land

---

[67] Interview with an official in Uasin-Gishu District Lands Office (Kenya 32), April 19, 2005.

[68] Interviews with an official of the Ministry of Lands (Kenya), February 14, 2005; a member of an NGO involved in activism on land issues (Kenya 2), February 15, 2005; a lawyer employed by and NGO involved in activism on land issues (Kenya 3), February 17, 2005; a member of a land control board in Nyeri District (Kenya 18), march 3, 2005; a divisional officer in Laikipia District (Kenya 40), April 27, 2005; an official of the Institution of Surveyors of Kenya (Kenya 56), May 5, 2005; a member of a lands office in Taita Taveta District (Kenya 58), May 11, 2005; and a member of a land control board in Nyeri District (Kenya 15), March 2, 2005.

[69] Kenya, *Report of the Commission of Inquiry into the Illegal/Irregular*, p. 189.

documents that was easily exploited by fraudsters and politicians intent on selling worthless or encumbered land documents for economic and political gain. The subversion of land documentation by these groups was only exacerbated by the reintroduction of democratization.

This effort at emphasizing the importance of the endogenous mechanism through which land documentation in Kenya contributed to its own downfall does not rest on a denial of all exogenous factors. In Kenya we have to note the landlessness and land hunger that led many to take the bait of fraudsters. It is partly for this reason that the more equitable redistribution of land rights is imperative in places such as Kenya, Namibia, South Africa, and Zimbabwe, which I briefly discuss below. We also must note the relative weakness of the police and judiciary that allowed fraudsters to operate on the margins of society even before state leaders embraced fraudulent activities and that curtailed the willingness of enforcement agencies to crack down on these practices.

Here I argue that, holding these factors constant, the rise of land documentation and the beliefs it engendered facilitated efforts by fraudsters to take advantage of lax policing and land hunger. How else can we understand the ability of one LBC executive to defraud tens of thousands of people across the country? Various laws, land documentation institutions, the Companies Act (Cap 486), and peoples' increasing belief in these institutions, all of which allowed for the creation and operation of LBCs, are invaluable for understanding the scale and nature of the fraud. Without these institutions and people's trust in them, it would have been extremely difficult for any one person to gather and defraud such a huge section of the population. The argument here is that the contradictory potential of land documentation enabled wily actors to exploit these exogenous contextual factors, leading to the subversion of land documentation.

The contributions of endogenous processes to the change of institutional arrangements laid out here require us to reexamine the conception of critical junctures. Critical junctures are defined as the moments at which change occurs and actors chose between various alternatives, unlike normal periods that are marked by the structural reproduction of paths.[70] The story told here about the contradictory potential of institutions, forces us to rethink the periods in which we locate historical significance and concentrate attention in research. It reduces the historical significance of critical junctures while infusing the periods of supposed stability with more historical significance. It does this by showing

---

[70] Mahoney, "Path dependence in historical sociology," p. 513; Thelen, *How Institutions Evolve*, p. 30.

that agency operates in many periods outside of critical junctures, even in some cases where institutions display positive feedback effects.[71] In the study of land politics in Kenya, the overwhelming focus on the re-introduction of multiparty democracy, to the detriment of earlier periods in the country's postcolonial history, might thus be mistaken.

Also, the analysis here offers an important corrective to the popular understanding of institutional change that tends to see change as the effect of mobilization by groups that are disadvantaged by and work to bring about the fall of institutions.[72] I show here that change can also be brought about unintentionally by parasitic subversives who harbor no grievances against institutions. Indeed, they often love and depend on these institutions. But cumulatively, their exploitation of these institutions over time can seriously contribute to institutional decline.

---

[71] Streeck and Thelen, "Introduction," p. 4; and Thelen, *How Institutions Evolve*, p. 32.
[72] See, for instance, Clemens, "Organizational repertoires," p. 757.

7

Conclusion

How well does the argument laid out in this work account for how leaders
handle property institutions in places beyond the cases considered in this
work? In this chapter, we use Zimbabwe to test the ability of the theory
constructed here to travel beyond the main cases considered in this work.

Zimbabwe is a good choice in part because it has become the "10,000-
pound gorilla" in any discussion of the politics of property rights in
Africa. Widespread media coverage of land occupations and political
violence there has placed it in the center of discussions of property rights,
democracy, and human rights around the world. Methodologically, it is
a good selection because, like the other countries in this book, it was also
colonized by Britain. In many ways, it is similar to Kenya. It experienced
settler colonialism with the widespread expropriation of black land for
exclusive European use, which resulted in a situation where "42% of the
country was owned by 6000 (white) commercial farmers" at independence in 1980.[1]

But the similarities between Zimbabwe and Kenya do not end there. As
in Kenya, the seizure of lands for use by Europeans was accompanied by
the construction of an institutional structure to facilitate the use of such
land for commercial agriculture by Europeans. Also similarly to Kenya,

---

[1] Bertus de Villiers, *Land Reform: Issues and Challenges* (Johannesburg: Konrad Adenauer
Foundation, 2003), p. 6; and Sam Moyo, "The political economy of land acquisition and
redistribution in Zimbabwe 1990–1999," *Journal of Southern African Atudies* 26 (March
2000), p. 6.

title registration had taken deep root by the time of independence in 1980. This independence was won under the leadership of a Zimbabwe African National Union-Patriotic Front (ZANU-PF) government, led by Robert Mugabe, through a negotiated settlement after a bloody liberation war.

The war had pitted African liberation movements against the racist white government of Ian Smith, who had formally declared independence from Britain in 1965. Respect for the property rights of white settlers was a significant element of the negotiated Lancaster House Agreement, which also included a sunset clause requiring noninterference with the rights of such settlers until the expiration of ten years in 1990.[2] The redistribution of land, to which the ZANU-PF government that has ruled the country since independence was committed, was supposed to proceed through a willing buyer–willing seller policy. Full market rate compensation was supposed to be promptly paid to settlers whose lands were acquired for redistribution, just as in Kenya.[3]

UPHOLDING AND THEN UNDERCUTTING INSTITUTIONS IN ZIMBABWE

Leading up to the late 1990s, ZANU-PF displayed a remarkable willingness to maintain the strength of institutions such as title registries that governed property rights in Zimbabwe.[4] Low-scale land redistribution was carried out, with the British government and other donors providing money with which to buy farms from white settlers for such purposes.[5] As in Early Kenya, this process was undertaken in a very orderly manner, with the beneficiaries receiving well-demarcated plots, and recorded and documented land rights.[6]

Land redistribution during this period was not an effort to undermine institutions that governed land rights. It redefined who owned land

---

[2] Ibbo Mandaza, "The state in post-white settler colonial situation," in Ibbo Mandaza, ed., *Zimbabwe: The Political Economy of Transition 1980–1986* (Dakar: Codesria 1986), p. 39; and Eric Worby, "A redivided land? New agrarian conflicts and questions," *Journal of Agrarian Change* 1 (October 2004), p. 487.

[3] Sam Moyo, "The land question," in Ibbo Mandaza, ed. *Zimbabwe: The Political Economy of Transition 1980–1986* (Dakar: Codesria 1986), p. 172.

[4] Human Rights Watch, "Fast track land reform in Zimbabwe," *Human Rights Watch Publications* 14 (March 2002), pp. 6–8.

[5] de Villiers, *Land Reform*, p. 11.

[6] The fact that land recipients got occupation permits that were subject to renewal and put limits on how they could transact in land created uncertainty of rights among some beneficiaries. de Villiers, *Land Reform*, p. 10.

instead of putting into question whether people owned rights at all. This redefinition was mostly achieved in ways that further reinforced, not undermined, institutions that govern land rights,[7] making Zimbabwe "a model of how land reform should be undertaken."[8] The ultimate arbiters of rights were still institutions for governing rights such as title registries and the courts. The redistributive consequences of this slow process were low,[9] and the beneficiaries from such lands were sometimes well connected ZANU-PF politicians and bureaucrats.[10]

From about 1999, ZANU-PF adopted a different approach to the process of land redistribution that not only redefined who owned what, but fundamentally challenged the ability of institutions such as land documentation systems, the courts, and enforcement institutions to guarantee any rights at all. Like elites in Late Kenya, ZANU-PF officials systematically reconfigured property institutions in ways that sapped the autonomous ability to define, adjudicate, and enforce rights and left them at the whim of state officials and local party strongmen. Recipients of land in the frenzied redistribution exercise often did not receive any document indicating their rights. When they got documents, they only received one-year temporary occupancy permits that the state was in no hurry to transform into 99-year leaseholds as required under the law.[11]

Sometimes the whole allocation itself was not recorded.[12] Further, the system of determining land recipients was so complicated that people often did not even know the right way of obtaining land as informal layers of local ZANU-PF party officials and their loyal war veterans[13] displaced formal state institutions for allocating land. This often resulted in the same plot being awarded to more than one person by different agencies.[14] The police took a back seat in the enforcement of rights as war veterans became the arbiters of who received and lost land.[15]

What explains this change?

---

[7] Good, "Dealing with despotism," p. 10.
[8] de Villiers, *Land Reform*, p. 5.
[9] Moyo, "Land acquisition," p. 9.
[10] de Villiers, *Land Reform*, p. 12.
[11] Human Rights Watch, "Fast track," p. 13.
[12] Ibid., pp. 15–16.
[13] The war veterans were fighters in Zimbabwe's liberation struggle against white minority rule and had an organization called the War Veterans Association. They have been seen as loyal to ZANU-PF since the 1990s.
[14] Human Rights Watch, "Fast track," pp. 28–30.
[15] Ibid., p. 28.

ACCOUNTING FOR THE SWITCH

As in Kenya, a drastic transformation in the political environment in which ZANU-PF operated led it to change how it exploited land and its consequent preference for institutions that govern property rights. Before the late 1990s, ZANU-PF leaders had drawn handsome rewards from land that was mediated by its productive use. Even though they did not own productive interests that were as vast as those of Kenyan leaders, there is evidence that senior ZANU-PF leaders had acquired some productive land interests.[16]

More importantly, commercial agriculture and its related industrial sector contributed significantly to the economy and government revenue, enabling ZANU-PF to secure its hold on the state.[17] The employment created by these farms also kept sections of the population placated that would otherwise have posed threats to ZANU-PF rule. Maintaining the property structures that supported these commercial agricultural interests made a lot of sense to them.

Beginning in 1999, ZANU-PF leaders began to exploit political gains from land that were unmediated by its productive use, just as elites in Late Kenya had done. In 1999, the Movement for Democratic Change (MDC) was formed by a variety of societal interests. Its broad base posed the first truly serious electoral threat to ZANU-PF control of the state since 1987 when a unity pact between ZANU-PF and the Zimbabwe African Peoples' Union had created a de facto one-party state.[18]

Importantly, the MDC drew substantial electoral and financial support from the white settler farmers and the Commercial Farmers Union to which they belonged.[19] These white farmers saw the MDC's less-confrontational approach to the process of land reform as less threatening than that of Mugabe. Beginning in the mid-1990s Mugabe had become increasingly involved in a tense confrontation with Britain over British funds to pay for the acquisition of farms from white settlers for redistribution. They also disagreed over the terms under which such farms could be acquired.

---

[16] Isaac Maposa, *Land Reform in Zimbabwe* (Harare: The Catholic Commission for Justice and Peace in Zimbabwe, 1995), pp. 95–102; Good, "Dealing with despotism," pp. 12–13; and de Villiers, *Land Reform*, p. 14.

[17] Moyo, "The land question," pp. 191–192.

[18] Good, "Dealing with despotism," p. 10.

[19] Human Rights Watch, "Fast track," p. 9.

Mugabe saw the British as having a duty to resolve land problems that they had created when they had robbed black communities of land for European settlers. The British had always sought to use any financial contributions toward resolving these problems as an instrument for safeguarding the interests of white settlers and influencing Zimbabwean politics. Things came to a head in 1997 when Clare Short, the U.K.'s Minister for International Development, formally wrote to the government of Zimbabwe denying that "Britain has a special responsibility to meet the costs of land purchase in Zimbabwe" since her new Labor government had no connections to former colonial interests that had created the problem.[20] Apparently, the death of the original British officials who expropriated the land must have absolved Britain of all responsibility for the expropriation![21] Mugabe's subsequent threat to compulsorily acquire farms without compensation to white farmers explains the zeal with which Commercial Farmers Union members threw their support behind the MDC, whose land redistribution policy was less confrontational and threatening.

Like KANU in early 1990s Kenya, ZANU-PF was soon in a fight for survival as MDC demonstrated its massive appeal. First, MDC successfully campaigned for the rejection of a constitutional referendum in February 2000 that would have increased the powers of the president and given him the power to compulsorily acquire land for redistribution without compensation.[22] Then in June 2000, less than a year after it was formed, the MDC won 57 to ZANU-PF's 63 seats during parliamentary elections.[23]

A month later, the government announced the fast track land reform program. The goal was to compulsorily acquire without compensation thousands of farms owned by white farmers, amounting to 9.23 million hectares for redistribution.[24] From the perspective of this book, what was remarkable about the program was not the intention to redistribute land, which is something that had to be done to secure Zimbabwe's long-term

---

[20] Ibid., p. 7.

[21] Many activists in debt-ridden countries would warmly embrace this Short Doctrine in their agitation against the debt regime if only countries such as Britain were truly tolerant of it beyond cases like Zimbabwe where it absolves them of responsibility for their wrongs.

[22] Amin Kamete, "The rebels within: urban Zimbabwe in the post-election period," in Henning Melber, ed. *Zimbabwe's Presidential Elections 2002: Evidence, Lessons and Implications* (Uppsala: Nordiska Afrikainstitutet, 2002), p. 32.

[23] Good, "Dealing with despotism," p. 24.

[24] Human Rights Watch, "Fast track," 11.

political stability. It was the new extraction of gains from land in ways that were unmediated by its productive use. ZANU-PF and its underlings had transformed the land redistribution exercise into an instrument for buying and keeping support and punishing and dissuading opposition in the face of MDC threats to their rule. The criteria for acquiring land now was not need or skill at farming, but demonstrated support for ZANU-PF.[25] In accordance with this, war veterans and ZANU-PF local leaders were often the ones who issued application forms for land parcels, and they often asked applicants for ZANU-PF identity cards before receipt of application forms.[26]

The criteria for seizure of farms for redistribution was no longer rational bureaucratic criteria concerned with promoting a rational political economy; it was opposition to ZANU-PF.[27] Those who had received plots in the redistribution process but had failed to render support, were punished by having their parcels repossessed.[28] To increase the amount of support that could be garnered using a fixed amount of land, the same parcel would be awarded to many different people who promised political support.[29] New land recipients thus felt insecure and decried the confusion that characterized the whole process, even though they were strongly in favor of land redistribution.[30] To prevent white settler farmers and the farm workers whom they controlled from supporting the MDC, they would be thrown out of their constituencies through farm seizures and the forcible dispersal of workers.[31] Most of these ways of exploiting land were eerily similar to activities of KANU leaders in Late Kenya.

Like state leaders in Late Kenya and Ghana, ZANU-PF leaders realized that, for land to be truly effective as such a political weapon and for them to engage in all of these activities, they had to undercut land administration, adjudication, and enforcement institutions to which they had been committed to in earlier redistribution efforts. Unlike in previous rounds of redistribution, they made allocation rules and procedures so cloudy that people given plots found it hard to prove that they had acquired those lands through the proper channels, leaving them dependent on protection from local ZANU-PF strongmen.[32]

[25] Good, "Dealing with despotism," p. 15; and Human Rights Watch, "Fast track," p. 15.
[26] Human Rights Watch, "Fast track," pp. 13, 29.
[27] Good, "Dealing with despotism," p. 15; and Human Rights Watch, "Fast track," p. 13.
[28] Human Rights Watch, "Fast track," p. 30.
[29] Ibid., p. 15.
[30] Ibid., pp. 14–17.
[31] Ibid., p. 20.
[32] Ibid., pp. 11–12.

Many who received land during this period were given no documentary proof of the grant. Those who got *one*-year permits were left with no doubt about the dependence of their continued enjoyment of rights on "correct" political behavior. Allocated plots were not well demarcated, causing disputes among claimants who had to resort to the magnanimity of ZANU-PF toughs to secure their rights.[33] The courts and the police took a back seat to ZANU-PF militias and the war veterans in adjudicating disputes and enforcing rights.[34] To top this off, Mugabe's presidential amnesty for political crimes apart from murder and rape committed in the first part of 2000 furthered the atmosphere of impunity, reducing hesitation by ZANU-PF activists involved in the violent exploitation of land rights.[35]

The general uncertainty that was thus fostered allowed ZANU-PF toughs to credibly threaten the property rights of those who engaged in opposition politics. It made it easy for them to prevent perceived opposition supporters like white farmers and commercial farm workers from voting in certain constituencies by expelling them. It enabled these toughs to buy more votes with land by giving out the same plots simultaneously to different people.

DECENTERING ZIMBABWE: SOUTH AFRICA AND NAMIBIA

Given the ways in which Zimbabwe parallels the case of Kenya and supports the overall argument of this work, there remains the question that I have faced often of why Zimbabwe is not one of the main countries studied in this work. The answer is that, at the moment, Zimbabwe is a problematic place to study. Some of this difficulty comes from very practical reasons. The process of land redistribution in recent years has been violent, and journalists, rights groups, and other researchers trying to document the violence have been targeted with threats and physically prevented from doing their work, especially in the countryside. With the limited time and resources that I had to conduct field research, I decided that a less difficult place such as Kenya, which tells a largely similar story, would do.

Much of the difficulty that comes with studying and discussing Zimbabwe these days is less practical and comes from the ideological

---

[33] Ibid., p. 15.
[34] Good, "Dealing with despotism," p. 15; and Human Rights Watch, "Fast track," p. 28.
[35] Good, "Dealing with despotism," p. 25; and Human Rights Watch, "Fast track," p. 23.

minefield that the country has become. Ideological struggle among scholars, politicians, and policymakers now makes any effort at understanding the country susceptible to various accusations either of imperialism or of despotic black nativism.

As Murunga[36] notes in an interesting, short piece, any comment on Mugabe's authoritarian rule and its disruptive and violent character is likely to draw condemnation of the author as at best an innocent victim of the imperialist machinations of Britain and other Western countries. But the same danger is present on the other side. Comments on violence by opposition supporters, the authoritarian character of MDC leader Morgan Tsvangirai, and the significant contribution of Britain to the crisis are likely to draw condemnations of the author as a supporter of despotic and backward black nativism.

It is in this regard that Kenya seemed to be a much better case to study. While the country has been embraced warmly by Western countries as a bastion of stability, it displays many of the problems concerning land rights that afflict Zimbabwe, but often in even grosser relief. Disputes over land rights, squatting, land occupations, and fighting over land rights are constant facts of life in Kenya. These disputes create little wars that often go unnoticed, because unlike events in Zimbabwe, they receive little Western media attention. One of these conflicts in Mount Elgon was so serious that, in 2007, the President deployed the Kenyan army and air force to pacify the Sabaot Land Defense Force, which was launching attacks on settlements in that district.[37]

As seen in this work, the naked political exploitation of land rights has a far longer and more illustrious history in Kenya than in Zimbabwe. Further, the human cost of such exploitation of land rights in Zimbabwe pales in comparison to that in Kenya. Human Rights Watch, which is not known to underestimate rights abuses, reports that, by the year 2000, seven white farmers and "several tens" of black farm workers had been killed in Zimbabwe in such violent exploitation of land rights.[38] By the year 2000, these activities in Kenya had resulted in the deaths of thousands and displacement of hundreds of thousands.

---

[36] Godwin Murunga, "Is anti-imperialism incompatible with pro-democracy in Zimbabwe," *Zeleza Post* July 1, 2008 http://zeleza.com/blogging/african-affairs/anti-imperialism-incompatible-pro-democracy-zimbabwe. (Accessed September 11, 2008.)

[37] "Army withdraws from Mount Elgon amid torture claims," *East African Standard* (Nairobi), September 2, 2008. http://www.eastandard.net/InsidePage.php?mnu=details&id=1143993969&catid=4. (Accessed September 11, 2008.)

[38] Human Rights Watch, "Fast track," p. 2.

Studying Kenya instead of Zimbabwe as the case of the settler colony can also be read as a deliberate attempt to decenter and "normalize" Zimbabwe in discourses on property rights, human rights, and democracy. It may be seen as an attempt to shift away from the widespread portrayal of Mugabe's government as a particularly evil and abnormal one worthy of special attention in newspapers, documentaries, panel discussions, outdoor performances, etc. However, the goal is not to minimize the problems in Zimbabwe. It is to cast them in comparative light so we can see what Zimbabwe's problems tell us about the politics of property rights in other former settler colonies such as South Africa and Namibia, which have thankfully not gone down the path of Zimbabwe *yet*.

This is not to say that South Africa and Namibia will go down the path of Zimbabwe and Kenya, but that there is a real possibility that they might. All of these countries share similar ingredients. They are all settler colonies with extremely unequal distributions of land that create a host of land-hungry people susceptible to exploitation by ingenious political entrepreneurs. Molutsi was correct in describing the land issue as a "landmine in Southern Africa" requiring immediate and serious attention.[39] de Villiers similarly notes that "the very democratic basis that took so long to be established could be threatened if land reform fails" in South Africa, Namibia, and Zimbabwe.[40]

Serious land redistribution in these countries would be a political master stroke in that it would take away one easily recognizable and powerful instrument for generating support through disruptive and violent means. A more equitable redistribution of land in these countries is necessary for their long term political stability.

Robert Mugabe enjoys considerable support among leaders in South Africa and Namibia, and many in these countries frustrated by the slow pace of land reform see Mugabe's fast track land reform as an alternative. In 2005 the then South African deputy president Phumzile Mlambo-Ngcuka commented that, since land reform in South Africa had been "too slow and too structured," the African National Congress "may need the skills of Zimbabwe to help [them]" and that South Africa should "learn lessens" from Zimbabwe.[41] Earlier in 2000 Thabo Mbeki had

---

[39] Patrick Molutsi, "Beyond the Zimbabwe mist," in Henning Melber, ed. *Zimbabwe's Presidential Elections 2002: Evidence, Lessons and Implications* (Uppsala: Nordiska Afrikainstitutet, 2002), p. 81.
[40] de Villiers, *Land Reform*, p. 1.
[41] "South Africa 'to learn from' land seizures," *BBC News*, August 11, 2005. http://news.bbc.co.uk/2/hi/africa/4140990.stm. (Accessed September 12, 2008.)

sent his Minister of Agriculture and Land Affairs to study the reform process in Zimbabwe.[42] Namibia's former president Sam Nujoma similarly expressed support for Zimbabwe's land reform in 2002.[43] And Mugabe has done his part to sell his model to the hordes of frustrated, land-hungry people of Namibia and South Africa. At a rally in Namibia in 2000, he told the gathered crowd that land inequality has "a simple solution." "If the other neighboring countries have problems similar to the ones we have encountered, why not apply the same solution as Zimbabwe."[44]

The stability and relative economic soundness of South Africa and Namibia should not lull us into a false sense of security. For years after independence, Zimbabwe was similarly stable and economically successful and was hailed as a unique success story in Africa.[45] Like the African National Congress in South Africa, the South West African People's Organization in Namibia, and KANU in Kenya to a lesser degree, ZANU-PF enjoyed tremendous support and popular legitimacy associated with its bitter and violent struggle against the racist regime of Ian Smith.

As we saw in Kenya and Zimbabwe, we should expect opposition parties over time to make greater inroads in South Africa and Namibia. If there has been no serious effort at land redistribution, land will most likely become a political weapon in both countries, with either the ruling party or the opposition seeking to gain an advantage from pervasive land hunger. If for no other reason, the redistribution of land in these countries should be pursued as a means of further stabilizing their systems by depriving political entrepreneurs of a potent and highly disruptive instrument of competition.

WIDER THEORETICAL PAY-OFFS

Why have national and subnational leaders in Botswana, Ghana, and Kenya handled institutions that govern property rights in such different ways in order to harness economic and political gains from rising land values? Two variables explain the divergence: the way in which elites extract value from land, and the extent of their capacity.

---

[42] Good, "Dealing with despotism," p. 27.

[43] "Namibia's worried white farmers," *BBC News*, September 6, 2002. http://news.bbc.co.uk/2/hi/africa/2240595.stm. (Accessed September 12, 2008.)

[44] "ANC backs Zimbabwe land policy," *BBC News*, May 28, 2000. http://news.bbc.co.uk/2/hi/africa/767261.stm. (Accessed September 12, 2008.)

[45] Moyo, "The land question," pp. 165–66.

The original contribution of this work lies in its employment of how elites extract value from land to clarify varying preferences towards institutions that govern rights in land. By deviating from the dominant view that all land market participants desire strong property institutions, I develop an argument that shows why some political leaders – but not others – benefit politically and economically from an environment of secure property rights in land. Borrowing from the rich revisionist literature, I combine this analysis of preferences with an account of leaders' capacity to explain the different ways in which leaders handle institutions that govern property rights in land.

The introduction of the variable of how elites exploit benefits from land is deeply rooted in the new institutionalism. A key insight of the new institutionalism is that, because institutions structure politics, they become the objects of intense political contestation.[46] Different property rights environments structure politics by facilitating or hindering different means of extracting political and economic benefits from land.[47] They thus enrich and empower different constituencies involved in different ways of using land, unleashing conflict in which elites try to fashion property rights institutions with these consequences in mind.

A significant payoff of this focus on how elites use land is that it gives us a clear and simple way of understanding why rational, well-informed, and capable actors would prefer weak property rights systems and how they would acquire resources to actualize their preference. This helps us go beyond simply asserting that some actors might benefit from weak property rights.[48] It also helps us make sense of North's[49] path dependency argument by showing why some actors seek to perpetuate weak property rights institutions in the face of rising land values and how they achieve the resources to do so.

A CORRECTION TO THE TRANSACTION COSTS LITERATURE

This book also exposes a serious but avoidable flaw in much of the existing transaction cost literature. By focusing on only a narrow subset

---

[46] North, *Institutions, Institutional Change*, pp. 47, 79; and Kathleen Thelen and Sven Steinmo, "Historical institutionalism in comparative politics," in Sven Steinmo, Kathleen Thelen, and F. Longstreth, eds. *Structuring Politics: Historical Institutionalism in Comparative Analysis* (Cambridge: Cambridge University Press, 1992), p. 9.

[47] North, *Institutions, Institutional Change*, pp. 47–48, 78.

[48] Feeney, "The development," p. 274.

[49] North, *Institutions, Institutional Change*, pp. 95–101.

of the ways in which people use land, it has adopted the flawed view that an environment of weak property rights always raises transaction costs, while an environment of strong property rights lowers transaction costs for all parties.[50]

If one focuses only on the subset of land users on which they concentrate analysis, this view is indeed correct. The problem, though, is that such analyses prevent a consideration of people involved in other ways of exploiting land from theorizing on property rights. As I show in this work, weak institutions, faulty record systems, and inefficient and corrupt courts are a godsend for people involved in certain ways of exploiting land. A weak institutional environment facilitates and renders certain land market transactions possible and profitable.

Such a hazy rights environment allows politicians to gerrymander constituencies by evicting opposition landholders and granting their rights to more friendly voters. It enables politicians to mobilize support by threatening the property rights of those who engage in opposition politics. Further, it allows politicians to exchange land for support by enabling them to credibly threaten the rights of those who receive land if they fail to render political support. Dishonest politicians who want to raise cash for political activity in an emergency can also exploit these weak institutions to sell nonexistent and highly encumbered rights.

Weak property rights do not raise transaction costs for all, just as strong property rights do not lower transaction costs for all. The question we must pose when we make proclamations about whether certain institutional arrangements lower or raise transaction costs is: "Whose costs?" This question reveals the conflict-ridden nature of struggles over the very issue of whether an environment of secure property rights in land is desirable in any society.[51]

This point is similar to that made by Yandle in his study of regulation when he noted that, "Regulation is a relief for some and a burden for

---

[50] Christopher Clague, Philip Keefer, Stephen Knack, and Mancur Olson, "Institutions and economic performance: property rights and contract enforcement," in Christopher Clague, ed. *Institutions and Economic Development* (Baltimore: Johns Hopkins University Press, 1997), pp. 68–69; Demsetz, "Toward a theory," p. 350; North and Thomas, *The Rise of the Western World*, pp. 19–23; North, *Institutions, Institutional Change*, p. 48; World Bank, *The State*, pp. 5–7; and de Soto, *The Mystery of Capital*, p. 58.

[51] This conflict is prior to conflicts over what design institutions should take once actors agree that they want a certain environment. Firmin-Sellers, *The Transformation*, pp. 11–12; Knight, *Institutions and Social Conflict*, p. 42; and Moe, "Power and political institutions," p. 1 deal with this latter conflict.

others, so that reform is a burden for some and a relief for others."[52] A situation in which the level of policing in a central business district in a city drops illustrates the point. Lax policing might raise transaction costs for shopkeepers who would be exposed to thieves and racketeers. But for the private racketeers, the lax policing lowers their transaction costs. It gives shopkeepers an incentive to pay protection fees. It also reduces the possible costs associated with their efforts at avoiding arrest and jail time for their activities. This reduced risk of ending up in prison also represents a lower transaction cost that the thieves operating in the business district would warmly embrace.

THE DISCOURSE ON INSTITUTIONAL REFORM

This account of how the ways in which political leaders use land affects how they handle property rights institutions is important partly because it resituates institutions in the discourse on development. One of the casualties of the renewed focus on the potentially beneficial effects of institutions instigated by the "new institutional economics" has been a focus on the prior structural factors that influence institutional choice and maintenance.

Not as much attention has been paid to exploring the causes of institutional arrangements, and we consequently know less about the sources of institutions than about their effects. Apart from reflecting on the causes of different ways of dealing with institutions that govern land rights, this book provides a further reason why renewed attention should be paid to those background conditions that explain institutional choice. As the products of more fundamental political economic structures, institutions should not be cast as ultimate explanatory variables but as important intermediate variables that are themselves the effects of deeper structural factors.

This resituation of institutions has significant implications for neoliberal efforts at property rights reform in Africa, Latin America, Asia, and post-Soviet countries. Two of the main instruments employed by international agencies such as the World Bank and UNDP in the promotion of what have come to be called "second stage reforms" have been proselytism and capacity building.

---

[52] Bruce Yandle, "Bootleggers and Baptists: the education of a regulatory economist," *Regulation* (May/June 1983), p. 14.

These approaches are undergirded by the belief that strong property rights institutions are in the interests of all, and that those who lack such institutions are either ignorant of the beneficial effects of these institutions or lack the capacity to put them in place. This is where the writings and activism of Hernando de Soto have been useful. His works on the benefits of strong property rights systems and the costs of weak property rights institutions render much of the market efficiency and revisionist literatures comprehensible to policymakers.[53] The UNDP has taken the step of sponsoring de Soto on speaking tours in developing countries to inform people of the beneficial effects of strong property rights institutions.[54] This present-day proselytism on the sweet fruits of institutions that secure property to the supposedly ignorant are not very different from eloquent sermons on the virtues of secure titles preached by state officials in early postcolonial Kenya to troublesome peasants who resisted title registration. Resistors in Lower Mbeere were branded as "laz[y] and backward ... people who do not understand the value of an individual freehold title."[55] Rabai elders who resisted registration were similarly accused of "chronic ignorance and conservatism."[56]

Those who oppose systems of secure titles just do not know what is good for them. They need to be educated. Little attention is given to the possibility that some of the leaders who listen to these sermons already understand economic arguments concerning property rights, but actually benefit from insecure rights. It is easy to see why such promotion of property rights reform might end in widespread failure if some leaders who are targeted by these sermons are indeed beneficiaries of institutional arrangements that perpetrate insecurity, as I suggest.

The situation here brings to mind Ferguson's interesting reflections on the massive failure of attempts by the Thaba-Tseka Development Project in Lesotho to transform the cattle sector in that country.[57] Despite efforts

---

[53] See de Soto, *The Mystery of Capital.*

[54] "A new kind of entitlement: Peruvian economist Hernando de Soto, has radical ideas about how to end world poverty," *Forbes.com*, December 23, 2002, http://www.forbes.com/forbes/2002/1223/320_print.html (accessed July 12, 2006); and "Ghana to solve mystery of capital," *Afrol News*, October 7, 2005, http://www.afrol.com/html/News2002/gha021_property_register.htm (accessed July 12, 2006).

[55] Mwaniki, "Social and economic impacts," p. 12.

[56] Letter from Assistant Regional Government Agent, Kaloneli to Regional Government Agent, Kilifi, August 18, 1964. KNA CA/10/120.

[57] James Ferguson, *The Antipolitics Machine: "Development," Depoliticization, and Bureaucratic Power in Lesotho* (Minneapolis: University of Minnesota Press, 1994).

by the project at encouraging the outright commoditization of cattle, villagers refused to sell their stock except under the most dire personal circumstances. Development officials blamed the refusal to sell cattle on the "lack of understanding" of villagers.[58] Officials repeated often that "villagers who opposed their schemes lacked education . . . If stock owners continue to refuse to convert to purebred stock and commercial practices, this only means, in the words of one official, that 'they must be educated, in order to understand.'"[59]

This insistence on the ignorance of villagers was in stark contrast to the statement by one villager that, "We understand very well what they are saying; we simply don't agree."[60] Indeed, the District Agricultural Officer in Thaba-Tseka was to admit that, "'It is not a matter of education.... There have been thousands of *pitsos* [public meetings in the villages]. People understand perfectly well what the issues are, what needs to be done – they just refuse to do it'."[61]

While no leader admitted to me that they benefited from and supported insecure property institutions, the brazen and fundamentally subversive statement by Kenya's Minister of Local Government in the 1990s that land titles were "mere pieces of paper"[62] should serve a similar role of alerting us to a preference for weak property institution. So should repeated moves by senior British colonial officials in Ghana to abort any reform efforts and suggestions by zealous junior officials.[63] They should alert us to the fact that preaching the good effects of secure rights might not be successful because some leaders benefit from insecurity.

Various capacity-building programs are the second and complementary element in these reform efforts, founded on the belief that people do not know the benefits of secure rights and/or lack the capacity to put title registration systems in place. In Ghana, for instance, the World Bank and other donors are funding an ambitious, 15-year Land Administration Project aimed at promoting title registration, introducing land tribunals, and undertaking other land administration reforms.[64] In Tanzania, with

---

[58] Ibid., p. 186.
[59] Ibid.
[60] Ibid.
[61] Ibid., p. 183.
[62] "The indigenous and the natives," *Weekly Review* (Nairobi), July 9, 1993.
[63] See Chapter 3 of this work.
[64] See the World Bank, http://web.worldbank.org/external/projects/main?pagePK=104231 &theSitePK=40941&menuPK=228424&Projectid=P071157. (Accessed June 25, 2007.)

major funding from the Norwegian People's Aid and backing from the World Bank and EU, de Soto's Institute for Liberty and Democracy is carrying out a large national titling program under the name MKURA-BITA.[65]

By refocusing on the causes of different institutional arrangements, my work shows why such capacity-building efforts might not always bear expected fruits. If weak property rights provide some leaders with real political and economic benefits, then such capacity-building efforts that construct institutions such as title registries might end up making rights more insecure in some places. Given the contradictory potential of these institutions, elites seeking to engage in the fraudulent sale of land and the use of land rights to gerrymander constituencies might transform such registries into instruments for the further subversion of property rights. The ability to print and issue titles might become an ideal instrument for creating conflicting interests through the distribution of multiple titles for the same piece of land.

As shown earlier, the Commissioner of Lands in Kenya was heavily involved in these activities in the 1990s.[66] The establishment of these title registries and other land administration institutions in postcolonial Kenya had been funded by the World Bank and the British government, among others, in an attempt to build the state's capacity to facilitate agriculture and markets and redistribute property in the 1960s.[67]

Distributive Conflicts

Importantly, this focus on how leaders employ land also sheds light on the limitations of the distributive conflict literature on the origins and transformation of property rights institutions. Why do people pursue distributive conflicts over land in divergent ways? Some create title registries, courts, and enforcement institutions through which they channel these disputes. Others employ highly disruptive and violent means and do not create such institutions.

As an important part of the revisionist response to market efficiency theories of property rights, the distributive conflicts literature argues that variations in the creation of property rights institutions in the face of

---

[65] "Poor people's wealth: plain language information about Tanzania's property and business formalization programme," *Mkurabita* (February 2007).

[66] Kenya, *Report of the Commission of Inquiry into the Illegal/Irregular*, p. 75.

[67] Kenya, *Report of the Commission of Inquiry into the Illegal/Irregular*, p. 123.

rising prices can be explained by distributive conflicts over rights. Where distributive conflicts persist, secure property rights are not created because no acceptable definition of property can be reached, and no actor has the capacity to impose his preferred definition. It is only in the cases in which these conflicts are settled that property rights are created.[68]

Thus framed, this literature does not shed much light on the puzzle of why people pursue these conflicts in different ways. Distributive conflicts over land are pervasive and are hardly ever resolved permanently. Disputes over land rights are common in Latin America.[69] In China there are frequent peasant revolts over land issues.[70] Disputes over land rights persist even in highly industrialized societies such as the United States.

In the 2006 mid-term elections in the U.S., ballot initiatives concerning eminent domain trumped all other initiatives, including those concerning same-sex marriages.[71] The pervasive and enduring character of distributive conflicts over land rights around the world advise a focus on the more pertinent question of why people pursue these conflicts in varying ways. Some create property rights institutions through which they seek to channel these conflicts in predictable and less-disruptive ways. Others pursue similar conflicts in disruptive and violent ways that fundamentally undermine existing institutions.

A key problem with the distributive conflicts literature is that it focuses too much on questions of ownership and control instead of how people benefit from land to gauge preferences for strong institutions that govern property rights in land.[72] The causal link is tenuous because the ownership and control of land do necessarily confer any benefits. These benefits have to be squeezed out of land through various means. Also, given the right environment, one can benefit from land without owning or controlling it.

---

[68] Knight, *Institutions and Social Conflict*, p. 42; Firmin-Sellers, *The Transformation*, pp. 9–14; and Riker and Sened, "A political theory," pp. 953–955.

[69] Thomas Skidmore and Peter Smith, *Modern Latin America* (New York: Oxford University Press, 2001), pp. 336–353.

[70] "For Chinese, peasant revolt is rare victory," *The Washington Post*, June 13, 2005. http://www.washingtonpost.com/wp-dyn/content/article/2005/06/12/AR2005061201531.html (accessed June 11, 2007); and "A real peasants' revolt," *The Weekly Standard*, June 1, 2006. http://www.weeklystandard.com/Content/Public/Articles/000/000/006/616ckhar.asp (accessed June 11, 2007).

[71] Arnolby, "Topping 2006 ballot initiatives."

[72] Firmin-Sellers, *The Transformation*, pp. 12–13; Glaeser, Scheinkman, and Shleifer, "The injustice of inequality," p. 200; Sonin, "Why the rich," p. 716; and Riker and Sened, "A political theory," p. 951. In noting that, "Formal property's contribution to mankind is not the protection of ownership," de Soto, levies a similar criticism against this orientation around a logic of ownership. *The Mystery of Capital*, p. 59.

By focusing on how actors exploit land, I am able to establish a more direct causal link to their preference for various levels of effectiveness of property institutions. The goal here is not to de-emphasize the significance of conflicts over the ownership and control of land. These conflicts over ownership simply have limited causal salience when it comes to determining whether political leaders prefer the strong public institutions that secure property rights in land discussed here.

In my analysis of Ga and Akyem Abuakwa, I show that the ways in which leaders choose to pursue distributive conflicts is explained by how they use land. Chiefs, *landguards*, and diverse con men in the Ga Traditional Area deliberately employ violent strategies and manufacture distributive conflicts to facilitate various fraudulent land deals. Akyem chiefs deeply involved in cocoa farming employ far less disruptive strategies to pursue similar conflicts because a secure and predictable environment is critical for cocoa production, from which they draw resources even to make and defend land claims.

NEW DIRECTIONS FOR RESEARCH

This book raises some critical and interesting questions that it makes no systematic effort to answer.

- Why, in some contexts, do politicians choose to exploit land directly rather than indirectly?
- Why do politicians seek to generate support and profit from land in one way rather than another?
- What determines politicians' choice among different means of mobilizing political support?

The lack of a systematic response to these questions does not constitute a shortcoming of this work. It does not make it merely descriptive instead of explanatory. This book poses the important question of how politicians handle institutions that govern property such as title and deeds registries, land tribunals, and so on. It provides evidence for an argument that emphasizes the causal impact of how leaders draw benefits from land and their capacity on how they handle property institutions. The theoretical payoffs stated above from this exercise are not negligible. But, like many works, this book raises new questions for research as it answers its *stated* question. It highlights the need to address another series of questions in a long and elaborate causal chain.

This work focuses on how leaders' strategies inform how they deal with institutions. The causal link is a strong one because each strategy requires an enabling institutional environment to be possible and effective. But at some point we must pay more attention to explaining the choice of strategy itself, which was never a goal of this book. Works on the adoption of particularistic as opposed to programmatic election platforms, vote buying, etc.,[73] already contribute to our understanding of this issue. But even more effort needs to go into studying this issue, especially as it relates to the exploitation of land.

There is a great suspicion that politicians facing stiff competition will tend to undermine rights for political advantage. But, as I show through the case of Moi's effort at consolidating his succession of Kenyatta in Kenya, securing property rights can also be a potent political weapon for leaders fighting for their survival. We also see the working of this logic in Akyem Abuakwa, Ghana, where chiefs' struggled to secure their autonomy in the face of efforts by Nana Ofori Atta to subject them to his rule. It is clear that undercutting rights is not always the best way of entrenching rule in the face of challenges, nor is it the one that politicians always follow. More systematic investigation of why leaders follow one path instead of another would be very enlightening.

Such investigations will be part of the wider and, as demonstrated here, insightful attempt at using land as a window to look into the wider question of uneven political and economic development across African countries. Because of the importance of land in all of these countries, politics in the land arena is often reflective of wider national political economies. Reflecting on the significance of land, Berry noted that, "Land has been a key focus of economic and political struggle in Africa throughout the twentieth century and shows no signs of diminishing in importance or contentiousness. . . . "[74] This makes the study of politics in the land arena in largely agrarian societies increasingly attractive for continuing research.

---

[73] Leonard Wantchekon, "Clientelism and voting behavior: evidence from a field experiment in Benin," *World Politics* 55 (April 2003); Brusco, Nazareno, and Stokes, "Vote buying in Argentina;" Wang and Kurzman, "The logistics."

[74] Berry, *Chiefs Know Their Boundaries*, p. xix. Also see Lund, *Local Politics*, p. 3.

Appendix

Notes on Field Research

The Enigma of Access

I conducted about 17 months of field research for this book in Botswana, Ghana, and Kenya between 2002 and 2005. I undertook archival research, participant observation, semistructured interviews, and many informal discussions with state officials, land users, land market racketeers, NGOs involved in land issues, etc. Given the sensitive nature of the subject matter that I was researching, I was always concerned about whether people would be willing to talk to me and whether they would try to mislead me. I quickly learned that, while some were unwilling to talk, many were very eager to. I also discovered quickly that learning the "truth," if anything like that does exist, would require clever investigative work.

Some government officials in Ghana simply refused to talk. A *land-guard* in Ghana asked me to bring USD 100 and a bottle of schnapps to appease the god he had erected in his backyard if I wanted an interview. He could only speak with the permission of the god, who had to be appeased before it would consent! Given the even more sensitive nature of land issues in Kenya, I expected only limited fruits on my way there.

My contact person in Kenya, who had worked with many other researchers, confirmed that getting a permit from the Ministry of Education to study land issues normally took weeks if one was fortunate. His view was that, in Kenya, state officials had a lot to hide when it came to land issues. The fact that I had earlier spent my first month in Botswana waiting for a research permit from the Office of the President further fueled my fears.

I received my Kenyan research permit in two working days! This was partly fortuitous and a function of the time during which I conducted my research, but it also demonstrated the motivation behind some people's willingness to reveal information on sensitive issues. In early 2005, the National Rainbow Coalition government that had succeeded in defeating KANU, which had ruled the country since independence, was in the middle of its first term. Revealing to the public all the facets of KANU's misrule was a significant part of the National Rainbow Coalition's agenda. Illicit land dealings constituted a big part of these public revelations, and my stay there coincided with the release of the report of the Ndung'u Commission of Inquiry's investigation into the illegal and irregular allocation of land by KANU officials. The official at the Ministry of Education was thus all too happy to provide me with a permit to dig into KANU's mishandling of land matters.

Despite the elements of luck involved, this story illustrates the larger point, that many were eager to be interviewed because it allowed them to state their own sides of sensitive stories. The airing of their side of the story was important for two reasons. It undermined the ability of opponents to monopolize control over the public record and so gain an undue advantage in land disputes. Further, it created evidence that could be used in courts of law in later litigations over land. Berry notes in this regard that "claims [on land rights] may be based, of course, on written deeds, wills, and/or witnesses' recollections, but people also draw on archives, scholarly publications.... Scholars may find their publications quoted in court...."[1]

Giving interviews and providing evidence was thus an integral part of the struggle over land rights. There were many instances in which interviewees slowly dictated whole lines, preceded by the request, "When you write the book, put it exactly like this." Some ended interviews by asking me to read back to them the content of specific sections of their interview. If they did not like what had been written, they would ask that some lines be erased and new ones inserted.

At other times, officials simply savored the opportunity to use a visit from a researcher from abroad as evidence of how well they were doing their work. In Botswana, I was sitting in a crowd at a land board allocation meeting one day when the board chairman suddenly called on me

---

[1] Berry, *Chiefs Know Their Boundaries*, pp. xxvii–xxviii.

to mount the stage and sit with board members. He then went on to announce to the people that the board was doing such a good job that a young researcher had been sent all the way from Ghana to study the workings of the board. While I benefited a great deal from the close relationship I had with this land board, the invitation to sit on the stage with board members ensured that some members of the public became unwilling to talk to me because they saw me as a close associate of the board.

As evidenced in the speech of the land board chairman, I realized very quickly during my research that, even when interviewees were not deliberately trying to present me with distorted information (many did this), "the truth" was always a matter of perspective. People that some regarded as poor landless squatters were seen by others as wicked land invaders. Key foreign exchange earners in the eyes of state officials were regarded by some peasants as evil land grabbers. What some saw as progressive efforts at title registration to promote market activity were seen by others as shameless acts of land expropriation. The tough guys who were seen as protectors of land rights by some communities were seen as evil threats to land rights by others.

In this environment of multiple narratives, making sense of information required, among other things, observing people in different settings, understanding the wider world in which they operated, triangulating interviews, and interviewing people multiple times and for long periods. Senior state officials in capitals sometimes knew only what subordinates in far-flung areas wanted them to know. As a result I had to get to some of those villages to interview lower-level officials.

Government officials also tended to start interviews by telling me how things were supposed to be (what the laws were) in response to questions about how things actually were. Fortunately, I had bought and read many of the legal instruments and could recognize these accounts. For instance, referring to customary and state land, many officials informed me that, "In Botswana, land is not bought and sold. Only developments on land are bought and sold." Forty minutes into an interview or during the second interview, when asked about impediments to their efforts at rationalizing land policy, these same officials would disparage the greed and avarice of people who sold land and talk about the difficulties involved in trying to prevent them from selling undeveloped land. Interviews with private real estate agents then revealed the existence of an extensive market in land (not developments on land) and the elaborate legal mechanisms that people have crafted to subvert state injunctions against the sale of land.

Anonymity

I have gone to great extremes to remove all marks that would identify interviewees in this work. I first made the decision to keep the identities of research subjects confidential while seeking permission to do research for this book from the Institutional Review Board of Northwestern University's Office for the Protection of Research Subjects. But the need for confidentiality was truly driven home only when I started doing interviews. Land is an extremely sensitive subject in the societies that I worked. Many people divulged information that could potentially result in their being fired from jobs, prosecuted, or even physically assaulted if what they said came to the attention of others. Such disclosures included people admitting to land rackets, physical assaults on land users, and even murder. It also included lower officials revealing the illicit dealings of their seniors.

To protect research subjects, I devised a system for keeping their identities confidential. I created a list stored in my email where names corresponding to the numbers which I used to identify interviewees in my notebook were stored. After the initial week, I also stopped tape-recording interviews. The wisdom of these elaborate measures soon became apparent when various interviewees began to ask to see my notebook and demanded to know whom else I had interviewed.

The Handsome Fruits of Archival Research

Archival research for this book proved invaluable in providing a historical background against which to make sense of current events in these countries. I conducted research at the national archives in Accra, Gaborone, and Nairobi. I also worked in the Akyem Abuakwa State Archive at the palace of the Okyenhene in Kyebi. The original government documents and old newspapers in these collections provided a rich source of information that prompted some of the theoretical innovation in this work.

Letters from the Okyenhene threatening or directing the seizure of the farms of lower chiefs, and letters from these chiefs pleading their cases, first drew my attention to the problematic nature of the claim that chiefs and citizens in Akyem Abuakwa invested in agriculture because of credible commitments to property rights security by the Okyenhene. It also provided an indication of the persistence of distributive conflicts in Akyem Abuakwa even during the era of relatively secure property rights under Okyenhene Ofori Atta.

These insights were key bases for the broad theoretical point that distributive conflicts over land rights do not explain actors' preference for institutions that ensure property rights and that the ways in which elites use land better explains this preference. Similarly, the rich accounts of the activities of land-buying companies in the *Weekly Review* issues of the 1970s inspired the theoretical insight that institutions display contradictory potential.

The Invaluable Contribution of Field Research: Identifying Assets in Kenya

Field research proved critical to this project. It was particularly valuable for gathering information about the landed assets of politicians. None of the three countries have had long-standing, effective laws requiring politicians to publicly declare their assets. In Ghana, the Public Office Holders (Declaration of Assets and Disqualifications) Act (1998) and the Public and Political Party Office Holders (Declaration of Assets and Eligibility) Law (1992) require politicians to declare assets. But these laws do not prescribe serious punishment for noncompliance or make declarations accessible to the public.

In Kenya, the Public Officer Ethics Act (2003) now requires politicians to declare their assets, but this information is also confidential and inaccessible to the public. In Botswana a bill introduced to mandate asset declaration was abandoned in parliament by the government.[2] Politicians have various reasons for keeping their assets secret. It minimizes the risk that people will recognize their corruption. It also reduces the possibility that opponents will confiscate these politicians' assets once they lose power. Acquiring this information was, however, critical to my work and required a mix of interviews, archival research, and some probing into title registries and the registry of companies.

In Kenya, things turned out to be even more challenging. I was under the impression that I would be able to tell who owned what by studying the registry of companies and land title registers. A Kenyan friend smiled at my naiveté when I told him of my plans. These documents had fallen victim to the deliberate subversion of institutions by politicians in the 1990s. Many pages had been torn out of registers, entries had been changed, and some transactions had not been recorded at all.

---

[2] "Botswana: government shelves Assets Bill, Liability Law," *Mmegi* (Gaborone), November 23, 2007.

Even the state-instituted Ndung'u Commission of Inquiry in Kenya was plagued by a "problem of missing records" when it sought information from the title registry and the registry of companies. It concluded that this "problem of missing records was just as pronounced in the latter registry as the former."[3] With regards to the disappearance of records at the Ministry of Lands, it was to conclude that, "in the view of the commission, this was no accident and no reflection on the general competence and accuracy of the Records Department. It seemed to be deliberate."[4]

Further, it is widely known that many politicians registered properties in the names of relatives. For instance, when various banks tried to foreclose on the properties of the influential Kenyan politician Paul Ngei who had defaulted on loans in the 1980s, they found it "difficult to trace any property belonging to [him]. Most of what is said to belong to him is registered under the names of members of his family. This makes it difficult for anyone to recover property from Ngei even through legal channels."[5]

In response to these challenges, I adopted the approach of travelling to farms, ranches, and game parks in various parts of the country to talk to local officials, farm workers, squatters, and local residents who lived near landed properties that newspaper reports and preliminary interviews had indicated belonged to politicians and bureaucrats. This turned out to be a highly effective approach. Locals always knew which politicians visited a farm frequently, hired and fired workers on it, determined who could live on it, and claimed to own it. Some local state officials even provided me with information based on requests made by politicians for administration police protection of farms and complaints lodged by politicians about squatters and theft. Being in the country, interacting with people there, and combing through archives turned out to be critical for this project.

Using these sources of information to make claims about land ownership patterns raises interesting issues. Because claims are not primarily based on information from title registers, the elites mentioned here can easily claim that they own no such properties, and that allegations that they do are mere rumors. As mentioned in the case of Paul Ngei, elites do make such rebuttals against those who accuse them of owning properties.

---

[3] Kenya, *Report of the Commission of Inquiry into the Illegal/Irregular*, p. 40.
[4] Ibid., p. 38.
[5] "Up for sale: Ngei's property to be auctioned," *Weekly Review* (Nairobi), April 11, 1980.

But understanding the wider politics of these societies allows us to see through such accusations of spreading rumors. Politicians deliberately hide their assets to create difficulty for those who seek to make "credible" claims about their wealth. Remaining silent about their wealth because of this lack of "credible" title registry information would be tantamount to handing them victory on a silver platter.

Index

28984812R00148

Made in the USA
Columbia, SC
19 October 2018